WEBER AND FIELDS

WEBER AND FIELDS

THEIR TRIBULATIONS, TRIUMPHS, AND THEIR ASSOCIATES

BY

FELIX ISMAN

With a New Introduction by Ken Bloom

EXCELSIOR
EDITIONS

Cover caricature of Weber and Fields by Al Frueh. National Portrait Gallery, Smithsonian Institution; gift of the children of Al Frueh: Barbara Frueh Bornemann, Robert Frueh, and Alfred Frueh Jr.

Printed in the United States of America

Excelsior Editions is an imprint of State University of New York Press
For information, contact State University of New York Press, Albany, NY
www.sunypress.edu

Library of Congress Cataloging-in-Publication Data

Names: Isman, Felix, 1873-1943 author. | Bloom, Ken, 1949- writer of introduction.
Title: Weber and Fields : their tribulations, triumphs, and their associates / Felix Isman ; with a new introduction by Ken Bloom.
Description: Excelsior editions. | Albany : State University of New York Press, [2022] | Series: New York classics | Includes index.
Identifiers: LCCN 2022006882 | ISBN 9781438490519 (hardcover) | ISBN 9781438490533 (ebook) | ISBN 9781438490526 (paperback)
Subjects: LCSH: Weber, Joe, 1867-1942. | Fields, Lew, 1867-1941. | Comedians—United States—Biography. | Vaudeville—United States—History.
Classification: LCC PN2285.I86 2022 | DDC 792.02/80922 [B]—dc23/eng/20220218
LC record available at https://lccn.loc.gov/2022006882

10 9 8 7 6 5 4 3 2 1

Contents

New Introduction

Ken Bloom

The team of Joe Weber and Lew Fields was the dominant musical comedy team at the turn of the last century. The team created classic comedic characters and routines that continue to influence the many comic duos who followed them. They also formed their own theatrical troupe, running a theater in New York City for many years where they produced successful revues that combined music, dance, and song. So famous were they in their day that they were a rare popular act that inspired a full-length biography published by a major publisher. This new edition brings this long-out-of-print classic to a new generation of theater lovers.

The team's first biographer, Felix Isman (1873–1943), knew them well. Isman was a colorful theatrical producer who got his start speculating in New York City real estate; he also amassed a large collection of fine art, some of which is now part of the Frick Collection. Married three times to three actresses, he made headlines as a bon vivant and man about town. Isman presented Weber and Fields on stage for a gala evening celebrating the Jubilee year (or fiftieth anniversary) of their partnership. So it's no surprise that, although this book was published in 1924, Isman concludes his book in 1912, the year of the Jubilee performance, making Isman one of the stars of the biography. His book, first published in 1924, was written less than thirty years after Weber and Fields first teamed up. In addition, many of the characters in the book were still alive and performing. It's as close to an eyewitness account of those heady days of the beginning of the US theater as you can get.

To set the stage, let's look at the earliest years of the birth of musical comedy and the theater in general. The last decades of the nineteenth century and the start of the twentieth saw great changes in US theater. These eras saw the beginnings of burlesque (then meaning topical spoofs of current shows and society), variety (later known as vaudeville), and the first steps on the way to an American musical theater. During this period, performers often based their onstage personas on the latest immigrant groups that were flooding into the United States. Reflecting the new emphasis on these characters, in 1912, Jean Schwartz and William Jerome composed the song "If It Wasn't for the Irish and the Jews." Mentioning noted theatrical producer David Belasco, one of the verses went:

I really heard Belasco say
You couldn't stage a play today,
If it wasn't for the Irish and the Jews.

Schwartz and Jerome were correct. In terms of writers and performers of early musical theater, there were two great teams that for all intents and purposes invented the American musical: The Irish team of Harrigan and Hart and the Jewish team of Weber and Fields.

The earliest were Edward Harrigan and Tony Hart, two Irish-immigrant gentlemen. Toward the end of the nineteenth century, they produced, wrote, directed, and acted in their shows. The comedy team celebrated the multicultural stew that was New York's Bowery. Their shows were paeans to life amid the new immigrants who strove to make a new beginning in New York City. They had an especial bonhomie for the residents of the Lower East Side no matter what their ethnic background. To them, the neighborhood melting pot made all men equal.

Following in that team's footsteps was another comic team, Joe Weber and Lew Fields. These two Jewish producers, directors, authors, and performers opened their first theater on Broadway in September of 1896. After years in the small time, they were ready for the big time. And so famous were their talents that they became the prototype of all the comedy partners who followed in their footsteps. Like Harrigan and Hart, the team based their characters as new immigrants. Weber and Fields were disguised as "Dutch" comics, taking the name from the slang term for Germans, "Deutsch." Of course, no mention of their heritage ever entered the act—it was just an excuse for the team to have a funny accent and a funny view of life in the big city. From then on, they always appeared as the characters Mike and Myer.

They usually made their entrances onstage with Fields pushing Weber, who complained, "Don't push me, Meyer, don't pooosh me!" Mangling the language was an integral part of their act, one that Americans new to the shores could easily identify with and that other entertainers could mine for their own characters. Weber and Fields's malapropisms forged the way to other comic acts like radio's Parkyakarkus (Harry Parke), the movies' Jack Pearl (aka Baron Munchausen, "Vass you dere, Sharlie?"), and Burt Gordon, the mad Russian ("How dooo you do!"), and on through the decades into television with Bill Dana as José Jiménez ("My name—José Jiménez").

Lew Fields played the taller and slimmer character and Weber the shorter and much fatter one (due to a lot of padding). Weber once said that "all the public wanted to see was Fields knock the hell out of me." That part of their legacy was handed down to the comics in characters like the tall, gangly Mutt and short and squat Jeff. The movies also emulated the team; Laurel and Hardy and Abbott and Costello both featured tall and short characters, as did the

Photo 1. Weber and Fields as Mike and Myer.

Three Stooges decades later. Television gave us the short, fat Toody and the tall, skinny Muldoon on *Car 54, Where Are You?*

Fields realized that their theater ticket sales would boost exponentially with a star at the helm. In 1897, Weber and Fields brought English music hall star and male impersonator Vesta Tilley to the Music Hall. To Fields, she reminded him of a teenage boy trying to act like an adult. She was charming, and audiences loved her. But Oscar Hammerstein also wanted Tilley for his theaters. A bidding war ensued, and Hammerstein lost, with Tiller receiving the astounding sum of $1,250 a week from Fields. In today's dollars, it would total to around $40,000 a week! She went on a tour of vaudeville theaters under the auspices of Weber and Fields. Her nine-week tour netted $50,000 in 1897 dollars!

Their shows weren't ramshackle, slapped-together stews of music, plot, and lyrics. They weren't afraid of paying top salaries to important stars. Typical of the kinds of shows at the Weber and Fields' Music Hall was *Helter-Skelter*, which opened on April 6, 1899. These shows included parodies of straight plays, with interludes of music, dance, and song. Julian Mitchell, the team's stage director, went on to greater fame as principal director of *The Ziegfeld Follies*. Included in the arsenal of performers was Bessie Clayton, wife of Mitchell (when they married she was sixteen and he was thirty-two). In September of that year, the team's next show, *Whirl-i-Gig*, played thirty-three weeks, with Clayton again exhibiting her terpsichorean talents.

Clayton was also featured in the subsequent show, *Fiddle-Dee-Dee*, which began a new season for the theater on September 6, 1900. In addition to Clayton, *Fiddle-Dee-Dee* had Weber and Fields and their regulars, Lillian Russell, Fay Templeton, DeWolf Hopper, and David Warfield, in the cast. The next September brought a new season and the première of *Hoity-Toity*, again with all the above mainstays of the Weber and Fields troupe. It played for thirty-three weeks and then toured the country for three more weeks. This would be the final show directed by Julian Mitchell for Weber and Fields. In 1902, Victor Herbert stole him away for *Babes in Toyland*.

In 1903, the Iroquois Theatre in Chicago burned down with many casualties. The fire laws in New York City and other big cities were amended, and the Weber and Fields' Music Hall was shut down. Disagreements between the partners about renovating the theater caused the team to break up in May 1904. It wasn't only the argument over the theater that caused the breakup. Fields wanted to branch away from burlesque and go into booking shows like the new offerings up on Broadway. But Weber hedged his bets, explaining, "I believe it is a good thing to stick to success and not go experimenting. Experience has shown us where our strength is. . . . Our style of show has made us a good deal of money and a big reputation. Why shouldn't we stick to it?" And there were even more reasons for the breakup. Their 44th Street Theatre was condemned, many of the stars had retired, and business was down. But, most importantly, perhaps, was that like many performing teams, each became jealous of the other.

Fields decided to produce a new musical at the Lew Fields Theatre, *It Happened in Nordland*, on December 5, 1904, with music by Victor Herbert and book and lyrics by Glen MacDonough. Naturally, Mitchell directed and Bessie Clayton was featured. The show was important in musical theater's evolution, with Mitchell attempting to further integrate the songs and dances with the plot. Meanwhile, Weber joined up with Florenz Ziegfeld to produce a Weber and Fields sort of show (part musical, part vaudeville) with Ziegfeld's star Anna Held in the lead. The show was *Higgledy-Piggledy* (1904). But Weber managed to alienate Ziegfeld, and Ziegfeld opened the show himself with Trixie Friganza starring instead of Held.

In August 1906, Fields produced *About Town*, with Fields himself sharing the stage with Vernon Castle and Jack Norworth. The following year, Weber reopened his refurbished Music Hall in the form of the old Weber and Fields burlesques, with *Hip! Hip! Hooray!* opening on October 10, 1907. But with all the new, up-to-date musicals playing, it closed after only sixty-four performances. Weber returned on January 2, 1908, with a satire, the aptly named *Merry Widow Burlesque*. Franz Lehar, composer of the show upon which it was based, gave his blessing for his music to be used in this satire. Many of Weber and Fields's stalwarts appeared, including Lulu Glaser, Bessie Clayton, and Mabel Fenton. When Glaser left, Blanche Ring took over and revitalized the production with her song "Yip-I-Addy-I-Ay," which became the hit of the show's six-month run. The next year, Fields cast Ring in his 1909 summer show *The Midnight Sons*. Ring stopped the show with her new song "I've Got Rings on My Fingers (And Bells on My Toes)." The show was a success, running through the summer and fall and into 1910.

In January 1912, Fields's father died, and Weber attended the funeral. Except for one brief meeting at a benefit performance, they hadn't seen each other for seven years. Riding back from the funeral, Weber sat with Fields in the back of the car. Each admitted they weren't doing so well, and Weber suggested they join forces again. On February 8, 1912, the team was back together on stage for *Weber and Fields 1912 Jubilee*. Fay Templeton returned to the fold to join the production. The show was a hit, with full houses for fourteen weeks at the New Amsterdam Theatre, grossing $405,000, at the time the largest gross ever for a musical. The engagement was cut short by commitments for the show to play across the country—a tour of thirty-three cities in one month! Marie Dressler joined the tour in Templeton's place, and after the tour, she appeared in a vaudeville revue with Lew Fields producing.

Toward the end of 1912, the partners mounted another show, *Roly Poly*. Audiences at the opening on November 21, 1912, flocked to the Broadway Theatre to see Weber and Fields stalwarts Nora Bayes, Bessie Clayton, and Marie Dressler. Frank Daniels and Jack Norworth, along with the two comedians, commanded the male contingent. The show sported two songs that achieved success outside of the production, including "Way Down in C-U-B-A" with music by Nora Bayes (Norworth's wife) and Antonio Torroella Chijo and a lyric by Norworth, and "When It's Apple Blossom Time in Normandy" by Harry Gifford, Tom Mellor, and Huntley Trevor. As usual for a Weber and Fields show, none of the original songs in the show became hits. But the houses were full for two months.

In 1913, Weber and Fields appeared on movie screens around the country. The film was *Popular Players of the Stage*, shot in an early color system, Kinemacolor. Other stage celebrities in the film included Lillian Russell, Anna Held, and Eddie Foy. The Weber and Fields All Star Company toured in 1914, with Nora Bayes and others of the team's stalwarts, but with war in Europe on the horizon, it closed after only three weeks.

In early 1918, Weber and Fields decided to reunite again and revise their early musical, *A Pack of Pickles*. Their new version sported the apt title *Back Again*. The show was booked into the Chestnut Theatre in Philadelphia, with the Dolly Sisters among the company, but it never came into New York City.

In 1921, Lew Fields toured the country with Nora Bayes and a young Fred Allen. That tour was conducted by Richard Rodgers, who was only nineteen at the time. Rodgers (and Larry Hart) had already collaborated with Fields by contributing songs to Fields's 1920 musical *Poor Little Ritz Girl*. In 1923, the partners were back before the film camera for an early talking picture. They memorialized their famous pool hall routine for a Lee DeForest Phonofilm sound short. On April 15, 1923, the film premiered at the Rivoli Theatre on Broadway.

In 1925, the team was enjoying one of their regularly occurring farewell tours. This one made it to the Palace Theatre as part of a nostalgia booking. On the bill with them were Marie Cahill, Cissie Loftus, opera star Emma Trentini, and the team of Blossom Seeley and Benny Fields. It was so successful that it was held over for a second week. But the team decided to leave the production when Marie Dressler, once their employee, got better billing than they did.

On November 15, 1926, the duo appeared with Will Rogers and Mary Garden on the November 15, 1926, debut of the NBC Radio Network. It was so well received that in 1931, NBC gave them their own series. Weber and Fields also reunited for the December 27, 1932, inaugural show at Radio City Music Hall, when the partners made what would be their last stage appearance as a team.

Lew Fields went on to appear in the film *The Story of Vernon and Irene Castle* as himself. The pair didn't appear together on stage again, but as partners they appeared in the films *Blossoms over Broadway* and *Lillian Russell*. Fields died in 1941. Joe Weber followed the next year.

Their legacy continued, however. Lew Fields had three children, and they all had a major impact on theater. Herbert contributed libretti for early Rodgers and Hart shows and went on to write scripts for several shows in collaboration with his sister Dorothy: *Annie Get Your Gun, Something for the Boys, Up in Central Park*, and *Arms and the Girl*. Dorothy wrote the libretti and lyrics for *Redhead, Sweet Charity*, and *Seesaw*, as well as over four hundred songs for theater, Tin Pan Alley, and movies with collaborators like Jimmy

Photo 2. Lew Fields and family in front of their New York City home. L to r: Dorothy, Lew, Frances, Mrs. Fields, Herbert, and Joseph. New York Public Library, Digital Collections.

McHugh, Jerome Kern, and Cy Coleman. Brother Joseph Fields, in collaboration with Jerome Chodorov, wrote the film scripts to *My Sister Eileen*, *Junior Miss*, and others and wrote the libretti to the musicals *Wonderful Town* and *The Girl in Pink Tights*. Joseph also collaborated with Anita Loos on the musical *Gentlemen Prefer Blondes* and with Oscar Hammerstein II on *Flower Drum Song*.

Weber and Fields's routines also influenced generations of performers. Their comedy might seem a little hoary to today's audiences, but at the time, their routines were up-to-the-minute. As the century turned, immigrants poured into New York City via Ellis Island. One of their routines spoofed problems in communication between the new Americans and established New Yorkers. In one routine, a newly arrived citizen asks the conductor, "Can you tell me where I get off to Watt Street?" The conductor replies, "What street?" And hilarity ensues. It's pretty creaky stuff—but think of Abbott and Costello's "Who's on first?" routine, which was a direct descendent of Weber and Fields's act.

This text was originally published in 1924 and includes terms that were in common use at the time to describe theatrical performers and genres. We have chosen to leave these terms unchanged to remain faithful to the original text.

Dedication

Broadway attracts the nimble wit of the world. There is its market. There the men who write, "We Have No Bananas Today," "I Would Leave My Happy Home for You," or a sentimental ditty such as "The *Shade of the Old Apple Tree," are to be found. The amusement purveyors in all forms of theatrical endeavor make it their home. They twiddle your heart-strings with laughter or tears, at will.*

It has seen many characters, but far outstripping all in point of energy, adroitness, nimbleness of wit and daring was the late Oscar Hammerstein, to whom this volume is respectfully dedicated. His office was his hat—it was a very large hat. His books were kept on the walls of the Victoria Theater—his reception hall a chair in the lobby. He knew the trend of realty values, keenly sensed the public's amusement tastes and was thoroughly at home whether he was presenting grand opera, Charmion, who disrobed on a slack wire, or Peter the Great, an educated monkey. Likewise, he was an inventor of great note and a musician of considerable ability.

Broadway has never known his like.

It was Oscar Hammerstein who gave Messrs. Weber and Fields their first chance on Broadway, together with scores of others who made their mark, one of whom, first known to great prominence, being Miss Mary Garden.

Acknowledgment

The author takes pleasure in acknowledging the great aid rendered to him by Mr. Wesley W. Stout in the preparation of the articles which appeared in the *Saturday Evening Post* and without whose valuable assistance, experience, and ability the work incident to the preparation of this volume would not have been undertaken.

List of Illustrations

Introduction

THE title of this volume belies its contents. Messrs. Weber and Fields are but the mediums to tell the story of two young American boys born in the ghetto, raised in the slums, with all the disadvantages of foreign parentage of that particular period, who by their lives and their living became shining examples of true American manhood. Through all the pitfalls and snares of life, Messrs. Weber and Fields came through untarnished and unstained, to rise to the greatest height of their profession. Well may it be said that neither before nor since has there been such a tremendous vogue for any theatrical organization in any branch of its many ramifications, as that enjoyed by the Weberfieldians.

It was the time and the place. When they started, America had no national theatrical institution individually its own, where the local atmosphere of this country found color and semblance, and through their and their compatriots' efforts, this country to-day has a strong, virile, national institution, recognized and copied throughout practically the entire world. They were opportunists from necessity, and subtleties born of desperation were also theirs. To the purist their evasions may be condemned—Oh, thou holier than I, these two boys had practically no education, absolutely no youth, their horizon very limited, their opportunities nil—excepting those which they could create for themselves. Little by little the responsibilities of their families grew upon their shoulders. The skirmishes they fought were but preludes to the little battles they won which culminated in their great and glorious victory with the Music Hall. No finer example can be shown by any general on any battlefield, of a campaign more skillfully and successfully conducted than that of these two undersized, underfed and underloved young Americans of the late '70s.

Chapter I

Rough Beginnings

Youth through Teen Years

Rickler? Sarah? Fanny? Golda? Bertha? Esther? Leah? Rae? Rebecca? Flora? Anne? George? Abraham? Solomon? Philip? Max? Joseph? And Joseph, youngest at the moment of the Webers, would pipe, "Papa, I'm here."

It was nose-counting at bedtime in a cellar in East Broadway, the time fifty years ago. A true cellar, too, in the New York ghetto; no half basement with windows to peer at the sun. In it were housed seventeen children in stepladder sizes, the father and mother; not infrequently the little nephew, Lawrence, now owner of the Longacre Theater; and, at intervals, a boarder to eke out the family income.

This cellar was the first stand on American soil of a Jewish family come to America from Poland by way of England, where, in Birmingham, they had halted long enough to acquire a working knowledge of English, a distinct advantage over the generality of their neighbors.

In the confusion of embarking at Liverpool, the family—then eleven in number—missed the sailing ship on which they had booked passage. The vessel, they were to learn in New York, was lost that voyage with all hands. In a ship sailing the following day, they were thirty-five days from port to port. On the thirty-third day, the youngest child, a babe in arms, died. For all the steerage passengers knew, they still were in mid-ocean; and they knew the burial customs of the sea. The family was gathered in prayer, a tallith, or Jewish ceremonial cape, spread over them, when the ship's surgeon entered the steerage. Sharks were following the vessel, a certain sign to an old-school seaman that death had come aboard. The surgeon demanded that the body be surrendered.

Mrs. Weber held the dead baby to her breast as if in suckling, and her ruse succeeded. Two days later the Webers carried their dead ashore with them, their first act in the New World a funeral. At once upon finding rooms in Mott Street, the senior Weber went to a synagogue. There, in an interval in which there was no prayer, he turned to the man next to him with some commonplace remark.

"You are a stranger here, no?" the man asked. "Whence come you? From Birmingham, in England? I have relatives there. Did you, by chance, know a family named Weber?"

At the next word the men embraced. They were uncle and nephew. The uncle, believing that his kinsfolk had sailed on the lost vessel, had said the prayers of the dead for them.

The flesh that orthodox Jews may eat, and the manner in which it may be killed, is laid down in the Mosaic code; and the kosher butcher is a lay officer of the synagogue. The senior Weber was such a schechter, paid at so much a head for the fish, fowl and flesh he prepared. As many as two hundred chickens were dressed in a day in the Weber basement. Rats, attracted by the odors, overran the rooms. The children were taught to think of them as household pets, the usual dependents of any well-ordered ménage, and had been known to boast that they had twice as many rats as the most favored of their neighbors.

Around the corner and up the block, on the second floor of a walk-up tenement, there was another roll call at nightfall, not quite so long in the saying. Papa Schanfield, by occupation a tailor, direct from a Polish village only a few versts from the former Weber home, would call:

"Max? Rene? Wenny? Solly? Abraham? Nathan? Annie? Lew?"

And little Lew, who was to drop the Schan from before his family name, and add an *s*, would pipe, "Papa, I'm here." Like his future partner, he had been born after his parents had crossed the Atlantic.

Papa Schanfield made twenty-five dollars a week some weeks. Below Fourteenth Street that was comparative opulence. Three rooms the Schanfields luxuriated in, and thought of Poland without regrets.

The Bowery then was the Bowery, from the Civil War to the 1890's a sanctuary for the devil and his work, linked in the mouths of sailors with the Barbary Coast of old San Francisco, and with Port Said. New York, after the lapse of a generation, inclines to think of it romantically. The glamor of its defiant diabolism is remembered, its vicious realities forgotten or sentimentalized. Its neighborhood shunned by the better class of trade, rents were cheap in its side streets, and the poor crept in to make a witches' caldron of bitter struggle and prosperous vice.

Out of this sink, and using it as a springboard, came Weber and Fields and other men and women to contribute unvarying decency to the American stage, and the sober honesty of their private lives to American society. The stubborn resistance of orthodox Jewish family life to its environment, the product of two thousand years of oppression, served them better than they knew.

Might was right, and every boy was on his own. Quickness of wit and limb alike stood him in stead. And on the sidewalks of the Bowery and the flagstone yard of Public School No. 42, in Allen Street, first was joined the team that was to become one of the classic partnerships of our stage.

A partnership of nimble legs and nimble minds they used to advantage one Monday morning in the '70s—their first joint appearance their ransacked minds recall. Baths were had at public bathhouses. A nickel entitled one to a towel and locker. Otherwise you stood in line and were herded through somewhat in the manner of cattle being dipped at a quarantine station.

With five other boys, young Joe Weber had set out for the nearest bathhouse before breakfast this Monday morning, a two-cent piece, then a current coin, tied in the tail of his shirt against the appetite a public-bath scrubbing made certain.

In the bath he lost his crowd and emerged alone, shining, hungry, in enemy territory, and two cents in his fist. As such, he was a lawful prize for the first eye to see him, and he knew it well.

Before such an eye could rest upon him, he converted the two-cent piece into a bolivar cake—a sandwich of gingerbread and coconut cake—at a street stand before him, and crammed the entire cake into his mouth. Nor too soon, for privateers bore down on him from all quarters and seized him. His mouth and throat crowded with dry cake, he could only wave his arms in frantic gestures. One of his boarders jumped to conclusions.

"Deaf and dumb!" he exclaimed. "Better leave him be. Them deaf and dummies are awful strong. If they hit you and kill you, they don't do nothing to them."

One of the enemy wrote on the sidewalk with a stub of chalk, "How long you been deaf and dumb?"

Weber borrowed the chalk and wrote, "All my life."

This distinction gave him a pass through the lines. When he had put a sporting distance between him and the enemy, the cake now swallowed, Weber spoke—spoke in jeers and insults.

"Get 'im!" shrieked the enemy in many voices.

Their cries and the rush of their flying feet rose above the clatter of horse cars and trucks. Running beside him, Weber became aware of a strange boy. With something like manslaughter as the penalty of failure, the two, after three hard-pressed blocks, just won into the Weber basement, where the stranger explained that he was an earlier victim of the privateersmen, having surrendered a ginger cake. His name, he said, was Lew Schanfield.

With no pastures, weedy lots or back yards in which to expand, the boy life of the East Side, fighting and frolicking in the streets, had a tendency to dilate upward in handsprings, cart wheels and primary acrobatics. With that alert opportunism of the slums, that thirst for elbow room in life, the more gifted youngsters saw there was a market for such wares and sought to turn them into cash. To-day, and much more so half a century ago, a child in the ghetto was expected to earn part of his keep. If it might be earned by posturing for the public's applause instead of by drudgery, so much the better. Parents were interested in the sum, not the source.

Hardly were these two putting one foot before another with any surety before they were performing flip-flops. At fifty-five, Fields still is doing it. He turned them in his latest show this year. Of the apprentices in the Allen Street school yard, Paul Salvin, former owner of the Palais Royal and other Broadway cabarets, was the furthest advanced.

As Master Paul, he already had been seen on Bowery stages; and as the owner of the only pair of clogs—made to order at a cost of three dollars—in the neighborhood, he was the monarch of a court of urchins anxious to follow in his steps. Francis Wilson, James T. Powers and other lads whose names later were to shine on billboards were of this court. An adjoining street housed Arthur and Jennie Dunn, a child team of some small experience.

In cellars, the haylofts of livery stables, and on a vacant lot in what then was known as Little Twelfth Street, the hopeful talent of the streets, led and bullied by Master Paul and the Dunn brother and sister, played theater and practiced ground-and-lofty tumbling, charging as much as two cents and as little as one pin. Other children in ten thousand other American communities were playing the same game no doubt, and grew up to earn livings everywhere but on the stage. Play for them was pure pretense. On the East Side play and reality were only one station apart. Again, the sources of the American theater were as near at hand as the courthouse to the youth of Greensboro, North Carolina, and one did not have to run away with a circus or a Tom show or borrow money to attend a dramatic school, in order to smell grease paint.

Ten cents was a respectable sum, better known to hearsay than to possession. Dimes were not given away either by parents or by benevolent old gentlemen. They were earned, won in crap games or by pitching pennies at a crack. Among the followers of Master Paul was one whose pockets never lacked a jingle. He had been known to show two and even three dollars, sums that seemed to merit the notice of the police. He made the money, he said, selling gingersnaps on Sundays in One Hundred and Twenty-ninth Street in Harlem. Joe and Lew shadowed him for two days until they learned where and at what terms he bought and sold his cakes. Borrowing thirty-five cents each from their fathers by describing this business opportunity, they walked the five or six miles to Harlem, with its peculiar susceptibility to ginger snaps, and cleared $1.30 between them the first Sunday. They repeated the following Sabbath, though tempted away from business every time the One Hundred and Twenty-ninth Street drawbridge opened for a passing tug and offered a free and novel ride. The senior Weber and Fields met and congratulated each other on their sons.

The third Sunday Weber perfected an imitation of a tongue-tied boy trying to say, "Please buy my gingersnaps," which promised to move the heart of every woman who passed. It was especially designed for ladies on the arms of their Sunday escorts, and it had not failed in three try-outs, when a heavy rainstorm broke. Before they could reach shelter, their gingersnaps were a sodden lump. Afraid to go home without even the original capital, they loitered back toward the Bowery afoot. All boys knew that a coin was to be found now and then in the street-car tracks, dropped by conductor or passenger. The story sounds unlikely, but it is a fact that by gluing their eyes to the tracks, they found almost a dollar in pennies, nickels and dimes in the path of the horse cars from Harlem to the City Hall. But Harlem had to get its gingersnaps elsewhere thereafter.

The rare dime that did not go toward feeding and clothing the families took them to the gallery of the Bowery Theater, now the Thalia, and one of the few New York theaters of half a century ago still in use. Ten cents' worth included a comedy, a drama, a pantomime and three or four specialty acts. Theater hours have shrunk now from eight-thirty or eight-forty-five to ten-forty-five or eleven o'clock. Then the curtain rose sharply at eight o'clock, not to fall finally until half an hour past midnight. To get a seat in the front rows meant gulping supper and dashing off to the gallery entrance to stand in line for an hour before the doors opened.

There are no galleries in New York theaters less than ten years old. The audiences have gone to the movies, and architects design only two floors. In the pre-Hollywood day, however, the gallery was the pulse of the popular stage. Actors played to the gallery literally, not figuratively. And the nigger heaven, as it was known in the West and South, voiced its likes and its antipathies just as the spirit moved it. It hissed and jeered the villain, shouted encouragement to the put-upon hero, guffawed and stamped at the clowning of the low comedian when it approved and stopped the show when it didn't.

A bouncer, armed with a rattan cane for boys and brass knucks, more than likely, for the older gods of the gallery, censored its comments. When he, in his own wisdom, thought that there had been enough of whistling and cat-calling, he would rap for order. The wise heard and obeyed. The foolish were snatched from their benches and whaled with the rattan. Fields has a habit of rubbing his legs reflectively when he describes the bouncer.

New shoes oppressed young Lew's feet one such winter night in the Bowery Theater. Off came the shoes. That was characteristic of the gallery; so was the sequel. In his pop-eyed absorption in the alarming fortunes of the harassed heroine of "Escaped from Sing," he forgot the shoes. When he reached for them at the final curtain they were gone. The boy had to walk home in his stockings, and caught both a cold and a licking.

The year was 1876 and the dollar was large in American pockets. It came hard and bought much. The whistles blew at seven A.M., and blew again at seven P.M. Store's opened before eight o'clock and closed after six, or as late as trade offered. Only bankers and brokers went to work as late as nine o'clock, and business men did not give two hours to their lunch and then telephone the office that they could be found at the golf club. The American home was something more than a dormitory, and the tired business man was tired. Woman's place was in that home, and she spent such money as her menfolk gave her.

The Centennial was on in Philadelphia, Grant was President, Colorado was the newest star in the blue field, and Moody and Sankey were evangelizing the land. The electric light was flickering its first commercial flutters, the telephone had not yet dispersed the armies of messenger boys, and young men were learning to write on the typewriter. The Brooklyn Theater had recently caught fire during a performance of "The Two Orphans," and two hundred and eighty persons had died in its ruins, and in New York the Rialto lay on and below Fourteenth Street.

New York is a world metropolis now, and a year-round playground attracting an average of fifty thousand visitors a day. These visitors are the mainstay of the city's first-class theaters. Fifty years ago New York was merely the largest of American cities, had few transients and supported its own theaters. Fourteenth Street was a boundary line as definite as the Hudson. Those who lived below it rarely crossed over. Above was another city that appeared to mock their clothes, their speech and their manners. Something of the same feeling exists below Fourteenth Street still, but now those teeming square miles are largely a foreign quarter, little affecting or affected by the rest of the city.

The growth of the transients pulled the theaters northward and away from the masses, until now the Broadway that typifies New York to the rest of America is more familiar to Denver and Birmingham than to several million who live only five cents away.

On a specimen night in 1876 a theater-goer might have chosen between Fanny Davenport, Charles Coghlan and Georgie Drew in the "School for Scandal" at Daly's Fifth Avenue; Edwin Booth as Richard II at the Lyceum; Lawrence Barrett as Lear at Booth's; Clara Morris and James O'Neill, father of Eugene O'Neill, in "Miss Multon," a forgotten drama, at the Union Square; Lotta as Musette at the Park; Dion Boucicault in "The Shaughraun" at Wallack's.

Or for another taste, there was cheap and violent melodrama to be had at the Grand Opera House, pride of Jim Fisk; Barnum's Circus at Gilmore's Gardens; variety at Tony Pastor's, with Fields and Hoey on the bill; variety at three or four other houses, including the Comique, where Harrigan and Hart were asking, "Are You There, Moriarty?"; burlesque of a low order at three, minstrelsy at two, a magician at Heller's. An orchestra played at the new aquarium in Broadway at Thirty-sixth Street, and Professor Cromwell gave magic-lantern slides of the Philadelphia Exposition, together with instructive comments, at the Masonic Temple.

Not a note of music in the first half of this list except "Musette." Light opera—"Giroflé-Girofla," "Wang," "Robin Hood," "Ermine," and the *bouffes* of Gilbert and Sullivan—had not yet wedded with burlesque to parent musical comedy. Nor had H. R. Jacobs yet originated his ten-twenty-thirty houses, and the Stair & Havlin circuit brought cheap and moderately good drama to the multitudes.

But no New Yorker needed to be told that this did not exhaust the evening's possibilities. Scattered about the city somewhat as the cheaper movie houses of our day, usually in converted storerooms, were half a hundred dime museums. From noon until midnight shillabers and barkers pleaded with all who passed in custody of ten cents to step in, be edified, electrified, instructed and amused; and perhaps as many heeded day by day as entered the doors of all the more pretentious theaters combined.

The museums varied little. The fronts were plastered with great crude-colored canvases, highly romantic conceptions of the wonders to be seen within. The entrances were crowded with lesser marvels to arrest the eye and stir the appetite. Stuffed mermaids; stuffed flying fish; the embalmed form of the very rat tamed and trained in his prison cell by Guiteau, the assassin of Garfield; the half-woman illusion; the war club that killed Captain Cook; a complete suit of clothing cunningly contrived of blown glass; electric battery shockers, then new; blood testers, fortune tellers, phrenologists, and the horse with the snake in his eye. Inside, a fat woman, a bearded lady, a giant, a dwarf, a living skeleton, a dog-faced boy, an India-rubber man and a snake charmer. The formula has passed down almost unchanged in the circus side show, where only Zuleika the Oriental Dancer, a novelty of the Chicago World's Fair, is new. Having stared and been stared at, bought a photograph of the bearded lady from that lady's own hands and earned a growl from the dog-faced boy, the spectator's attention was invited to the splendors that for a merely nominal sum, an additional nickel, would be unfolded in the theater, in the back room or on the second floor. At the signal of the ballyhoo, a Punch and Judy would start its shrill clamor inside the second barrier, the shillabers would crowd about the ticket seller, tendering imaginary nickels, the barkers would shout and the crowd would be stampeded into parting with an extra five cents.

These splendors proved to be a variety show, a haphazard mixture of amateur and smallest-time acts.

A sorry cradle for talent, it might be thought, but from the stages of the dime museums came Harry and John Kernell, Kelly the Rolling-Mill Man, Jimmy and Bonny Thornton, Maggie Mitchell, Maggie Thome, James T. Powers, Sam Bernard, Peter F. Dailey, Joe Coyne, James F. Hoey—Young Mule—Francis Wilson, and a long line of others whose names have not yet lost their magic.

This was the theater of America to the first-generation immigrant from non-English-speaking lands. His unfamiliarity with the language kept him away from the more pretentious entertainments. Here he was on a par with all others, his eyes supplying whatever he missed of the lecturer's harangue. And with the more unsophisticated of the native born and the Irish, he provided the museums with a large and sure public.

This lowliest and most frugal of the stages was the obvious goal of two such calcium-blinded young urchins as Weber and Fields; obvious to Joe and Lew, not so patent to the managers of the museums, who laughed at their nine-year-old presumptions.

Among the other young passengers bound from the Bowery for the same destination were the Standard Four. The Standard Four never had been seen on any stage, and it was, just now, only three—the Rosin twin brothers and Joe Fields, who was no kith or kin of Lew's.

Lew, at the moment, was tending a street soda-water fountain for a man named Gump, half a glass for one cent, a full glass for two cents, and three cents for a glass with cream in it, cream being an East Grand Street trade name for milk. The first ten days Fields drank glass and glass for every order he served, and drank alone when business was dull. Thereafter he became a teetotaler, one who shudders yet when he passes a soda fountain. Joe was at work in a cigarette factory.

While Lew, all unknowing, went on dispensing penny sodas, Weber got himself elected the fourth of the Standard. Joe Fields knew one trick dance step which he taught Weber. When Fields awoke three days later he abandoned Mr. Gump's strawberry and vanilla syrups and promised the thirty-five cents of wages due him to Joe Fields if he would teach him the same step.

The Standard Four promptly threw Weber out and named Lew Fields in his stead. Weber and Joe Fields fought; and though Weber won a moral victory, he didn't get back into the Standard's fold. But Lew went the same way within a week. A boy known as Master Williams, who had made two or three professional appearances, offered to join the Standard, and the team of Weber and Fields was reunited, free agents both, and destined, it happened, to reach the stage before the others.

Among the various youths who called at the Weber home in homage to the older daughters was one who was high in the Elks Serenaders Social Club, whose balls and entertainments in the Turn Hall in East Fourth Street were social events in the district. Feminine pressure led the young man to introduce Joe and Lew to the chairman of the entertainment committee as a promising young black-face acrobatic song-and-dance team, and brought their first engagement. Their pay was two complimentary tickets.

At six o'clock of the momentous night Mamma Schanfield, Mamma Weber, Lew and Joe appeared at the Turn Hall, an hour in advance of the first stage hand. Mrs. Schanfield and Mrs. Weber chose the two front-row seats nearest the stage door and settled down in pleased anticipation. The latter carried an old-fashioned bouquet with a tin-foil handle and a white-paper-scalloped border.

Their sons went backstage to prepare. Knowing nothing of make-up, they had begged two lumps of charcoal from a peddler. They crushed the charcoal and tried to smear it on their faces. It left only a faint soot. Water was added, producing a tear-and-coal-dust effect. An hour's untiring effort left them looking unquestionably dirty, but unmistakably Aryan. There were other hours until they were to go on. Nervous thirst set in and they drank all the water in the fire buckets.

At last a shout of "You kids are next!" and they were shoved onstage. They had agreed beforehand to make their entrance backward that they might be the less confused by the lights and the audience. This they remembered; but without waiting for their music cue, they burst into song badly off key. They danced where they should have sung, sang where they should have danced. The orchestra attempted to overtake them, but never quite caught up. At one point the act called for acrobatics in time with the music, Joe to hold his fingers locked in the familiar alley-up gesture, Fields to vault lightly into the hands and be somersaulted in the air. They missed the count, Fields failed to turn completely over and landed on his head with a force that stirred a cloud of dust from the stage planks. Dazed, he bounced up again and danced frantically, but to no purpose.

The curtain fell suddenly and the boys were yanked off demanding explanations. A stage hand with compassion, a sense of humor and a poker face told them that the curtain man, in his breathless interest in their act, had let the ropes slip through his hands.

"It's too late to do anything about it now," he added; "but you kids have a great act. Come around and see me sometime and I'll introduce you to Tony Pastor." The reader of 1924 may not know—but the boys did—that Tony Pastor was then the great man of the variety stage.

Photo 3. Tony Pastor, c. 1880. National Portrait Gallery, Smithsonian Institution; gift of Francis A. DiMauro.

They washed the charcoal smears from their faces and joined their mothers.

"Why," Mrs. Weber wanted to know, "did the curtain come down so quick? I didn't get time to throw the bouquet to you."

She heard the stage hand's soothing version and glowed.

The theatricals over, the chairs were cleared away and dancing began. Mothers and sons promenaded the floor, pridefully acknowledging all salutes. Joe and Lew held the bouquet in turn, amicably at first, then to be bitten for the first time by the serpent of professional jealousy.

"Give it to me!" shrilled Joe. "You've held it long enough. Didn't my mother bring it?"

"She brought it for me as much as for you," Lew protested.

Their partnership might have withered and died with the bouquet had not the jocular stage hand, no longer in overalls, danced their way in the throes of a schottish. They halted him.

"Say," they demanded, "what's the best time to find Tony Pastor?"

"Let me see—he pretended to ponder—"I should say about seven o'clock in the morning." And he resumed his schottish with a heavy wink for his partner.

"I'll be at your house at 6:30 to-morrow morning," Lew decided on the instant, and led his mother homeward.

Tony Pastor's New Theater stood at 587 Broadway, near Prince Street. At seven the next morning two boys posted themselves in front of the deserted theater and asked every white male that passed if he were Mr. Tony Pastor. Four hours later the interrogation still was going on, unmindful of rebuff or insult. The question was put for the thousand and second time.

"Yes," was the answer, and the answerer kept on into the lobby, where they overtook him.

"What can I do for you?" asked the great Tony.

"We're actors and we want to go to work," they shouted in unison, and began forthwith to turn flip-flaps the length of the lobby.

Antonio Pastor tossed them a chuckle.

"Come and see me again in four or five years," he said as he turned away.

Well, if Tony Pastor didn't know talent when it was thrust under his nose, there were other theaters. The rest of that day they tramped the streets between City Hall and Twenty-third, and at every theater and museum they showed their flip-flap repertoire and bespoke an opportunity. At nightfall they staggered back to East Broadway and fell asleep over their suppers.

The attack was resumed at dawn. In Chatham Square a new museum was being opened in quarters vacated by a secondhand clothing shop. The manager, Morris by name, was new to the business, and poorly armed to defend himself against the assault the two launched at him. He watched their cart wheels dubiously.

"I guess you boys will do," he admitted finally and with no enthusiasm. "But three dollars a week each is all I can pay."

If he hoped to escape them in that fashion he was an amateur hoper. When the new Chatham Square Museum opened Weber and Fields opened with it. They were nine years old. The Turn Hall stage hand's jest had turned sour and fermented. It would take more success than this to turn their heads. Weber's feet were so firmly on the ground that he kept an anchor to windward and stayed on his cigarette-factory job.

"You do the act by yourself in the afternoon," he suggested to Fields, "and I'll slip around as soon as the factory quits work."

As their act called for an entrance, singing "Here we are, a jolly pair," Weber's absence promised to be a strain on the imagination of the audiences. Fields solved the dilemma ingeniously by adopting a stray kitten and leading it onstage by a long ribbon at the afternoon shows. In the bustle of opening the new house, the manager was several days in learning that he was not getting all his three dollars a week called for.

Weber was sent for.

"Are you working for me, or aren't you?" The manager was indignant.

"Well, if I was sure it was a steady job——" Joe temporized.

"Steady for the little fellow, anyway, who's been doing the work, and who gets four-fifty this week to your dollar and a half," was the reply; "and steady for you if you behave yourself."

With that assurance, Joe returned to the cigarette factory to resign. Nothing so drab and unimaginative as merely asking for his pay was in his mind. Going straight to his bench, he lit a cigarette with elaborate ostentation. Smoking, he knew, was expressly forbidden. A hushed silence at this effrontery, a silence broken by the foreman's roar. The rebel breathed a smoke ring in the foreman's direction and flicked a feather of ash with an insolent finger.

"Are you addressing me?" he inquired in the disdainful accent commonly used by the hero on the villain at the Bowery.

He was not mistaken. The foreman indubitably was addressing him. Joe waved the waspish words aside with a splendid gesture.

"Give your job," he declaimed, "to your mother-in-law's half sister. I resign. I now am an actor." He turned to Joey Sand, a schoolmate who worked at the next bench. "Boy," he ordered, "bring my wages down to the Chatham Square Museum."

He reached the door unassaulted before the astounded foreman could summon his wits.

Eight to nine shows a day, as many runs as a program picture gets in a continuous movie house, was the order of the day at the Chatham Square; and when the two were not onstage performing, they were offstage hammering away at new steps, new gags and new gymnastics. The morning was not far off when they were to report at the museum to find the doors closed and its brief career ended. It had served its purpose in the career of Messrs. Weber and Fields, though that comforting reflection may not have occurred to the bereaved manager. Rough-and-ready professionals of four weeks' continuous experience they were now, no longer backing onstage to escape the paralyzing eye of an audience.

Sauntering placidly along the Bowery, they came to No. 298, the abode of the Globe Museum, and recognized in the porter a former friend of the Chatham Square. Were any actors needed?

"Ask him," said the porter, jerking a thumb at a man leaning negligently against the lobby wall, one hand in the front of a chinchilla overcoat. It took more assurance than they could command at once to address a being in so royal a garment, and they fell to studying the lobby posters until their pulses should recover, one eye each on the chinchilla lest it vanish. It remained stationary even when they approached, leaning against each other for support.

The owner and occupant of the chinchilla, they were to learn, was George Middleton, afterwards of Kohl and Middleton, first proprietors of a string of museums in the West, later important factors in vaudeville. Years afterwards, Middleton confided in them that the eye-filling overcoat concealed a linen summer suit, the worse for wear, in which he had arrived from a circus the week before.

Middleton turned them over to the stage manager, Frank Hoffman, who still lives.

"Let's see what you can do," he commanded.

The two rushed home, gathered up their homemade costumes and dashed back to the Globe, there to find that they had forgotten their burnt cork. Another performer on the bill offered to lend them a supply of lampblack.

The boys thanked him feelingly, while the onlookers grinned. A veteran trouper, on the down grade, interfered.

"Give the kids a chance," he growled. "They're trying to get on, and we may be glad to get a job from them some day."

He offered them his burnt cork and explained that lampblack would not come off for days. They went through their act furiously and finished in a spray of perspiration.

"Uh-huh," Hoffman grunted. "I can't pay you much."

"How much ?" they shouted, as if a rehearsed line.

"All I could pay you"—he paused and studied a finger nail—"is twenty-five-dollars a week for the act."

Lew burst into tears. Joe thought quickly. Pretending to comfort his partner, he put an arm around him and said with heavy unction, "That's all right, Lew. We'll take it until Tony Pastor is ready for us."

One act, little varied, had served them week by week at the Chatham Square; but the Globe, they found, required a complete change every two weeks. Their second fortnight they put burnt cork aside and burst upon a Bowery audience in Little Lord Fauntleroy suits of velvet to ornament a dance-and-paper-tearing turn known to the trade as a neat.

"Ladies and gentlemen," Weber would announce, "your attention is invited to our difficult achievement of performing three separate and distinct feats at one and the same time—dancing in unison, keeping time to the music and tearing these sheets of paper in in-trick-ate designs."

At the final crash of the tin-panny piano, pummeled by a bored youth with a cigarette drooping from the northeast corner of his mouth, and the concluding pat of their feet, the paper would be unfolded with a snap in its completed design. Old newspapers sufficed the first week. They cost nothing.

The second week virgin-white letter sheets from a stationery shop across the street were scattered prodigally on the Globe's stage. The act was looking up in the world.

The sunshine of their success was interrupted by the shadow of their old enemy, Joe Fields, once of the Standard Four, at the stage door. With a partner named Furman, he asked for a try-out, went through a German comedy skit and was engaged—to the chagrin of Joe and Lew. The house was packed with relatives and friends of Fields and Furman at the Monday matinée when they opened, with results the reverse of the intended. The familiar faces frightened instead of reassuring them; they lost their heads, as Weber and Fields had at their Turn Hall début, and flopped badly. The curtain was dropped on them and the act refused.

Joe and Lew were telling the stage manager that they could "do a better Dutch act than that" before the other pair were well out of the stage door.

"I never knew you kids had a Dutch number," Hoffman said in surprise.

"Sure!" they chorused.

"Could you go on with it to-morrow?"

"Sure!"

"Trot it out then," Hoffman agreed.

The truth was that they had no German act, and never had thought of one until they watched Fields and Furman's failure from the wings.

"But we 'yessed' them all in those days," Weber explains. "Had we been asked if we could do Antony and Cleopatra or Uncle Tom and Little Eva, our answer would have been the same. We strove to please. 'Yes' took no more breath than 'no' and had a lot more possibilities."

On this overnight order the youngsters threw together a patchwork of knock-about nonsense that grew eventually into the Weber & Fields of tradition. The reader will recall the tall, thin Fields and the short, dumpy Weber of the turn in its final development. Actually, they were much of a size in 1877, Weber a shade the taller.

An old suit of his father's, padded out with pillows from the family beds, and built-up shoes for Fields, formed the ground-work of the illusion. It was completed by Harry Seamon, now of Hurtig and Seamon, burlesque producers, then the son of a neighboring house painter. Seamon borrowed all his father's working equipment except his ladders and applied a make-up that threatened never to come off. The German accent came easily to boys from homes in which Yiddish, a corruption of German, was spoken. It was crude and juvenile, but the none too critical Globe audiences laughed. The management asked nothing more.

Toward the end of their sixth week at the Globe George Middleton asked them if they cared to go on the road. He could book them in Paterson, New Jersey, at six dollars a week and expenses. The word went around in East Broadway that two of their own were going "out West." A papier-mâché trunk, straps painted on it as trees are painted on a back drop, was bought that afternoon and packed with all the spare clothing of the two households. This did not crowd the trunk. In two kitchens special dishes were baked and roasted. For three days the rest *of* the Weber and the Schanfield families ate when and what they might, and wore such clothing as was left to them.

The day came. The train was due to depart at 11:30 A.M. At eight o'clock they were at the station in Hoboken, sitting on their papier-mâché trunk, holding two huge parcels of food and surrounded by excited relatives. Tears and cheers as the wheels turned. In the day coach two boys whose hearts pounded. Others might trust their trunks with the baggage man. Theirs stayed in the aisle alongside, despite the protests of the train crew to the contrary.

They flattened their noses against the windows to peer at the Jersey meadows and the Orange hills in the distance. The Great Plains and the Rocky Mountains, given a dash of imagination. Had Sioux and Comanches ridden Indian file through the rank grass, and herds of migrating buffalo blocked the Erie tracks, there were two passengers who would have believed their eyes. Just how far west Paterson lay they had not thought to ask.

In the ecstasy of that morning's dawn they had been too nervous more than to peck at their breakfasts. Now the knowledge of food in the luggage rack overhead intruded. The packages were opened. In the midst of their first drumstick a brakeman poked his head in the door and shouted, "Paterson! Paterson! This station is Paterson!"

Was this some other Paterson, or was the brakeman a practical joker? Neither, apparently, for someone was saying, "Come on, you kids; here we are." Bundling the food together in one motion, each grabbed an end of the trunk and followed the other performers down the aisle, through the station, and afoot to the Passaic House, a typical one-night-stand hotel.

The name and look of that third-rate hostelry is as vivid in their minds to-day as it was forty-five years ago. It was their first time away from home, their first hotel, their first train ride. A red-hot, pot-bellied, air-tight iron stove glowed in the center of the plank-floored room that was the lobby, ringed with wooden chairs, each convoyed by a chewing-tobacco box filled with dark-stained sand, serving as a cuspidor.

After the last show of the night, the performers, freaks and all, gathered in the hotel barroom. Neither boy had any money. They never did; their pockets were as empty when they worked as when they loafed. Little or much, their wages went into the family exchequers with no deductions. Fields was partial to candy. Weber already was chewing and smoking. He still argues that the habit had nothing to do with his five-feet-four, pointing to a six-foot brother who did the same at a like age.

"And how much taller would the big brother have been if he hadn't?" Fields is in the habit of asking.

Fields had no candy and no prospect of getting any. Weber had one cigarette, soon smoked, but better prospects. There was no closed season on snipe shooting on the Bowery. Among the pipe and cigar smokers at the bar was a lone cigarette devotee, one of the nervous types who flip the weeds aside after inhaling three or four drafts. Standing close beside him, Weber saw the man turn to discard his cigarette. Instead of dropping it where the boy could salvage it, the smoker abstractedly opened the stove door and tossed it on the fire.

At this dismaying juncture the night clerk sang out that a boy was wanted to carry a message. Lew beat Joe to the desk and was bade in five minutes with a penny, one of those fat copper-nickel-alloy one-cent pieces looking something like a dime, with which the mint experimented for a while after the Civil War. A penny would buy two cigarettes, but Fields had earned it, and he voted for candy. Moreover, he had the penny. Two doors away was a notion shop with a case of cheap sweets. A girl in short dresses, her hair down her back, was in charge at the moment. The child had attended the museum earlier in the day with her mother, and flustered at recognizing in her customers two such romantic objects, she gave Fields nine cents change for his white penny. Fifty-fifty was the unwavering rule of the partnership, but nine cents was an uneven sum. Lew gave Joe four cents and kept the Shubert end himself.

The Buffalo Bill Wild West Show, then in its inception, was billed for Paterson on Saturday, and the advance man had arranged for part of the troupe to be housed at the Passaic House on Friday night. To accommodate them it would be necessary to persuade the museum performers to find other beds for one night. Some ingenuity was needed. The plot used on the boys was immediately effective.

"I've been worrying all day what to do with you lads on Friday night," the clerk told them on Wednesday. "The house is going to be full of Indians, and Indians, they tell me, are specially partial to boys' scalps. I hope nothing happens. Of course I could send you over to a friend of mine who's got an extra bed."

They begged him to speak to his friend at once. On Friday night the clerk in person escorted them to their temporary lodgings and introduced them to the owner as Mr. Weber and Mr. Fields, to the gratification of the two misters. The owner led them by light of a tallow candle to a garret, pointed out the bed and left them in utter darkness.

It was a blustery, wintry night, with snow and sleet falling. The window sashes rattled in the warped frames, the sleet clicked on the panes and the weary timbers of the old house groaned and sighed. The two boys clutched at each other under the covers, their hearts knocking on their ribs and their ears straining for each new noise. It may have been half an hour that they held out—no longer. Fleeing from the garret, down the rickety steps, and out into the shivering night, carrying most of their clothing, they burst into the Passaic House as if pursued by the devil himself. There were worse fates in their imaginations than Indian tortures.

On the lobby floor, circled about the stove, most of the museum troupers slept, and the night clerk rustled two additional blankets. The boys missed the gaunt and familiar outlines of Doctor Brandy, the living skeleton, from among the sleepers. The doctor, it happened, was reclining comfortably on a shelf of the linen closet. He had roused at their coming in, and heard their trembling tale. Waiting until the boys had settled in their blankets, he demanded in a voice from far down in his chest, "Where are those two papooses ?"

The two froze in their blankets.

"Indians!" Lew whispered hoarsely.

"I smell the blood of two palefaces," the voice insisted. "You can't fool me, old Chief Horsetail!"

At the convulsive movements under the blankets, the living skeleton, unable to contain himself longer, broke into a shrill cackle that, quite beyond his intention, sounded like nothing ever heard before on land or sea, and froze the very marrow of their bones. But in the enjoyment of his own joke the doctor rolled off his shelf and exposed the hoax.

The traveled ten-year-olds returned to New York to a family welcome worthy of a Livingstone back from the sources of the Nile, and found an engagement at a museum headlining Jo-Jo the Dog-faced Boy. Jo-Jo, forerunner of seven hundred other dog-faced boys, was a fresh importation from Europe. History does not record who or what the original Jo-Jo really was, nor by whom invented; but he was a happy inspiration second only to Barnum's Tom Thumb, White Elephant and Siamese Twins.

New York showed such an interest in this phenomenon that the museum managed to crowd twenty-three shows into each day. Audiences found themselves back on the sidewalk before their dimes had lost the warmth of the fingers that tendered them, and Joe and Lew and their fellows backstage dared not step into the alley for a smoke for fear of missing their next cue.

In the midst of this success Jo-Jo was called back to Europe to fulfill contracts. Weber and Fields were unprepared to find him on the bill with them again in Jersey City two weeks later. It was the true, the only Jo-Jo, they agreed after close scrutiny. He came onstage with the same lecturer as before, his head rocking, eyes rolling and jowls slathering, while the lecturer described how he had been captured at great expense of life, limb and money in the wilds of Some-thing-or-Other. The lecture concluded, Jo-Jo would bark savagely or bay mournfully, as the spirit moved him.

But there was one sceptic backstage—Bob Knowles, of a team called Martin and Knowles. They, too, had played with Jo-Jo two weeks previously; and Knowles had noticed at the time that an animal-call imitator, also on the bill, never took his eyes off Jo-Jo. Knowles drew his own conclusions. Now, at Jo-Jo's every appearance he would station himself in the nearest wing and comment in a voice too low to reach the audience, but perfectly audible to the dog-faced one:

"I know you, you bleeding English animal imitator," he would begin. "I'd know that bark of yours in a cemetery in Cape Town in the dark of the moon. Calling yourself a dog-faced boy, are you—and taking honest folks' money? Ain't you ashamed of yourself, you lime-juice humbug you? You're no more a dog-faced boy, you ugly fraud, than I'm the town hall of Jersey City. Where did you get that mop of hair, anyway? Come on now and tell the truth for once in your swindling life. How do you think your old mother would like to see her son frothing at the mouth and palming himself off as a cross between an ape and a laughing hyena for a few dirty dimes? Snarl for the nice ladies and gentlemen, you whelp!"

The game went on all week. The sceptic lay awake at night devising new insults and sly sallies intended to provoke Jo-Jo either to laugh or fight, but the hairy hide of the dog-faced boy turned indignity as a duck's back sheds water. Jo-Jo spoke only in barks and growls, nor turned his head toward the wings. Knowles began to be regarded backstage as slightly touched, a man with an obsession.

When he had growled his last acknowledgment of Jersey City's approval on Saturday night, Jo-Jo jerked off his wig and was revealed as the animal imitator Knowles had said he was all along.

"You nearly got a snicker out of me Thursday night, Bob, when you called me Ba-Ba the Mutton-faced Lizard," he acknowledged, "and I choked when you pulled that one about the sausage."

Arm in arm, Knowles and the dog-faced one vanished between two swinging doors across the street.

For six years Masters Weber and Fields went the rounds of the New York museums, with an occasional date out of town and an infrequent engagement on the better-paying variety stages. They did not average twenty weeks' work a season, and odd jobs were needful at times to weather the long gaps between engagements.

The booking agent, now the middleman between actor and manager, like prohibition and the flapper, had not been invented. Out-of-town engagements were written for, usually on stationery borrowed from the writing room of the Fifth Avenue Hotel. The boys had a regular letter-writing schedule. Uncle Billy Harris, proprietor of the Howard Athenaeum in Boston, and father of Henry B. Harris, who was lost on the Titanic, were on their list. Uncle Billy's invariable answer was a post card reading, "Sorry. Nothing open." To vary the monotony, they sent Uncle Billy a post card one day. It read:

"Sorry. Can't accept engagement. Booked solid. Masters Weber and Fields."

Wherever work offered they accepted. Harry Hill ran a resort at the corner of Houston and Crosby Streets of which men talked in barber shops and smoking rooms the country over. It really was a saloon with amusements—the cabaret in its earliest form. Anyone who bought a drink was welcome, and the keys had been thrown away years before. After even the Bowery had gone to bed, Hill's place remained open to catch the farmers and drovers coming in from Jersey and Long Island before dawn. Hill had trained John L. Sullivan for one of his bare-fisted battles and had a pugilistic stable across the East River in Astoria.

This was no atmosphere, admittedly, for two adolescent boys; but too nice a discrimination was no part of getting ahead in the popular theater. Theirs not to reason why, but to perform their three specialties a night and mind their own business. After all, the street-car company did not demand a certificate of character from its passengers, nor the city refuse to pipe water into a questionable address.

Their program at Hill's consisted of the Irish song-and-dance-number, a wrestling burlesque and a boxing burlesque. The business of the latter necessitated Weber's taking considerable punishment.

"Why don't you stop some of those blows?" a voice inquired one night. Weber turned his head.

"None of them's passed me so far," he rejoined.

The late Harry Kernell thought the answer so apt that he used it as a gag for years after.

The free-for-alls at Coney Island, where they found intermittent work in the summer, were patterned after Hill's place. Coney Island was largely sand, a few sketchy bathhouses, saloons and concert halls. For two dollars a day and five beer checks each, Weber and Fields worked from ten A.M. until midnight at Duffy's and other Coney resorts. The beer checks were sold to waiters at the standard price of fifteen cents for five, bringing the team's weekly income up to $30.10.

Duffy owned three race horses, which he ran on Long Island tracks. When one won, the saloon closed early, but a losing race meant staying open until midnight or later that he might get back part of his money from the bookmakers and track followers. Coney being a slow and costly train or boat ride from Manhattan, the boys lived at the shore. To bed after midnight, they would rise with the dawn to watch the horses being exercised on the Brighton Beach track. Inevitably, they fell victims to a stable-boy tout who promised a killing. Holding out their entire weekly wage, which was supposed to be sent home with deductions only for board and lodging, they gave the tout thirty dollars to lay on the good thing. The horse lost, of course, but it developed that the stable boy had not even bothered to bet the money. Joe and Lew took their troubles to Duffy.

"Do you think you could lick this boy?" Duffy suggested. Joe thought it likely that he could whip John L. Sullivan for thirty dollars. "I'll get the kid over here," Duffy planned. "When he comes in you jump him, and if you lick him I'll see that you get your thirty dollars." A grudge fight would be a tasty appetizer to the usual evening program of an amusement saloon. With any ferocity at all, it would be worth all of Duffy's thirty dollars, and more than likely the spectators would pay it themselves if the hat were passed. Weber supplied the ferocity. The battle was hot and bloody. Weber won, the barroom audience, as expected, made up the thirty-dollar purse and the Weber and Schanfield families went in ignorance of the bad bet.

Next door to Duffy's a man named Trebor opened a rival saloon and made overtures to Duffy's talent. When Weber and Fields told him Duffy was paying them two dollars a day and five beer checks each, Trebor offered three dollars and seven beer checks. They accepted. Their act done at Duffy's they would step out the back door and in Trebor's back door. Duffy had no idea they were playing next door—Trebor assumed that they had quit Duffy's.

In the midst of an imitation of Harrigan & Hart singing "The Market on Saturday Night," and made up as two market women in clothes lent them by Mrs. Duffy, that lady's husband found them performing for his enemy. Someone had told Duffy, and he came down the aisle swinging a rawhide. The song never was finished. Joe and Lew made for the surf, wading out until each comber submerged them, and breathing between waves. Duffy turned back and tried to use the whip on Trebor. The contest was undecisive, but Weber and Fields were seen exclusively thereafter at Duffy's.

Duffy's place was built on stilts over the beach, and in their off moments the boys played in the sand underneath. The floor behind the bar was slatted as a drain for water and beer slops. As the two were throwing up the ramparts of a sand fort one night they caught the flash of a silver coin dropping through the slats. As they watched, another coin fell. A little heap of halves, quarters and dimes lay in the sand, and grew slowly. Looking up through the slats, they saw the cashier directly overhead. Before closing time there was five dollars in the pile. The sum was not guesswork. The boys had counted it—and pocketed it. From a hiding place later they saw the cashier scratching perplexedly in the sand. Talking it over in bed that night, they decided to tell Duffy on the morrow.

"Keep it for being honest," Duffy growled. "I'll take five dollars out of that cashier's hide, anyway."

There were laws in New York governing the appearance of children under sixteen on the stage. The state left their enforcement very largely to the semi-official activities of Elbridge T. Gerry and his Society for the Prevention of Cruelty to Children. Sooner or later, Masters Weber and Fields were certain to run afoul of the S. P. C. C. It came in their eleventh year.

Summoned before Judge Gerry, the senior Weber appeared with a Hebrew volume in which he said he had recorded the birth dates of all his children. He began reading from the right-hand corner of the page in Hebrew fashion, and came to a line which, he avowed, proved his Joseph to be sixteen years old last Passover. Gerry adjusted his spectacles and scanned the unintelligible passage, and having a sense of humor, he dismissed Weber.

But Fields's mother was without guile. Confused and frightened in the magisterial presence, she admitted that her Lew was but eleven. Lew was officially denied the freedom of the New York stage; and, without his partner, Joe was finished as effectually as if Elbridge T. Gerry had read Hebrew as readily as English.

When a New Yorker collides with the law he turns first to political influence. This phenomenon, it is understood, has been observed in forty-seven other states. Lew's father had a cousin who was a lawyer; and lawyers, as everyone knew, all were mixed up in politics. On being consulted, the lawyer cousin thought that, for a five-dollar fee, he could get a special dispensation from Mayor Grace. So the Webers and the Schanfields were mustered before his honor. That bluff old steamship magnate was moved at the spectacle of two beggared families denied the support of these sturdy sons, and signed a limited permit entitling Lew and Joe to sing one song three times a day at Worth's Museum on the Bowery at Hester Street.

When the lawyer cousin called for his five dollars the senior Fields protested that his son was earning only five dollars a week on the limited permit given him, that only an unlimited license was worth five dollars, and offered to compromise on two dollars paid in two weekly installments. The lawyer talked about suing.

"Would you, then, have his honor the mayor know how you lied?" Fields, Sr., asked. There was no suit.

Chapter II

"A Jolly Pair"

Breaking In and First Road Trips, Early 1880s

Here we are, a jolly pair,
With no troubles or care.
We are here once more
To make the people roar,
Before we go to the ball.

When first we landed over here
The people said we looked so queer;
But we leave that to you;
It's the best thing we can do.
We are going down to the fancy ball.

MASTERS WEBER AND FIELDS now were in their teens, with five years of song and dance in dime museums, variety theaters and beer gardens behind them. The words above, need it be said, were their own, the tune borrowed from something they once had heard. They first piped it in the cellars and livery lofts of East Broadway, tried to sing it at their Turn Hall debacle, made their entrance with it at their Chatham Square Museum professional debut.

Serviceable lyrics, those. For a black-face act, they sang, "Here we are, a colored pair"; for an Irish act, "Here we are, an Irish pair"; for a German number, "Here we are, a German pair." The rest of the words needed no alterations. They fit any figure, as did the second-hand suits in the Bowery schlockshops. The costumes and make-up were expected to carry the illusion. The Irish turn was decked out with green satin breeches, black velvet coats, green bow ties and green derbies. With this, they threw in a song that went, as nearly as they remember:

Success to the shamrock,
And soon may it be
Entwined with the violet
And the emblem of the free.

Ireland for the Irish.
May God give freedom to their isle,
Acushla Gall Machree.

What the last meant they did not know then, and have not learned since. And all the Acushlas in Erin and all the green in the spectrum could not conceal the flamboyantly Semitic cast of their faces. As a random shot one night at Miner's Bowery Theater, they put their hands over their noses as they sang, "Here we are, an Irish pair." The house howled, and no Jewish comedian from that day on has failed to use that gesture.

The German knockabout number they had devised overnight at the Globe Museum to humble their old enemy, Joe Fields, had been put aside to be used now and then in an emergency. They had little love for it; it left too many bruises. Their stock in trade continued to be the original black-face turn, and the Neat Irish Songs and Dances and Paper-Tearing; This Act Must be Seen to be Appreciated—as their billing read.

A standard and inexpensive kid act for any hard-pressed manager to fall back upon to round out a bill. They had won this measure of recognition, a certain feeling for the theater, a sense of ease with audiences, a little facility at give and take, and some mastery over their limbs and voices. These are the A B C's of the stage. But they had lost their momentum. Their song and dance was much the same act with which they had begun. Much smoother, make-up and costumes no longer amateurish, a bit of new business here and there; but instantly recognizable to anyone who had seen them in 1876 at the Globe. Old stuff, in other words.

They were at that critical point when the child actor is about to lose his childhood, and to discover coincidently that a little precocity was all the theatrical baggage he ever had. There are many notable actors and actresses on our stage who memorized lines before they did their letters, but they are a small company alongside the prodigies who walked out the stage door arm in arm with their youth; actors with a future become hat salesmen with a past.

The backwashes of the stage, too, are cluttered with the hulks of men and women who made their hit, then dropped their oars overboard. Get out your programs of fifteen years ago and call the roll. They will answer from the boarding houses of the Forties. To-morrow they will go the rounds of the booking offices again, peddling the "knockout that stopped the show in 1908," showing a book of press clippings that began to grow thin about 1912 and deploring the lowered standards of the day. Many of them had sweat for years to make that one big success; and having made it, sat down, while the theater went on. It is a spectacle familiar to other trades.

Weber and Fields had been out of work for months, and loafed the days away in the saloon that was a part of Miner's Bowery Theater, a sort of unofficial club for variety actors. The dues were paid over the bar and delinquent members were posted by being thrown out the door. As neither drank, they justified their presence by playing pool. Billiards was charged for by the hour, but pool went by the game at two and a half cents a cue. Long experiment had proved that rotation pool, with the last ball banked, could be made to last almost indefinitely. If either player had the ill luck to pocket a ball at which he was presumed to be shooting, the other was ready with a cry of "Scratch!" and the ball was returned to the spot. It isn't to be found in the sporting annuals, but Weber and Fields claim the American endurance record of three hours and sixteen minutes in pocketing fifteen balls on one of Mr. Miner's tables. This game actually never was finished, a billiard marker who had been watching out of the corner of his eye having declared a foul and stopped it.

The stage manager strolled through the barroom on a Friday night, saw the two at their endless pool playing and offered them twenty dollars to play the house the following week. They grabbed at it, but in a theater where fifty dollars for teams and thirty dollars for singles was standard pay, twenty dollars was a sorry price for a team, and their misgivings increased. They had sent in their stock Irish-songs-and-dances billing, but Lew suggested that it might be well to drag out the old German knockabout act and work it over for this engagement. It was so decided, and they toiled all Saturday and Sunday on the turn, practicing in a bedroom and taking fearful falls.

Sore and stiff, they reported at the theater on Monday morning to find that the show was the Ada Richman burlesque, one of the first American burlesque troupes, and the only one then traveling. The bill consisted of first and third parts of burlesque, with three or four specialties in between. All specialty acts in that day were expected to double as a matter of course. At a Brooklyn theater, when they were making their first appearance, Weber and Fields once found themselves cast as the hero and villain respectively of the afterpiece. They were agreeable; but the manager, who had assumed from their billing that they were grown, took one look and made hasty substitutions.

What contribution the specialty people made to the balance of the show was left largely to their own judgment. For their part in the opening burlesque the boys made up in grotesque tights, and were dubbed, at first sight, Tom and Hattie, names that clung to them until they were grown. Virginia Ross and Ed Connelly had a duet in the first part. Miss Ross had a coloratura voice of which she was properly proud. She was using it to full effect, supported by Connelly's barytone, the rest of the company grouped behind them. In the mistaken belief that something more than respectful silence was expected of them, Masters Weber and Fields launched a broad pantomime of the singers behind their backs. The audience sniggered. Miss Ross missed a note and Connelly said something out of the corner of his mouth which the boys mistook for approbation. They kicked each other and took two comedy falls. The house laughed aloud. At the curtain, Miss Ross gave herself up to hysterics; and Connelly, stage manager of the troupe, demanded their blood. The house manager, after a stormy time, succeeded in persuading the barytone that he had mistaken ignorance for malice.

In rehearsing with the orchestra that morning, Charles Pettingell, of the American Four, another specialty on the bill, and a big drawing card of the '80s, had interrupted with a demand to know where they had gotten their music.

"We wrote it ourselves," they told him.

"Did you now?" There was sarcasm in Pettingell's voice. "That is interesting. But it so happens that that music belongs to us, and we won't need any help in singing it."

This was one night, evidently, when "Here we are, a jolly pair"—a colored, Irish, German or any other pair—was not to introduce them to an audience. Pettingell's injunction took away the only tune they knew for their home-made lyrics. They never had made an entrance otherwise, and without it they were as lost as a hymn book at an Elks clambake.

Without any of the three being aware of it, Pettingell had understudied for fate that day. Five years of give and take had schooled Weber and Fields well in taking care of the unexpected on the stage and off. There was no time now to rehearse a new entrance. In lieu of the lost song, an experiment was agreed upon. They would walk onstage talking excitedly in broad German-English and mispronounce every word as ludicrously as possible. It would be necessary to make up the dialogue as they went along. Vamping and ad libbing, it is known to the profession. When they had killed the time usually given to the song, they would take up the old act at the knockabout.

As the cheapest act on the bill, they opened the variety program. At the last moment Weber had varied his original costume with a coat borrowed from a sister-in-law. It was the day of puffed sleeves and flaring tails in women's coats. This absurdity drew a laugh from the house the moment it saw him.

They came out from the wings shouting and gesturing furiously, and flinging the mangled corpses of murdered English words at each other. There had been German-dialect comedians before, but no such interchange of twisted, strangled speech as this. Each mispronunciation was echoed by a roar from out front. Heartened by such a reception, they worked the harder and more confidently, and shaded off into the knockabout.

In a climax of seeming fury, Fields reached out with his crooked cane, hooked it around Weber's neck and threw him. Weber arose, hooked his cane around Fields's neck and dragged him across the stage, while the house rocked with glee. Fields kicked Weber in his padded stomach and hit him murderously over his padded head. They did everything in their own repertoire and improvised from their memory of other acts. Weber's pillow padding got knocked askew and made him even more ridiculous. Here was true slapstick and in a new dress, the most primitive and the most effective of humor. Others in the company hurried from their dressing rooms to learn what had set off the audience. Masters Weber and Fields had stopped the show.

The management was suspicious. Packing the house at Monday openings with neighbors and kinsfolk was a familiar artifice. There was a Tuesday afternoon show at Miner's Bowery called the actors' matinée, from the number of the profession, their Tuesday afternoons free, who were accustomed to attend.

Here would be a critical house and a more convincing test. But Tuesday matinée was a repetition of Monday night. Tuesday night the curtain man blistered his hands hauling the drop up and down for the calls at the finish of the knockabout. The management was persuaded.

That night the house manager, Sheldon, sought them out.

"How would you boys like to play our Eighth Avenue house next week?" he asked with the air of one bestowing largess.

"We'd like to—for fifty dollars." Joe did the answering.

Sheldon lifted his eyebrows and shifted his quid of tobacco.

"Whoops, my dear!" he exclaimed. "Got the big head already, eh? Back to the pool tables for you, my sons! I don't think you finished that game last Friday night."

The discussion ended without Lew having spoken. Outside, he had much to say.

"I've got a business man for a partner, I have," he opened. "We lay around six months looking for work, and just when we get it, and have the Bowery talking about us, you kick the manager in the face. Who do you think you are? Booth and Barrett, or somebody? It's a good thing for me I've got you around to look after my interests or I might have missed a chance to get a nice job scaling fish in the Washington Market next Monday." And more to that effect. Joe thought of no adequate reply.

But Sheldon looked them up again on Thursday night.

"It's a lucky thing for you two whipper-snappers," he began, "that I couldn't find another act for the Eighth Avenue next week. You get the fifty dollars. Now swell up like two poisoned pups and bust. It'll ruin you for good, probably. I'll have that satisfaction."

It was their first time at Miner's uptown house and rarefied air after one hundred and eighty nights in a barroom. Colonel Hopkins, owner of the Theater Comique at Providence, was in town looking for acts for his house. Edward Talbot, on the bill with them at the Eighth Avenue, had been booked for the Comique two weeks hence and would be unable to keep the engagement. He told the boys that Hopkins would be in to see the show some time during the week and promised to suggest them as a substitute.

"If he wants you to go cheap, laugh at him," he warned. "Ask for a yard and a quarter," by which he meant one hundred and twenty-five dollars a week.

That was a fantastic sum, but Masters Weber and Fields were in an asking mood by now. Eighth Avenue was as flattering as the Bowery, and presumably a more fastidious public. Colonel Hopkins came, saw and was impressed. Would they like to come to Providence? They would—for one hundred and twenty-five dollars a week.

"All right; send in your billing," the colonel concurred, just like that.

Here was something rotten in Denmark. In their two-by-four dressing rooms, they talked over the colonel's all-too-ready compliance. A manager who would agree without a struggle to part with one hundred and twenty-five dollars very likely was one who had no intention of paying anything. The Bowery was a long walk from Providence. They would devote next week to seeking an engagement at a figure there was a chance of getting.

But they failed to find it. Better Providence, and trust to Providence, than back to the pool tables. The cheapest route to the Rhode Island capital was by steamer to Fall River, thence by rail. Saturday noon they bought two tickets and checked their trunk. The boat would sail at six P.M., the ticket agent said. At half past five they approached the wharf in company of Weber's brother and a friend whom they remember only as Jersey Sam. A steamer's siren was hooting. It had the sound of a boat pulling out. A boat, in fact, was pulling out—their boat, and their trunk, containing their all, aboard. That day the Fall River Line had shifted its schedule and the absent-minded ticket agent had forgotten.

Between them Weber and Fields had possibly sixty cents. Weber's brother had nothing. But Jersey Sam, in an ill-advised confidence, had admitted ownership of five dollars. That would buy two half-fare tickets by the all-rail route to Providence, but Jersey Sam had other plans for his five dollars. Lew wept, Joe pleaded, his brother promised, and Jersey Sam was lost.

At the old Grand Central Station Joe sidled up to the New Haven ticket window, stooped low, his eyes just showing above the counter, and gave his best imitation of a frightened small boy asking for half-fare tickets to Providence for himself and baby brother. The ticket agent hissed the act.

They waited until another ticket agent came on duty. This time Lew toddled to the window, and in a lisping treble asked if this was the place where little boys bought half-fare tickets for Providence. He lacked only a rattle.

The ticket seller rose, peered over the counter and said, "Not with that face!"

The board of strategy met again. When half-fare tickets were bought in connection with full-fare billets, the railroad was not so inquisitive. Why not locate some adult bound for Providence and persuade him to act as their purchasing agent? Taking stands at the station's busiest door, they grabbed at the coat tails of every man who passed in, clamoring, "Mister, are you going to Providence?" New York's manners have not altered greatly since the early '80s. Nine brushed by without answering, sensing a snare; the tenth would be a man down to meet his aunt from Moosup, or a furniture salesman returning to Grand Rapids.

At twenty minutes to train time the prospects of ever learning whether Colonel Hopkins talked in Union or Confederate money were poor. At nineteen minutes to, the Three Herbert Brothers, acrobats, and Nellie Parker, wife of one, came through the door. Providence was their destination and they would be glad to accommodate. The boys sat up all night in the day coach and listened to one of the Herberts describe the glories of the Freeman Hotel at Providence—dollar a day and ice cream every noon.

From the Herberts they borrowed make-up stuffs and money with which to buy two canes. The only curved sticks to be had at the price were blackthorns, hard and knobby. Pillows for padding were sneaked from the hotel. A fellow actor, Alex Zanfretta, lent Weber a skullcap. Coated heavily with flesh-colored grease paint and a handkerchief stuffed beneath as a pad, it would have to serve instead of the steel reenforced wig in the trunk presumedly at Fall River.

Joe coached Lew carefully on the location of the handkerchief, but early in the knockabout at the opening show the makeshift pad slipped out of place. At the first clout over the head Fields's blackthorn cut through the skullcap and laid open his partner's scalp. A trivial scalp wound bleeds alarmingly, and this was to require four stitches. The audience, which had been enjoying itself moderately, exploded. In the violence of the knockabout and the elation of their first important out-of-town engagement, Weber had felt no hurt. Accustomed to end the act in a drench of perspiration, he mistook the wetness of his scalp. Weber raised a hand to his forehead to wipe away the obtruding moisture as they took their second curtain call before an uproarious house. His hand came away covered with blood and he fainted in full view of the audience.

Colonel Hopkins, who had looked in from the box office to see what his patrons were exciting themselves about, was backstage by the time Weber had revived.

"Where are those two kids?" he shouted.

Lew was pouring a trickle of cold water on Joe's head. They set themselves for bad news. Here would be the alibi for not paying that one hundred and twenty-five dollars a week.

"Great!" yelled the colonel. "Wonderful!" He danced and waved his hand. "I don't see how you worked it! Looked just like real blood! Most natural thing I ever saw! It wasn't in the act when I saw it at Miner's. When did you think it up?"

Joe still was too weak to talk. The thing to do was to tell the boss what he wanted to hear. That was Lesson One in "How to Get On in the World," as they had read it. Lew did the telling.

"Why, last week," he invented, "when we hadn't much to do, we tried soaking a little sponge in carmine and putting it underneath Joe's wig. It worked pretty well, so we thought we'd try it out here and——"

"Bravo!" the colonel cut in, oblivious of the fact that the "sponge" still leaked. "You actors do get an idea now and then. Keep that in the act, whatever you do. You've got a gold mine." And then as an afterthought, "You might rehearse that faint a bit. It looked kinda forced to-night."

This was a horse on the colonel; so good a one, it was thought backstage, that no one disabused his mind. It was not by design that Fields's blows reopened the cut on Tuesday night. But if he must bleed afresh, Weber meant to bleed to some purpose. Intentionally now he wiped his forehead, stared at his hands as Lady Macbeth at hers, and swooned to the queen's taste.

Wednesday the trunk came from Fall River and Weber recovered his armor-plated wig. Hopkins had been bragging the act the length of Providence, and Wednesday night he enticed three politicians down from the State House to see it.

"The first time the tall one hits the little fellow over the head with his cane, watch what happens!" he coached them.

Lew whacked Joe's head once, twice, and many times, and nothing happened. The colonel, denied his evening's blood, came backstage in a rage. It seemed a moment for the truth, and they told him.

"You kids deserve to get on," was his tribute. "You've got nerve."

Monday was New Year's Day, and there was an extra matinée. On Saturday the house treasurer paid them not one hundred and twenty-five dollars but one hundred and thirty dollars. They counted the roll four times to make sure, then turned five dollars back. The treasurer waved it aside. It was for the extra matinee, he explained. Here were men who were above taking advantage of unpracticed youth. Champagne was being opened in the box office in honor of the year 1883, and the treasurer even invited them to join him. Not with one hundred and thirty dollars in their pockets did they intend to dally with the mocker, wine. The treasurer was insistent and the bubbles flirted with them. To humor him, each took a sip. When they were outside they exchanged impressions. Vinegar was cheaper and tasted the same, they agreed.

With Colonel Hopkins and his one hundred and twenty-live dollars as a reference, the firm laid in a new stock of Gilsey House and Fifth Avenue Hotel stationery and gave their afternoons to letting the out-of-town managers know what they were missing. No answers came, and they were reduced to taking thirty dollars at Col. Bob Waring's German Beer Garden in Hoboken. The name to the contrary, it was merely a theater in which beer was sold during the performance.

An act was an act to the Hoboken colonel, and he had one price—thirty dollars for teams, fifteen dollars for singles, take it or leave it. The first four acts to apply were as apt as not to be hired, and all turn out to be acrobatic turns. It was said that he once had engaged four separate and distinct ventriloquists for the same bill. Joe and Lew never doubted it, for on viewing his program that Sunday night the colonel discovered that three out of the four turns were Dutch comedy numbers. As the two others were better known to him, he paid the boys two dollars and fifty cents apiece after the Sunday show and fired them.

Within a month they had descended from one hundred and twenty-five dollars and wreaths of bay leaves in Providence to thirty dollars and the hook after one performance in Hoboken. A neat morsel for the Bowery to roll under its tongue; the Bowery, which had had to listen for two weeks to Providence this and Providence that. Not if they could prevent it would the Bowery know.

Monday night they returned to Hoboken as usual. There was a rival beer garden down the street. The manager was not interested, but they quoted bargain rates. He closed with them at a dollar and a half a night for the team and a night-to-night contract. After the last performance Saturday night they carried their trunk to the ferry—a trunk with genuine leather straps now. On the Manhattan side they hefted the trunk again and set out afoot for the Bowery. It was 1:30 A.M. and three miles or more to go, but there was no place in the budget of a dollar and a half a night act for baggage-hauling charges.

Two partly grown boys carrying a trunk through the streets in the dead of the night was a spectacle that could not escape the eye even of a New York policeman of the '80s. They were halted before they had crossed West Street.

Actors, eh? A likely tale, that! No nonsense now, and open up that trunk!

At Ninth Avenue a second patrolman stopped them, at Bleecker Street a third, as sceptical as the first, and not to be convinced under twenty minutes. And with only eight blocks to go, a fourth copper not to be convinced at all.

"Here, look in the trunk and see for yourself!" they pleaded.

"I'll look well into the trunk, but it'll be at the station house," he answered, and took them there.

It was a dull hour, and the drowsing sergeant thought he might believe their story if they should put on their costumes and dance for him. Dawn was creeping over Williamsburg when they came home to East Broadway. The taste of Hoboken is bitter in their mouths after forty years.

Those afternoons of letter writing bore their first fruit the next day. A note from Gilmore's Grand Central Theater, 809 Walnut Street, Philadelphia, was in the letter box back of the bar at Miner's saloon. It ordered them to come on for a try-out at eighty dollars a week.

Gilmore's was a byword in the variety world. Its owner was a tart, irascible character, as tough a customer as ever bought goods. Playing his house was both an ordeal and a speculation as uncertain as a horse race. He held himself privileged to fire an act as the spirit moved him. Invariably he sat in the first entrance at rehearsals and the opening show, looking his hired hands over sourly. To survive a rehearsal was a feat, to last out the opening performance entitled one to wound-and-service stripes, and to finish the week was a patent of theatrical nobility. Gilmore found his justification in the box office. There were no empty seats in his house.

One story told of him was characteristic. A man with a trained dog played his theater. The man recited Paul Laurence Dunbar's poem, "A Yellow Dog's Love for a Coon," and the dog did the rest. When the actor applied at the box office on pay day, Gilmore yelled in a voice that all Walnut Street could hear, "Send in the dog. I'll pay him. He did all the work."

There were other actors on the train for Philadelphia. They recommended Mother Bunger's boarding house, good board and clean rooms, six dollars a week.

Mother Bunger greeted them with, "Vere is you kids playing at?" At the mention of William J. Gilmore she started. His caprices had cost her many a defaulted board bill. She could not be sure of Gilmore's reception of an act that was unknown to her, and she would gamble on no novices. "Funny," she said, "dey ain't got your names on de bills vat I see, und besides I ain't got some more rooms left. Better that you go by the Irishman's. For four dollars he has fine grub and beds."

The Irishman's was Murphy's boarding house. Murphy took them in and his faith was justified. Gilmore watched them without comment, and put them next to last on the bill, where they remained the week. Eddie Foy had been loaned that week to Gilmore by John L. Carncross, the minstrel man. Foy liked the Weber and Fields act and spoke of it to Frank Dumont, who was to succeed to Carncross's minstrel mantle at the latter's death. A letter followed them back to New York. Carncross asked their terms.

The letter caused a small sensation among the professionals gathered in Miner's saloon. Privately and publicly the crowd didn't believe it. Carncross never had been known to play a white-face act. To be the first to break that precedent was to be made, they were told with much back-slapping which called for drink buying. They named seventy dollars a week in their reply and got an acceptance the next week.

This time whatever Mother Bunger had was theirs. That lady posed as the actors' best friend and never ceased to ask her boarders to pause in astonishment at her greatness of heart. Her life, as she described it with each dinner, was one long succession of sacrifices and distinterested services for "mein children," as she was pleased to call her patrons. Against any possible scepticism, she had at hand a clinching case in point with which she always closed.

Years before, an actress had abandoned her infant son in the boarding house, and Mother Bunger had reared the boy, now half grown.

"Lou-ee," she would call to him as she approached her peroration—"Lou-ee, tell the ladies and gentlemen what did I take out of my ears and send them to the pawnshop for to lend that poor lady, Mrs. So-and-So."

"Your earrings, mamma." Lou-ee knew his one line well.

The golden age of negro minstrelsy was on, and Carncross had the pick of the land at his peculiar institution at the Eleventh Street Opera House. A churchman himself, he kept his entertainment immaculately clean and attracted a clientele all his own. Quakers and other religionists made a sharply drawn distinction between the theater, which they regarded as a halfway house to perdition, and minstrelsy. Philadelphia was not alone in this discrimination, though Carncross's was its most notable example. Throughout America, until the prejudice against the stage began to relax, the minstrel show was sure of an audience no other form of the theater except the circus could attract.

The first half of a Carncross show was the conventional farrago of quip, quirk and sentimental ballad. In 1883 he had as end men, tambos and bones such comedians as Lew Dockstader, Eddie Foy, Hughey Dougherty and Dick Turner. Such tenors as Chauncey Olcott sang the ballads dear to the hearts of mid-Victorian Americans. The second part was a burlesque of some folly or sensation of the moment and a pot-pourri of the current theater, a mild approximation of the topical revue of to-day. Carncross is dead, Frank Dumont is dead, Lew Dockstader has recently departed, minstrelsy is all but dead; but in its early stock form it holds out feebly still in Arch Street, Philadelphia.

Photo 4. Chauncey Olcott, c. 1902. Bain News Service, George Grantham Bain Collection, Library of Congress.

Weber and Fields went on with their Dutch knockabout at the Eleventh Street Opera House on Monday evening and made the flattest failure of their lives. The audience gave them dead silence from entrance to exit. They finished with the feeling of having rehearsed in a morgue. In their dressing room they waited for a knock on their door, and dismissal. The knock came, but not the "Sorry, boys, I can't use you" which they had looked for.

"If you are not doing anything else about ten: o'clock to-morrow morning, you might drop in at the theater," was the owner's message. It was a rule that an act must be discharged after the first performance or be paid for the week. So there was hope.

"Don't let last night discourage you," Carncross told them in his office the following morning. "I have a peculiar public here, unlike anything you ever met with in the theater. My patrons are very conservative. Few of them ever attend another theater, and the more familiar a song, a joke or a piece of business, the better they like it. You must give them time to get used to you.

"There is another thing or two. They thought you really were hurting each other, and were uneasy. Why not shake hands and kiss exaggeratedly when you finish? I think that would do the trick. Those loud check suits you wear no doubt are just the thing for your usual audience, but if you will permit me, I will buy you other clothes that will suit my people better. I know them, you see."

Carncross took them to a secondhand shop on South Street and bought them two full-dress suits, the first use of formal evening dress by a comedy act on the American stage. Tuesday night they embraced and exchanged a loud smack. Carncross's diagnosis was perfect. His peculiar public warmed to them, and took them to its heart the second week. Their engagement ran eight months without a break, the first and one of the few white-face acts ever seen in this home of burnt cork.

All rules failed at Carncross's. When they had flopped he had told them not to worry, and set them aright. Now that they were an established success, he called them in and amazed them by saying, "I'd like to keep you the balance of the season, but I don't want to pay you the same salary."

They retired to consider. Their conclusion was that a long run would be so good an advertisement that they could afford to cut their price as low as fifty dollars.

Reporting back, they said, "You have been so decent to us that we will leave the salary to you. Whatever you think fair will suit us."

"Good!" he agreed. "Your wages will be sixty-nine dollars after this week."

They could only look at each other stupidly, and put it down as the Carncross idea of a practical joke. He was, however, entirely serious. Among the superstitions he practiced, but did not like to admit, was one that it was unlucky to pay out an even sum. All accustomed to doing business with him—actors, stage hands and tradesmen—were prepared to receive $1.99 or $2.01 for two dollars, and were expected to accept it without comment, as a normal business practice.

Eight uninterrupted months of well-paid work—a new high-water mark for Weber and Fields. Six dollars each for room and board, a few dollars for incidentals, a few more for ads in the theatrical weeklies, and the balance flowed back to the East Side to raise the Weber and Schanfield families to comfort.

From the time they were twelve until they were sixteen a duel of wits with the railroad companies went with every out-of-town engagement. Long before Sir James Barrie invented and named him Peter Pan, the boy who never grew up was arguing with New Haven and Pennsylvania ticket agents and trainmen. For all railroad purposes, Joe and Lew turned the calendar's face to the wall and hugged their eleventh birthday as a woman does her twenty-ninth; clung to it until the pretense would not have passed in a home for the blind.

On their first trip to Baltimore to play at Herzog's Museum for fifty dollars a week, and to live with the freaks at Hancock's boarding house, they began a contest with one Pennsylvania conductor that went on for a year. In the opening skirmish Fields took a seat in the forward end of the smoker, Weber in the rear. The conductor looked at Fields, then at his ticket, and asked his age.

"Going on twelve," was the answer.

The same question and answer when he reached Weber.

"Do you know that boy up front?" the conductor demanded.

Did he or didn't he? Maybe Lew had referred the conductor to him in support of his age. Joe flipped a mental coin and it came down heads.

"Sure!" he said. "He's my brother."

The wrong answer!

"How does it happen then," the conductor wanted to know, "that he is going on twelve also?"

One reply only to this embarrassing inquiry was possible.

"We're twins," Joe exclaimed, as if that fortuity had just occurred to him.

"Twin liars, at least," the trainman commented dryly. "I'll let you by this time."

Baltimore liked them so well that Herzog booked them to return in three months. Homeward to New York they rode with a strange, and, they suspected, a nearsighted conductor. But on the second journey to Maryland they were so unwise as to take the midnight train as before. The same conductor found them in the same relative positions in the smoker.

"How old are you now?" he asked Fields.

"Going on twelve," Master Lew replied.

The conductor punched a check, slipped it into Fields's hatband and passed on.

"And how old are you to-day?" he inquired solicitously when he came to Weber.

"Going on twelve," Joe thanked him.

"And going off at the next station unless you pay full fare," was the rejoinder. "I let your 'twin brother' up there ride on a half-fare ticket. It's my guess that neither one of you ever will see fifteen again, but I'll compromise with you. One half and one full. Are you going to pay?"

Joe had eighty cents and a package of cheap cigarettes. He tendered them. The conductor replied in the manner of France to Germany. The train was pulling into Newark, and he saw Joe to the station platform.

Railway coaches were not vestibuled in the '80s, and Joe swung onto the open platform of the last coach as the train pulled out. Near the rear of the coach a buxom negro woman slept, her limp body slumped toward the aisle. Joe slipped past her noiselessly and curled up in the shelter of her bulk, his face averted. The car lights were dimmed and his presence went unnoted by the trainmen.

Toward four o'clock in the morning, Weber thought the train near enough Baltimore to risk going forward to reassure Fields, whom he pictured in a frenzy of anxiety. This picture was not to be reconciled with the facts. Lew he found snoring unfeelingly. Joe woke him with a jab. Fields rubbed his eyes and registered surprise.

"I thought they put you off," he managed to say.

"And what were you going to do about it?" Weber asked.

"Oh, I had all that figured out," Fields assured him. "As soon as I got to Baltimore I was going to look up Herzog and ask him to wire you an advance on our salary."

"Wire it where?" Weber persisted.

Lew began to be annoyed.

"I could have sent it to the depot and asked them to call out your name, couldn't I?"

"What depot?"

"Why, at Elizabeth, where they put you off, of course!"

"I thought as much," Joe retorted.

It appeared that the conductor had waited a station before telling Lew that he had lost his partner.

Again Baltimore encored their act. When they set out on their third trip to Maryland, in another ninety days, they took the precaution of asking questions at the Jersey City terminal. Their old enemy was taking out the midnight train, they learned.

"If anybody gets put off at Newark to-night, it's not going to be me," Joe gave notice, and bought a whole ticket for himself. So fortified, they claimed seats together in the smoker.

"Still going on twelve, I suppose," the conductor greeted Lew, who sat on the aisle. "A fine big boy for twelve! I'll bet your mamma is proud of you."

Lew thanked him for his friendly interest.

"And you?" He turned to Joe.

"Going on fourteen," Weber chirped, and surprised the conductor with a full ticket.

"My, how you have grown in a couple of months!" the man with the punch and lantern exclaimed. "I'm afraid my putting you off at Newark aged you considerable. Maybe if I put your 'twin' here off at Newark to-night he would be going on fourteen, too, the next time he rides with me. It'll be worth trying anyway."

Lew was not put off at Newark, but only because he made up the balance of a whole ticket in cash. In Baltimore they heard that Hallen & Hart's road show would be returning to New York the next Saturday night. Traveling troupes were granted greatly reduced rates by the railroads. The boys persuaded the manager to elect them members of his company for the duration of the trip. Their pro rata was less than two half-fare tickets, and fingers could be snapped at the race of conductors. Most of the company spent the night in Pullmans. Joe and Lew sat up to save two dollars, and wondered if they would travel with a road show some day.

The Pennsylvania conductor had his counterpart on the New Haven. They clashed first with him on the memorable occasion when they missed the Fall

River boat, and he had been making pointed comments at every meeting since. It was getting so any trip to New England was good for a garland of insults.

Bound for Providence to play at Drew's Museum, they received an ultimatum one Sunday night.

"What, again?" The conductor shook his punch under their noses. "Get this, now!" he told them. "This is the last time you ride on my train at half fare. It's a wonder one of you doesn't sit on the other's lap and ask me to believe he is an infant in arms. I'm warning you now! The next time I'm going to reach for the bell cord and put you off ten miles between stations."

One week later the night train from Boston picked up at Providence, among other passengers, Masters Weber and Fields, the Big Little Four, consisting of Harry Kelly, Charles Buckley and the Callahan Brothers, and the Parker Twins, all kid acts familiar to variety audiences.

The eight crowded into two seats turned face to face. The most commodious suitcase in the party was laid across their knees, the Parker Twins passed cigars around, Harry Kelly shuffled a deck of cards and a penny-ante poker game began.

"Tickets!" a voice commanded.

Eight poker players smoking eight big cigars laid down eight sets of five cards, fished in eight pockets and brought out eight half-fare tickets. The conductor they looked up at was the one of the week before. As a comedy situation none of the eight ever surpassed it on the stage.

Fifty years of education in applied profanity went for nothing. The conductor's cuss words melted on his tongue and he laughed through his set teeth.

"I'll frame these," he said when he got his face straightened out. He put the eight tickets in a special pocket and went on.

Weber and Fields had played every dime museum in New York save one, but that one was the aristocrat of the lot—G. B. Bunnell's, at Broadway and Ninth Street. Bunnell looked somewhat like P. T. Barnum, the father of the dime museum, then still alive and a circus proprietor, and he cultivated that resemblance assiduously.

The team had finer feathers in its cap than this, but there would be a gap in the record until Bunnell's had been conquered. For five years they had failed to catch his interest. When Doctor Cole, whom they had known as lecturer on the freaks at the New York Museum, 210 Bowery, was promoted to the lectureship at Bunnell's, they tried again—and got a curt refusal. They would show this man Bunnell.

The wild talk of a drunken sailor on the Bowery was the seed of the plot. The sailor claimed to have shipped from Chi-fu with a Chinese helmsman who had one eye, and that in the center of his forehead. Days later it occurred to Lew and Joe that the yarn had practical possibilities.

Dropping in at Bunnell's, they spoke casually to Cole of having seen such a Chinaman in Doyers Street sometime before. They described him with great detail. His peculiarity, it seemed, was little known even in Chinatown because of his habit of pulling his hat far down on his forehead. A slit in the hat fitted over the single eye.

Cole declared excitedly that the Chinese Cyclops was a phenomenon without parallel in his experience. Bunnell would pay three hundred—four hundred—even five hundred dollars, perhaps, just for the tip.

A pity they had not thought of Mr. Bunnell at once. Meanwhile, unfortunately, P. T. Barnum had opened negotiations with them and would have the first call.

Bunnell was with them within the minute. Just the two boys he had been hoping to see. Lucky chance that they should happen in. Would they like to play the museum next week? The pay would be forty dollars, Bunnell's top. Nothing was said of a one-eyed Chinaman.

Bunnell booked them for a second week. By the by, Doctor Cole had said something about a Chinaman with an eye in his forehead.

To Joe's and Lew's expressed sorrow, Mr. Barnum had first call on the marvel and had all but closed with them. Bunnell thought he could meet Barnum's offer—possibly better it. Would they give it their best thought? They would indeed.

Bunnell had two other museums, one in Brooklyn, the other in Jersey City. The third week he sent them to Brooklyn, the fourth to Jersey City, the fifth he brought them back to Broadway. A funny thing, it was being said in Miner's, this sudden popularity of Weber and Fields with Bunnell.

Bunnell began to be pressing. Where was the Chinaman to be found? Couldn't he see the man himself? What word from Barnum? Were they certain that there was only one eye, and that in the center of the brow?

Their little jest was beginning to grow claws. Practical jokes and tiger whelps have their similarities. Amusing pets in their infancy, awkward playfellows as they approach maturity. Joe and Lew conferred and decided to break with Barnum. The next day, in Bunnell's presence, they denounced the circus man's lack of good faith. They had learned that while he pretended to dicker with them he was attempting to go behind their backs and deal independently with their property. All that he had accomplished was to frighten the Chinaman away. He had fled to a cousin's in New Orleans, and they now were trying to coax him out of retirement. As soon as they succeeded he would be Bunnell's for the asking.

When they had played twenty consecutive weeks at the three museums, and had been booked for the twenty-first, Bunnell demanded a showdown. Lew ducked around the corner and sent a message by an A. D. T. boy to himself and Joe in care of Bunnell. The Chinaman had returned.

Bunnell sent for his carriage and the three started for Doyers Street. Doyers Street was around the corner from the old Chatham Square Museum where they had begun their career. In half an hour now, when the cat got out of the bag, their career might end there too. They pointed at random with nervous fingers. Bunnell alighted and led the way. The house which their fingers had chanced to indicate proved to be a warren of Orientals, all of whom at once protested utter ignorance of English. When in doubt, Chinatown always fell back on "No savee," and such cryptical talk as this of eyes in foreheads was suspicious.

Out of the jabber of Cantonese, at length a voice suggested in perfect English that they address their inquiries to the Chinese consul in Clinton Street. Objections by Joe and Lew. A consul could not be expected to concern himself with museum freaks. He probably was very busy on matters of state, and anyway the only sure method of locating a Chinaman was to wait him out. Patience—that was it! They had unlimited patience, and Bunnell could return to the museum. He went, however, to the consul's and took them with him.

The consul was a Princeton graduate. He listened politely and gave it as his opinion that his callers had been imposed upon.

"You Americans are an incurably romantic people," he philosophized, "and you insist on inventing and believing weird and devious fictions about our quarter. You will have it that we are an enigmatical race given to strange deviltries. This, I judge, is another of these nursery tales. At any rate, I can assure you that every Chinese in Greater New York reports to me and that there is none such among them. Were he here, I would be compelled by your immigration laws, no doubt, to return him to China."

Bunnell's twenty weeks of delusion ended abruptly while the consul spoke. He had believed in the existence of the Chinatown Cyclops because he had wanted to believe, and these young scoundrels had played shrewdly on his obsession of outdoing the great Barnum. He stopped outside the consul's door.

"Tell me the truth," he asked. "There was never any one-eyed Chinaman, was there?"

It had come. They suddenly felt very sorry for their victim and for themselves. They looked at each other. Which one should tell him? They began the confession, now one talking, now the other, then both at once. The drunken sailor; how they had tried so long to get on at Bunnell's; how the joke had got out of hand, an Old Man of the Sea clinging to their backs.

Bunnell only stared, with a look half hurt, half quizzical. In their remorse they seemed more undersized, more underloved than ever; two of necessity's children, faces wistful with an age beyond their years. It was long before he spoke.

Then it was to say, "An old showman taken in by a pair of kids? I'd be a poor sport if I hollered. Shake hands on it, and no hard feelings." He stared at them longer. "You two ought to go far," he said, half to himself.

It was on their first trip to Boston.

"All for the insignificant sum of one dime, two nickels, ten coppers, one-tenth part of a dollar—the price of a shave or a hair ribbon! The greatest, the most astounding——"

A lean, black-haired, steely-blue-eyed young man with a throaty, insistent voice fixed the passer-by with hypnotic stare and chanted his ballyhoo.

"The greatest, the most astounding aggregation of marvels and monstrosities ever gathered together in one edifice. Looted from the ends of the earth. From the wilds of darkest Africa, the miasmic jungles of Brazil, the mystic headwaters of the Yang-tse-Kiang, the cannibal isles of the Antipodes, the frosty slopes of the Himalayas, and the barren steppes of the Caucasus! Sparing no expense, every town, every village, every hamlet, every nook and cranny of the globe has been searched with a fine-tooth comb to provide this feast for the eye and the mind. A refined exhibition for cultured ladies and gentlemen. No waiting, no delays. Step up, ladies and gentlemen, and avoid the rush! Tickets now selling in the doorway!"

The New England decorum of Washington Street, Boston, in the early '80s—then as now the city's busiest retail artery—was violated by the black-haired youth and his background. He stood in front of No. 585, formerly occupied by a hatter. The twenty-five-foot front of the three-story building was swathed in great brawling canvas twelve-sheets in violent reds and blues that did assault and battery upon the eyes of all who passed; a sign painter's nightmare of moss-haired girls, Circassian beauties, snake charmers, African pygmies, Bornean wild men, Siamese Twins, tattooed ladies, sword swallowers, human-faced chickens, and the original cow of Mrs. O'Leary, kicker-over of the lantern and setter of the Chicago fire.

The façade of the building was lost in the swirl of poster and banner, even the name, Keith & Batchelder's Dime Museum, obscured. Circus men both, B. F. Keith and George H. Batchelder had set up shop in downtown Boston in 1883, with a job lot of freaks gathered from the side shows, against the eight lean, idle months of the trouper season. The circus never knew them again.

In 1885 they divided, Batchelder going to Providence and Keith soon buying the Bijou Theater, next door to No. 585. In later years he joined forces with Fred F. Proctor, originally a barrel kicker from the circus, and Percy G. Williams, one-time medicine man, and they invented and organized American vaudeville as it is to-day, and the twenty-five-foot storeroom grew to be the B. F. Keith circuit, mightiest of theatrical syndicates.

The lean, black-haired, steely-blue-eyed ballyhooer was Ned Albee, now Edward F. Albee, with B. F. Keith from the first year of the museum, immediate successor to him and his son, and now absolute overlord of vaudeville.

Here at No. 585 Washington Street one morning in 1883, Masters Weber and Fields reported for work in the concert section on the second floor at forty dollars a week. They went on eight times a day, alternating their Dutch knockabout and their neat song-and-dance acts. Freaks and performers slept, ate and dressed in the attic, and paid six dollars a week to Mom Keith, who oversaw that floor and waited on table, assisted by a chubby, eight-year-old boy—their son Paul. Eight-by-ten partitions in which the actors both dressed and slept lined the walls and opened upon the dining-room table, occupying the center of the attic floor.

The Reed family—father, mother and three children—opened the bill with a black-face act. The variety show began at ten A.M. The youngest Reed was not yet five years old. Lew's and Joe's clearest memory of that first time at Keith's is of the father letting his youngest sleep until 9:45, waking him with a cup of strong coffee and rubbing the burnt-cork make-up on his drowsy face as he held the boy in his arms.

Eleven years later, the senior Keith called Weber and Fields to Boston to play twice instead of eight times a day, and in a new $1,000,000 theater, much the most pretentious vaudeville theater in America. Both he and the Skull Crackers, as they sometimes billed themselves, had climbed many rungs of the ladder meanwhile, with many more to go.

Another eleven years saw them back at Keith's Boston house on their last vaudeville tour.

The late A. Paul Keith, grown from passer of the rice pudding in the attic at No. 585 to be manager of the Boston theater, called them into the office and opened the ledger with a flourish. They read:

	A WEEK
Weber and Fields, 1883.....................	$40
Weber and Fields, 1894....................	$400
Weber and Fields, 1905...................	$4000

During one of their early Boston engagements, at Austin and Stone's Museum this time, the act was canceled abruptly in midweek and the two returned to New York. Joe's family would need his earnings more than ever now. His father was dead.

Chapter III

Mike and Myer Are Born

Hitting the Road, the Mid-1880s

MIKE: I am delightfulness to meet you.
MYER: Der disgust is all mine.

MIKE WAS WEBER, Myer was Fields, and these two lines the opening salutation of the Dutch knockabout with which they first convulsed the patrons of Harry Miner's Bowery, and this was expanded ultimately into the Weber and Fields of tradition. New York, Philadelphia, Baltimore, Providence and Boston knew it now, and encored it.

MIKE: I receivedidid a letter from mein goil, but I don't know how to writteninin her back.
MYER: Writteninin her back! Such an edumuncation you got it? Writteninin her back! You mean rotteninin her back. How can you answer her ven you don't know how to write?
MIKE: Dot makes no nefer mind. She don't know how to read.
MYER: If you luf her, vy don't you send her some poultry?
MIKE: She don't need no poultry; her father is a butcher.
MYER: I mean luf voids like Romeo und Chuliet talks.
If you luf you like I luf me,
No knife can cut us togedder.
MIKE: I don't like dot.
MYER: Vell, vot do you vant to say to her?
MIKE: I don't vant you to know vat I'm saying to her. All I vant you to do is to tell me vot to put in her letter.
MYER: Such a foolishness you are! If I don't tell you vot to say, how vill you know vot to write if she don't know how to read?
MIKE: I don't vant nobody to know vot I'm writteninin to her.
MYER: You don't vant anyone to know vot you are rotteninin?
MIKE: No.
MYER: Then send her a postal card.

MIKE: Send her a postal card? If I do she'll think I don't care two cendts for her.

MYER: Are you going to marry her?

MIKE: In two days I vill be a murdered man.

MYER: A vot?

MIKE: I mean a married man.

MYER: I hope you vill always look back upon der presendt moment as der habbiest moment uff your life.

MIKE: But I aind't married yet.

MYER: I know it, und furdermore, upon dis suspicious occasion, I also vish to express to you—charges collect—my uppermost depreciation of der dishonor you haf informed upon me in making me your bridesmaid.

MIKE: Der insuldt is all mein.

MYER: As you standt before me now, soo young, soo innocent, soo obnoxious, there is only one void dat can express mein pleasure, mein dissatisfaction——

MIKE: Yes, yes?

MYER: Und I can't tink of der void.

MIKE: I know I vill be happy.

MYER: I know you vill be. (*He shakes* MIKE's *hand feelingly.)* Und later on, ven you lose all your money, und your vife goes back on you, und your house burns down, und your children get run over, then I, your best friendt, vill take you by der hand——

MIKE (*wiping a furtive tear away*): Yes, yes!

MYER: Und say——

MIKE: Yes, yes!

MYER: Und say, "I told you so!"

MIKE: Say, vot is dis going to be, a vedding or ein funeral?

MYER: A wedding, in course; und remember also dot vile I vish you plenty uff mishaps, I also vish you lodst uff misfortunes.

Old stuff? To be sure, in 1924, after it has been hacked and hawked about the stage for a generation by imitators, good, bad and indifferent, though worth a few laughs yet. In the early '80s such an exchange of hashed English never before had been heard in the theater, and its inventors were two thirteen-year-olds.

Weber and Fields's dime museum days were ending. Both they and the American theater were on the eve of great growth.

What Walt Whitman, then living in Brooklyn, had written of the native stage in 1845 still was largely true. In the Brooklyn *Star* in that year Whitman had asked:

"Would we have a theater? With all honor and glory to those immortals who have shone before the world in plays, we answer, 'No.' As at present conducted, no man or woman of taste can care much for theaters, or wish one in Brooklyn. Of course our readers will grant that we do not suppose that a playhouse must be bad *per se.* But until some great reform takes place in plays, acting and actors, nothing can be done in this country with the theater to make it deserve well at the hands of good men. It has worn the tinseled threadbare robes of foreign fashion long enough. It must be regenerated, refashioned, and born again. It must be made fresher, more natural, more fitted to modern tastes—and above all, it must be Americanized, ere we say put up more theaters. For what person of judgment that ever has spent one hour in the Chatham or the Bowery Theaters in New York but has been nauseated with the stuff presented there? And though the Park claims higher rank, yet even the Park is but a respectably stupid imitator—a bringer-out of English plays, usherer before us of second-rate foreign performers and the castings-off of London and Liverpool."

Whitman was writing of the first-class stage, and forty years later that stage still was strutting in Europe's hand-me-downs. The theater never had got its roots into the American soil. Of a necessity, it had begun by importing its plays, manners and conventions from London and the Continent! But after a century it still was a droopy, hothouse exotic. Negro minstrelsy was our single home product. There were no American playwrights worthy of the name, and therefore no American plays. The European theater was in the doldrums itself, and the stuff that was brought across the water, Shakespeare and the classics excepted, bore no relation to life—least of all American life. New York has been laughing this spring at a revival of one such mummery of highfaluting speech, preposterous asides, affectation and artificiality. This particular drama chances to have been the work of a New Yorker, and was hailed in the '40s as a bit of realism, a fresh wind in the theater, indicating how banal the usual fare of our largest city's stage must have been.

The Civil War jarred the nation into a new realization of its destiny and the ferment reached the theater. Like all great, popular movements, this revolution had its unnoticed beginnings with the masses. Here and there the legitimate stage had produced native actors of distinction, but they stifled in its fusty air. Not until a group of men and women began to push their way up from the beer gardens, the dime museums, the honkytonks and the variety saloons, bringing something racy of the soil and characteristically American, did the stage awake and take its place in society.

Such were Joe Weber and Lew Fields, and because of it their story is the history, in miniature, of the rise of the American theater. That rise was unguessed when Gus Hill saw their act in New York in the middle '80s and signed them for a season with his traveling show. Gus Hill since has made a fortune with popular-priced musical comedies, such as "Bringing Up Father"; shows that never see Broadway, but flourish on the road despite the blight of Hollywood. Trunk shows, they are known to the profession, from the fact that the scenery folds into specially designed trunks, making an extra baggage car unnecessary. By such economies Gus Hill has become one of the wealthiest theatrical men in the country.

Gus Hill also was an East Side product. He began as a club swinger, and continued to twirl his Indian clubs in his own show. They were of a staggering weight. He exhibited them in the lobbies where men and boys tugged and hauled at them to little result. Only a donkey engine could have hoisted them freely.

On-stage Gus toyed with these same clubs as airily as if they had been bamboo walking sticks, the explanation lying in the false bottoms that disgorged the lead weights with which the clubs were loaded.

This trick is associated in Fields's mind with a story of the old Guttenberg race track near Weehawken. One of the owners of the track, a New York gambling-house proprietor, owned the bookmaking privileges and a racing stable as well. His word was law at the track with bookmakers, starters, judges, weighers and all.

Little Fred, one of his horses, had won so consistently that it was posted to carry the terrific handicap of 156 pounds in a selling race. Despite this impost, the bookmakers were ordered to accept no bets on the horse. Little Fred won going away, and all the bookies but one turned in sheets showing heavy winnings. The exception had the reputation of being the wisest head in the betting ring.

"I'm usually in the habit of taking orders as they are given me," he apologized to his boss; "but I like to use the brains God gave me, and I'm darned if I can see yet how Little Fred could carry 156 pounds and win."

The owner gave him a withering look.

"And who in Haverstraw told you that Little Fred carried 156 pounds?" he barked.

This season with Gus Hill was Weber and Fields's first continuous contract engagement. It was for thirty weeks' work at fifteen dollars each a week, board, room and transportation—with the emphasis on the "work," they were to learn. They performed three times in each bill, as Weber and Fields in the knockabout, as Smith and Way in a neat song and dance, and in the afterpiece. Smith and Way was compounded of the names of the advance man and the angel, or financial backer.

The afterpiece was the ensemble, in which every member of the company must appear, and without which no entertainment was thought complete. It was chosen at random from among a dozen hackneyed skits known forward and backward by actors of any experience; such forgotten trifles as "Murder at the Old Toll Gate," "Ghost in the Pawnshop," "The Coming Man," "Oh, Ma, Look at Him," "Kiss in the Dark," and "Razor Jim." The last was typical. The rise of the curtain disclosed a theatrical manager about to cast a minstrel show, his office boy, and the negro roustabout, Razor Jim. One by one and two by two the office boy ushered in the others of the company. They sought parts. What could they do? In answer, they danced, sang or clowned until the manager signaled to Jim, who flourished a grotesque property razor, to chase them out. The soubrette entered last, smirking and flirting with the manager. She chucked the office boy under the chin, tickled Razor Jim, sang horribly in a purposely cracked voice, and was hired on the spot. Curtain! Audiences cried for it.

Three appearances in each show was not all of it. From seven until eight o'clock the boys collected the ten-cent tickets at the gallery door. Backstage they shifted scenery—stage hands carried no union cards in that day—ran errands and answered to the name of "Boy!" They ate when, where and what Gus Hill permitted them, and slept in the same room with him. The company was paid on Wednesday night as of the preceding Saturday, with the result that the boys, who sent all but a pittance home, were either broke over Sunday or borrowed from Hill, who generally charged a pretty stiff rate of interest, deducted in advance. If Hill ransomed their laundry he added his usual interest charge.

Gus Hill's show carried them west of Baltimore for the first time, their initial date on the far side of the Alleghanies falling in the old Academy of Music in Pittsburgh. The backstage accommodations of secondary theaters, and of most first-class houses of the time, were those of a barn. Only the star's dressing room contained a washbasin. The others sloshed their make-up off in long troughs, one for the women, one for the men. Frequently the actors' quarters were bitterly cold in winter and suffocating in summer; but in the Academy no one shivered. The dressing rooms were under the stage, surrounding the house furnace.

An old theater usually is rife with rats, but the Academy was a rat heaven; sleek, pompous, arrogant rats that strolled about as casually as a house dog. The owner, Harry Williams, would permit no cat in the building, and had blacklisted actors for killing his pets. The rodents thrived on another superstition, one invented possibly by Williams for his own purposes. Any actor who ever played the Academy, Weber and Fields among them, will swear that no rat could be coaxed into the dressing room of an act that had flopped. It followed that to have a rat on your calling list was a certificate of merit, two a patent of success, and a family nest equivalent to flattering press notices in every paper in Pittsburgh. Old friendships had been wrecked on the accusation of luring away another's own rats. The Academy's mascots favored grease paints above all other delicacies, cheese included, and the shrewder players purposely kept an open box on the floor night and day. The results were uncanny. Gorging on the grease paints, the rodents' noses and whiskers were perpetually smeared with reds and yellows as if they had been made up for some rat-hole masquerade, a spectacle that had sobered some men instantly and driven others into delirium tremens.

Cincinnati and the People's Theater, still in use, followed Pittsburgh. The Ohio city had an anti-Sunday theater law, enforced as were some other municipal ordinances. No attempt was made to interfere with performances; but toward ten o'clock of the opening Sunday night a squad of police would appear, arrest the entire company and take them before the old German police judge who officiated at midnight court. His honor would fine each one five dollars, which would be paid by the manager. That ended the incident. In effect, it was merely a license fee of five dollars a performer for a Sabbath show.

Actors looked forward to Cincinnati for this opportunity of hazing the rookie. Weber and Fields were the destined victims this trip. On the train, Gus Hill had called them to one side and warned them that Cincinnati was a peculiar community.

"They won't stand for that knocking and dragging each other around," he predicted. "They'll run you in sure if you use that rough stuff."

As Fields explains: "The knockabout was the best thing in our act. We would fall off a house for a dollar at that age, and we refused to be frightened. The story sounded fishy anyway. The show opened on a Sunday afternoon. We went through our act as usual, and nothing happened. But when we finished the afterpiece Sunday night we found three policemen in the wings. 'What did I tell you?' Hill yelled at us. We ducked for the dressing room, washed up, jumped into our street clothes and tiptoed toward the stage door. Apparently we were getting away. The three cops had their backs turned, but on the outside steps we ran into the arms of a fourth policeman."

The boys thought it odd that the rest of the company were herded along with them to the station to suffer for Joe and Lew's crimes. All the others pretended to be greatly cast down. There was no need for the boys to pretend. Haines and Vidocq, the headliners of the company, wrung their hands and protested that never again could they look their poor mothers in the face. Both boys were rubbing their eyes before they reached police headquarters.

The company was marched directly into night court. "Name?" demanded the clerk. "Age?"

"Five dollars," pronounced the judge. "Next case!" No charge, no defense, no comment.

When the roll call reached the boys, Joe piped up in a quavering voice, "Honest, we were just fooling, judge, your honor. We don't really hurt each other. It's just part of the show. We really love each other like brothers." As proof, he kissed Lew noisily on the forehead.

When the court had had its fun, in that kangaroo fashion still common with police magistrates, the joke was diagrammed for them. As balm for their lacerated feelings, their backs were slapped, they were told that better men than they had suffered the same initiation; and they heard the story of Lottie Gilson, then a favorite of the music halls, with her, "There never was a minute little Willie wasn't in it, for he knew a thing or two" song. Lottie was arrested annually in Cincinnati for violating the Sunday law and never could recall the age she had given in court on her previous visits. When she had made her latest estimate, the judge delighted in reading the record on her. Last year she had been twenty, the year before twenty-seven, this year twenty-two. The quotation fluctuated like Erie Common in a disturbed market.

The judge enjoyed his newest victims so heartily that he sent for them on Monday night to entertain his midnight court with their knockabout act. His was a royal command, and they went. His honor being German, as an elective official was apt to be in that German city, he found Mike and Myer's dialect comicalities vastly amusing. Wednesday night, and again Thursday, there was another command performance. Royal favor ever is apt to become oppressive, and what first seemed a distinction now was a nuisance. Friday the boys slipped away early to their beds over Peterson's concert hall.

Cincinnati, despite its beer-and-sausage flavor, then liked to call itself the Young Paris, and strove determinedly to live up to the name. Vine Street, or Over the Rhine, as it was known affectionately, was a street to be named in italics; seven and eight concert halls to the block, all noisy past dawn. A city more wide open even than Frisco, as Weber and Fields remember it. Such a community was sure to take its practical jokes strong and straight.

When the royal courier reported back that Masters Weber and Fields had left the theater, his honor paused in the midst of lecturing a plain drunk to remark, "Go and find them." The policeman was back in an hour with the word that he had found them in bed, and that they refused to get up.

"Bring 'em in and lock 'em up," the judge ordered jovially.

At 2:30 A.M. Joe and Lew were shaken awake by two men in blue coats and brass buttons, commanded to rise and dress in the name of the law, and marched away.

"Which would you young fellows rather do—dance for me or sleep in the calaboose for contempt of court?" his honor asked with a chuckle. They danced—danced in the spirit of tenderfeet sashaying to the music of six-shooters aimed at their feet. In after years when they returned to Cincinnati, the judge was sure to be in the house the opening night and back-stage later to recall, with much leg-slapping, the time he had hauled them out of bed—always, that is, until their last visit, the year of their jubilee. They missed his honor's wrinkled face and learned that he was dead.

In the summer between the first and second seasons with Gus Hill, Joe and Lew made their debut as producers, an enterprise that tossed no bomb in the producing world, however. It took the form of a commonwealth tent show playing South Brooklyn and Williamsburg. They tried it in Harlem, but that superior environ would have none of it. A commonwealth show was one in which the gate receipts, less expenses, were divided equally among the performers after each show, and in this case the only expense was the rental of a tent with benches. The advertised admission was ten cents, but at matinées, which were patronized exclusively by children, they compromised on pennies, knives, tops or what-have-you. Joe sold tickets and Lew collected them.

They managed and produced, and appeared twice on the bill first under their own names in the knockabout, and second as Smith and Way in combination with the Rogers Brothers. Max and Gus Rogers were neighborhood kids on the East Side. Gus, now dead, had appeared at occasional benefits in imitations of Pat Rooney, one of the favorite comedians of the '80s. Max had yet to lose his amateur standing. Weber and Fields had taught them what they knew of dancing and lent them a hand.

Since there were but two dressing rooms, Joe and Lew took one by right of their dignity as managers, and the rest of the company used the other. Being the youngest and least experienced, the Rogers Brothers suffered a continual hazing until they appealed in tears to be permitted to dress with the stars. The boon was granted, and Joe and Lew began to notice, without giving it much thought, that their pads and wigs were never exactly as they last had left them. These props of their knockabout act had been contrived ingeniously, not only to protect their heads, limbs and trunks from injury but to give off a maximum of sound when whacked. Without them, the act was impossible. Two years later when they beheld an imitation of the knockabout that its own parents could hardly distinguish from the original they could not help suspecting that perhaps they had been too hospitable with Max and Gus.

The second season with the Gus Hill show was much like the first. A variety show could play only the cities having variety theaters, and the list was not long. New York, Brooklyn, Paterson, Philadelphia, Baltimore, Washington, Pittsburgh, Cincinnati, Indianapolis, St. Louis, Chicago, Milwaukee, Cleveland, Buffalo, Rochester, Syracuse, Albany, Worcester, New Haven and Providence exhausted it. Twenty theaters all of a pattern; drinking and smoking during the performances in each, and men-only audiences. But the season is remembered for having brought them two new jobs.

In Chicago, in the spring, they played the Lyceum Theater. Tom Grenier, the owner, recently had bought the Burr Robins circus. He asked the boys if they would care to go out with the circus the coming summer. They wanted to know what they could do in a circus. Grenier thought that their knockabout would go well in the concert or after show, and that he could use them as clowns in the big ring; something simple, such as hanging onto the tails of galloping horses, falling off a horse now and then and making faces at the ringmaster. He would pay them twenty dollars a week each and expenses, and throw in a songbook-and-concert-ticket-selling privilege netting 10 per cent of sales. It was at a time when they could procure no other work. What two boys in their early teens ever hesitated over such an offer? Not they, anyway.

Later in the season, the Gus Hill show played Hyde & Behman's Theater, Brooklyn. Hyde & Behman was a great name in the variety world and when Richard Hyde noticed their act and offered to raise Gus Hill's thirty dollars to fifty dollars a week if the boys would join his Hyde's Comedians, managed by his brother Jim, the next season, they accepted. The fifty dollars would not include board, but they at least could eat when, where and what they liked. Hill was irate; but as his displeasure took the form of making them sleep by themselves and depriving them of all their extra work for the remaining ten weeks of the season, they survived.

Grenier's was a two-ring railroad circus, in contradistinction to a wagon show. Until ten years previously, all American circuses had moved overland under their own horse power. In 1872, despite the stubborn opposition of P. T. Barnum, his partner, and the indifference of the railroad companies, W. C. Coup had pioneered by putting his show on railway trucks. A wagon show's daily jump was limited to twenty to twenty-five miles. This low mobility made it necessary to play villages of a thousand persons or fewer, or to skip a date. The railroads could shift all equipment a hundred miles or more in twenty-four hours with ease, and Coup's experiment was so immediately successful that most of his competitors imitated his move in the next few seasons. The smallest shows continued to straggle through the mud and dust of Southern and Western roads for forty years more, growing fewer each year, until to-day another revolution is in full swing. With the spread of hard-surfaced roads, the perfecting of the gasoline motor and the soaring costs of railway transportation, the carnivals and all but the largest circuses are turning back to the highways with motorized shows, already a commonplace of the sawdust world.

The American circus has altered little in half a century, looked at from within the tent. It is larger, more elaborate and infinitely better organized; but old troupers will tell you that the substance of the entertainment is the same and the personnel of performers and roustabouts unchanging.

Outwardly, there is another story to tell. The circus has turned respectable. The old circus had a dual nature. It was both an entertainment and a guerrilla band levying war and tribute on the countryside. Its entertainment offended none, but with it and of it, licensed and protected by it, traveled a rough crew of pickpockets, sneak thieves, burglars, short-card gamblers, confidence men, short-change artists and the like.

Circus day was a day of high carnival in the rural community, followed, as high carnival usually is, by the cold gray dawn of the morning after. "War, pestilence, famine and the circus," was a rural adage, and there is no exaggeration in saying that one day's passing of these locust swarms often was equivalent in its effects to a partial crop failure in the afflicted vicinity.

The mender, or fixer, traveled ahead of the show, calling on the local police authorities. He was a silk-hatted, swallow-tailed personage, with a bulge in his right trousers pocket. A gentleman of infinite resource, of suave and unctuous or bluff and hearty address as the occasion seemed to demand. He left behind him more than a memory of his engaging personality.

Circus-ticket sellers were not paid. They paid the governors, as the owners were known, for the privilege of doing their work. The main ticket-wagon concession was worth one thousand dollars a season with the ordinary show, the lesser ticket concession smaller sums, and they paid splendid returns to men who knew their business. The ticket seller, an adept at palming and double counting, had the aid of cappers who jostled the buyer and shoved him along before he could check his change.

The clothesline concession was as standard a byproduct as the peanut-selling privilege. The first blast of the calliope at parade was the signal for the pillage of back yards and homes to begin, and the quest of the little pea in the shell game, and the black ace in three-card monte to open on the street corners.

The man who guessed your weight—"No charge if I fail"—spoke in a code intelligible only to his accomplices. As he ran his hands over a candidate he talked, seemingly to no purpose, but his "I think your weight is," translated, meant "His money is in his right trousers pocket." "I guess your weight to be" located the victim's purse in the hip pocket, and "I say your weight is" the inside coat pocket.

The free tight-rope-walking exhibition announced to take place on the lot immediately after the parade was no philanthropy. A crowd pushing and craning its necks to follow the swaying fortunes of a girl in white tights overhead was one made to order for pickpockets.

As the crowd gathered on the show lot, a capper would mount a convenient wagon, sweep off his hat and deliver a solicitous warning against thieves.

"Ladies and gentlemen," his harangue ran, "the management desires to caution you to protect your money and your valuables from pickpockets. The great John Doe show makes every effort, even to carrying its own police and detective force, to guard its patrons from these gentry; but the most elaborate precautions sometimes fail. There may be pickpockets among you now, and we implore you to cooperate with us by exercising reasonable vigilance."

A fair speech, indeed—the only purpose of which, however, was to lead every towner within hearing to reach instinctively for his wallet and watch, thereby telegraphing to the dips in the crowd the exact location of what they sought. If a man here and there discovered that he already had been robbed, his clamor only created the confusion in which pickpockets work best.

The rural American of an earlier day was a belligerent and free-spoken citizen, and he was not in the habit of taking such treatment lying down. A holiday customarily was celebrated in corn liquor. He was apt to signalize his arrival in town by whipping some ancient enemy of a neighborhood feud, and a stranger was a fair mark at any time.

By nightfall, a pooling of injuries, drink-inflamed resentment and local pride, time and again came to a head in a furious mob descent upon the circus with knives, sticks, stones and firearms.

No sham battles these! The circus well knew the harvest it sowed daily, and was prepared for the crop. It not only was perpetually on the alert, but it exercised a certain discipline and method in its ranks that gave it the advantage an organized force always has over a mob. And much practice made for perfection on the circus side.

Clems, such shindigs were known in circus argot, and their battle cry, "Hey, Rube!" That shibboleth brought every able-bodied man forth to do battle with tent stake, feet and fists. They were a rough-and-ready crew, and there is no record in show history of such a battle having gone against them. Homeric affairs, some were, celebrated in an Iliad of their own, a song of endless verses, the first and last of which will suffice here:

"'They'll eat yer up in this here teoun,
The boys'll tear yer cirkiss deoun.'
Thus spoke a man with hoary head.
The main guy winked and softly said,
'Hey, Rube!'

Gawks, guys and rubes, another day,
Whene'er a circus comes your way,
And you are sp'ilin' for a clem,
Be sure they haven't learned to sing,
'Hey, Rube!'"

The Burr Robins circus opened in Chicago in May and played that city continuously for six weeks, moving to a new location each day—an unknown procedure now. It is Weber and Fields's impression that they played every vacant lot in that sprawling young giant of a city and repeated on some without recognizing them. The first day's stand fell in the vicinity of the stockyards. Loyal Chicagoans were proud of Back of the Yards, and backed it against all comers for handiness with fist, boot, brickbat or write your own ticket. Whence the sporting expression, Packing House Rules.

Reporting on the lot for the first parade, the boys were ordered to make up as clowns, ride atop a circus wagon and act funny. The circus had traditions, customs, rigid class distinctions and a language all its own; its people were as clannish and as aloof as gypsies. Joe and Lew sensed this, and were homesick and ill at ease. Their constraint was not lightened when a rock hummed past their heads within two minutes after the parade set out. Back of the Yards was amusing itself, and every lad was a sharpshooter. Weber and Fields clung to the swaying deck of the lumbering red-and-gold animal wagon as it lurched over Chicago's cobblestones. They ducked, dodged, took it, and hung on. The Yards whooped its delight. The new clowns were being funny all right, but not according to the blue prints.

They resigned three times to the block, but they had to wait on the parade's return to the lot to tell Grenier. They yearned for that sweet Sabbath calm of the Bowery and they were going back.

"What?" Grenier hooted. "That's all part of the game. You'll get used to it. Is that the sort of lady fingers you New York kids are?" And he shamed them out of it.

Other sections of Chicago were less demonstrative, and they did get used to it. As part of their parade clowning they early devised a burlesque crap game. The second day of it the game was on in earnest, the third it gathered recruits. After that as many clowns as could hold onto the roof of the wagon shot craps the length and breadth of Chicago. Grenier pointed with pride to his recruits. He no more suspected than did the spectators and the corner policeman that the stakes were real and the cries of the dicers heartfelt. It was the old, old circus story. Beneath the clown's painted grimaces and the carnival vestments lay breaking hearts—and broken pockets.

For the period of the Chicago stay Grenier boarded out his troupers by contract. Joe and Lew were assigned to a boarding house with the freaks. The bearded lady sat at Lew's left and drank her coffee from a mustache cup. The fat man occupied the next three chairs on Joe's right, and never missed the middle one when Joe removed it, as he did at every opportunity. Directly opposite, on a high chair, sat the armless wonder. What that unfortunate lacked in arms he made up in the prehensile cunning of his feet. With these he helped and fed himself, and manipulated knife, fork and spoon as matter of factly as the elephants used their trunks. The bearded lady had a reputation as a wit to uphold and it was her pleasure to shout, "Hands off !" at least once at every meal when the wonder reached for some dish.

At the first breakfast Lew asked that the biscuits be passed. They lay nearest the wonder. He thrust forth a leg with a biscuit clutched in his foot. Lew did his own reaching from then on. Lemon meringue pie was the dessert the following noon. The wonder's struggle with the elusive pie gave the boys a lifelong distaste for that dish. Before night they besought Grenier to give them the three dollars their board was costing him and let them find themselves. He did, and in their reaction to the wonder they ate their dinners sometimes at the Palmer House, Chicago's pride, where a jar of stick candy stood beside the catchup bottle and the vinegar cruet in the center of each table, and there were nineteen choices of meats on the seventy-five-cent table-d'hôte menu that read like an inventory.

As youngsters and outlanders, they were targets for every gust of humor, good or bad, that blew. They were ordered to hold up a tent pole and left holding it until their arms throbbed, or until another joker happened along to order them to drop the pole and fetch a bucket of stake holes. They were blamed for their own blunders and any other stray stupidity. The best they got was ignoring. Their answer was, "Yes, sir; no, sir; thank you, sir," and a smile. They sirred even the canvas men. Before the show was out of Chicago, that time-tested system had accomplished its ends. They belonged. Special favors even came their way, and when the boys left the show before the end of the season the entire troupe paraded to the station.

Their venture at the concert-ticket-and-songbook selling privileges Grenier had promised was brief—and instructive. Theirs, they discovered, was a subsidiary concession in the first instance. That is, a highly competent salesman with a satchel of tickets and change strapped over his shoulders stood at the gate of the concert tent. Only when the crush was so heavy that he could not handle it all did a stray customer filter through to Lew and Joe.

The main concessionaire was not selling tickets for any paltry 10 per cent commission. The boys, standing idle behind him, had both time and a vantage point to study his short-changing tricks. His glib rascality and the simplicity of his victims struck them as funny. This snickering so got on the short-changer's nerves that his hands lost their cunning. Turning in exasperation, he asked the boys how much they were making a day at the gate. They thought fifty or sixty cents would cover it.

"I'll give you each a dollar a day to stay away from here, and be glad to be quit of you," he snapped. It was a bargain.

At 10 per cent commission the songbook job did not pay for wear and tear on the lungs; but Joe and Lew kept at it until a day in Iowa when a band of blanket Indians from a near-by reservation attended the circus and stayed for the concert.

It was the custom to pass the songbooks among the after-show audiences for examination, and to return to collect either the book or its price. The first Indian shook his head and grunted a refusal to have a book. The boys had heard somewhere that a redskin and his money soon were parted by a paleface. Hadn't the teacher in Public School No. 42 told them how the Dutch traded the Iroquois out of Manhattan Island for a string of beads and a bottle of firewater? Here was the biggest opportunity since 1626, and our young salesmen rose to it.

They pressed books upon the unwilling aborigines. They called them all chief, and further flattered them by addressing them in their own, their native tongue or so Lew conceived "Look 'em pretty pictures, chief," to be. One Indian reached for a book, then another. The ice was broken. Every Indian wanted a book. Lew's supply was exhausted, then Joe's. They returned with fresh loads.

When the market was saturated, they held out open palms.

"Wampum," they said."Two bits, twenty-five cents! A quarter! Savee—money? Mazumah! Geld! You catchem book, me catchem wampum! Nice book! Pretty pictures! Squaw heap like! You buy?"

Stony faces among the Indian delegation.

"No wampum, no book," ruled Lew.

He reached for the nearest book. The Indian drew away. Joe grabbed and his Indian sat on his book. They grabbed at other books. Other Indians sat on their books and stared stonily ahead. As he missed his next snatch, Lew perceived, out of a corner of an eye, a redskin unsheathe his hunting knife and test the blade absently upon his thumb. He became aware that he was in the midst of several hundred blanketed Indians, and that more knives were coming out of their sheaths, abstractedly to be sure, but emerging all the same. His next step was backward. All his next steps were backward, and Joe passed him, stepping faster. At a distance, a considerable distance, they checked up. They were out one hundred and seventy songbooks for which they had paid cash to Grenier. It went down to profit and loss, and they retired forthwith from the songbook trade. Not a sound had been uttered or an expression changed by the one hundred and seventy redskins. The American Indian has a dry sense of humor.

When the circus took to the road everyone save those bespangled aristocrats, the cat tamers, the equestrian and the acrobat families, helped in tearing the show down, loading, unloading and setting it up again. It was rise and shine at eight o'clock. From the bunk cars in which they slept two and three to the berth, the troupe rolled out for breakfast: food of the coarsest, thrown at them scrambled in tin plates. Parade assembly was at nine. While the performers teased the populace with hints of greater glories to be unfolded, the canvas men got the tents up. Rarely was there time to wash the make-up off or change to street clothes between parade and afternoon show, afternoon show and night. The tearing down started before the night performance was over, and it was two or three A.M. before the last car was loaded and the train under way. A hard life in good weather, a dog's life in bad. Joe and Lew found eight or nine shows a day in the museums a bed of roses by comparison. Often the prairie sun beat down so hotly on the big top that the grease paint on their wigs melted and ran down their faces in blistering trickles. At What Cheer, Iowa, a tornado stood the circus on its head just before an afternoon performance. The boys ran into a near-by home in their clown make-up. An old woman was alone in the house and hysterical in the knowledge that her daughter and grandchildren were somewhere on the show lot. They forgot their own fright comforting the old lady. In the wake of the wind came a torrential rain that left the lot a swamp, but the tent was up again and the bands blaring by night.

The respect and deference shown the women of the circus, no matter what the stress and strain, impressed the boys. Lumber jacks and navvies by winter; canvas men, teamsters and razorbacks by summer—this whisky-swigging, hard-bitten crew leashed its tongues and doffed its hats for the humblest of the women. There was a girls' band with the Robins show. These band women were shown the same respect as the haughty young princesses of bareback and the flying rings.

All this, to those to the circus born, was a matter of course. That was trouping. They met hardships as indifferently as seasoned sailors. If they grumbled it was only by way of assuring themselves and others what rough-and-ready fellows, what born troupers, they were. And they looked with ineffable disdain upon the yokels and towners who were content to follow their dull little cow paths through life. The sharp pungency of trampled dog fennel in the hot summer air, the odor of the animal cages and the cool smell of sawdust were incense in their nostrils.

Once exposed to it, circus folk liked to believe that there was no cure but to go on trouping until age bent and slowed the legs or one died in the ring.

Joe and Lew did not find it so. Rather was it an antitoxin. Weber never cares to see, and Fields never has seen a circus from the day they left Grenier in Nebraska in August, 1887. Fond grandfather that he is, Fields has avoided even Madison Square Garden in the spring when the biggest show opens its season and the children of New York mark the calendar.

A startling adventure he and his partner underwent at David City, Nebraska, had much to do with this aversion, but that is another chapter.

Chapter IV

On the Road

Circus and Variety Days, 1887–1896

The Burr Robins Circus, trouping westward from Chicago in August of 1887, had pitched its tents at David City, a county-seat town of Eastern Nebraska, for a day's stand. The Missouri Valley was on the boom in '87 and business was flush.

There was a fight on the lot in the early afternoon. A townsman who had lost twenty dollars at a three-card-monte pitch attacked the card sharper. Three circus followers rallied to the latter's rescue and the townsman was beaten unmercifully. He was able to hiss a threat through his cut and swollen lips before he limped away.

Whispers of impending trouble ran about the lot at supper. Swapping of yarns in an infrequent idle hour with the show was certain to include a reminiscence of some epic battle between trouper and towner. On long Sunday jumps, the circus's one breathing spell, Weber and Fields had heard such tales of clems and Hey, Rube; had listened and laughed as one does at a good yarn.

The show's cars lay on a siding fully a mile from the lot. In coming in for the parade and again for the evening show, the troupe had used the road which led through town. There was one other route, down the single-track railroad, but the boys were not familiar with it.

As they were making up for the night show old Pop Davenport, the principal clown, a veteran of the day when the clown was the circus and all the rest little more than background for him, peered at them from beneath his shaggy eyebrows.

"Do you boys know what 'Hey, Rube' means?" he asked shortly. They grinned and said they had heard some talk.

"Talk, eh?" he retorted. "You're likely to hear more than talk to-night. Laugh, will you? Well, I've seen a sight of 'em in my time; but none that was funny, leastwise until a long time after the bruises healed. Take the advice of an old-timer. If trouble breaks it'll come about the close of the concert when they're taking down the main top. Don't put on any make-up for your concert turn. Put your costume coat over your regular clothes, and throw the funny stuff away the minute it pops. When you hear 'Hey, Rube,' no matter what you're doing, leg it for the cars as fast as your kid legs'll carry you. Take to the track. They'll murder you if you go through town. Don't bother your heads about what's going on; just light out for all you're worth and keep going. It's not your row; you're youngsters, and you ain't circus folk, and you'd only get in the way and need looking out for if you stayed."

The old man's earnestness gleamed through his clown's make-up, and they were sobered. His advice was remembered.

Three hours later the boys were in the midst of their concert turn when Grenier's brother-in-law, who traveled with the show, pushed back a tent flap and beckoned to them. They ran off the platform, shedding the costumes that branded them of the circus as they went. At the flap Grenier's brother-in-law seized each by a hand and started for the railroad right of way.

The night was overcast and sultry, its blackness broken only by flickers of heat lightning on the horizon and the guttering of the kerosene torches on the show lot. A band still played inside the tent, and they heard close by the soft whoosh of an invisible elephant blowing dust. In the distance a town dog barked, and the south wind rustled the ripening corn in a field across the track.

No other sound for the first hundred yards they ran. They asked themselves if they were fleeing from a fancy. Then, as they cleared the show grounds and struck the railroad embankment, a single shout awoke the night—"Hey, Rube!" A rattle of pistol fire; a confused and waspish buzz of voices, growing louder; a woman's scream, shrill and horripilating. A burst of flame. The main tent was afire, fed by coal oil. Horses stampeded past, their hoofs drumming on the hard prairie. An elephant's trumpeting was answered by a berserk roar from the lions' cage, setting off the menagerie. The thud of animal bodies beating against bars and wooden walls, the screech of monkeys and tropical birds, more shots, the clamorous pealing of an alarm bell in the town.

The circus forces were beating back the first shock of the mob's attack, laying about them with tent stakes in close formation. Women and children huddled in the shelter of overturned wagons. Blows thudded and thwacked, men cursed, groaned and breathed in gasps and grunts. An elephant, flailing a tent pole in his trunk, was prodded forward by the bull keeper into the enemy's ranks. Their center broke and fell back in panic. The glare of the burning tent rent the dark, under cover of which the attackers had at first swept everything before them, and now disconcerted their straggling lines. Others, satisfied with the blows they had struck, and mindful of their own heads, were slipping back into the town singly and in pairs.

The circus had won; but Weber and Fields and their escort, panting up the railway grade, could not know it. The tumult, rising in volume, seemed to be coming nearer. The burning tent lit up the landscape, and in their minds they were as visible to others as the show lot was to them when they stole a fearsome glance over their shoulders. Joe stumbled on a tie and fell. Grenier's brother-in-law kept on and was swallowed in the darkness ahead.

Lew helped his partner up and they ran side by side again. They came to a long trestle. Here lack of breath and the peril of a misstep forced them to slow to a walk. As they felt their way tie by tie over the shadowy skeleton of timbers the headlight of a train flashed round a curve ahead and bore down upon them on the single track. Now they saw only too well what lay ahead, behind, beneath and to either side. They were halfway across, below was the gleam of water, and there was not a foot of clearance on either side of the rails. They ran frantically and recklessly for the far end, and saw—or in their terror thought they saw—that they could not make it. The rails were singing, the pop of the engine's valves was in their ears now. Turning, they fled backward. The engineer saw them and loosed a staccato shriek of the whistle that completed their panic.

Darkly glinting waters lay beneath. Joe could not swim a stroke; Lew was an indifferent swimmer. One resource remained. They could hang by their hands from the outer edge of the trestle, possibly, until the train had passed. Down they swung. The train was upon them. The engine rocked past, hot coals spilling from the fire box and falling with a hiss into the water below. Then the pound and clank of freight cars; a string of empties and too evidently a long one. It was slowing for the yards, and sparks flew from the brake shoes. These children of the tenements clung desperately to a string piece in an agony of fear and aching arms while the train roared on endlessly. They prayed and shouted encouragement to each other, but their words were smothered. Finally the flash of green and red lights on the rear of the caboose and the train had passed.

But when they tried to pull themselves up again their overtaxed muscles would not respond. Each straining effort weakened the relaxing grip of their numbed fingers. They screamed for help and the echoes mocked them. Bullfrogs croaked a requiem in the reeds.

Between sobs, Joe managed to say, "I guess we're goners, Lew."

Fields, choking on his tears, protested to a last despairing hope.

"There's one chance left, Web," he argued. "We can drop while we've a little strength left and swim for it."

"I can't swim," his partner reminded him. "Give my clothes to my brother Muck, and don't tell mamma it was this way. Call it pneumonia or something."

"Maybe I can you out, Web." Lew tried to put conviction into his voice, but it broke on him. "If anything happens to me and you pull through, just take my things home."

"When I count three we'll drop," said Weber.

"Good-by, Lew."

"Good-by, Web."

"One—two—three——"

They let go, falling like plummets, and landed with a great splash in a foot and a half of stagnant water, their legs sinking softly into a deep cushion of ooze. A cow, taking her cud-chewing ease on the bank, clambered to her feet with a startled snort and a fling of her heels and scampered away.

Death in a dozen forms had clutched at their throats continuously for fifteen minutes, to end in this ludicrous anticlimax. In their reaction, they laughed and cried hysterically and hugged each other ecstatically. The circus riot, it came to them, had been forgotten utterly for the past five minutes. Now it seemed a memory of another life. The west, they saw, was dark again. The tent had burned out and the night had recaptured its hush. The crow of a distant cock at midnight was borne on the soft south wind.

Four men were dead, casualties of that brief hot clash between trouper and avenging towner—two citizens, the boss canvas man and a razorback—but the boys would not know that until they had waded out of the stock pond and made their way to the show train, where the circus was beginning to bind its wounds and to count the cost of swindling a free-born Nebraskan.

Grenier had other worries that night, but Joe and Lew forced both themselves and their resignations upon his attention. The season was nearing its end and they must be back in New York to open with Hyde's Comedians—it had occurred to them since suppertime. Grenier's large and varied stock of profanity had gone to the well once too often since that same meal. He hadn't a curse left and only waved them aside wearily.

At sunup the circus was on its way again. Grenier and a few others stayed behind for the inquest, and to hire every lawyer in David City.

The circus did not show that day at its next stop; but the following morning brought a new big top from Omaha and Grenier from David City. He heard their resignations a second time and paid them off. Just then he was as weary of his circus experiment as were they, and sympathetic with their yearning for home.

"You've got something to tell them on the Bowery," was his only comment.

The troupe paraded the boys to the Chicago train and the girls' band played "The Girl I Left Behind Me." Their circus days were over once and for all.

The fare to New York in that day of five cents a mile would make a hole in their summer's earnings, so they stopped in Chicago in the hope of picking up a stop-gap engagement. The season had not opened and Kohl & Castle's Olympic was the only theater running. They knew Castle only by reputation, and repute gave him the name of being a Tartar. Outside his door, each pushed the other forward. They entered together, eventually, and spoke as one. Castle cut them short.

"What can you do?" he demanded.

They began a lengthy catalogue of their talents and were interrupted again.

"How much?" he growled.

"Sixty dollars," Joe quoted.

"Fifty dollars," quoted Lew, in the same breath.

"You kids better rehearse that number some more and come back when you know your lines better," Castle commented.

They conferred outside the door and were back again in the time it took the theater man to light a fresh cigar.

"Fifty dollars," they harmonized.

"Forty," was his reply, and that was what they got.

Hyde's Comedians opened in Baltimore at Kernan's Theater in September. Hyde played the same cities, the same theaters and at the same ten to fifty cent prices as the Gus Hill and all the other variety road shows; but Weber and Fields now did only one act—their knockabout—outside of the aftershow. Hyde boasted an all-star show that included such favorites as Kitty O'Neill and Helena Mora, whom old theater-goers may remember for her barytone voice and her practice of planting someone in the gallery to sing the refrain of her numbers. That season the gallery voice was that of Gus Edwards, then a boy, now a producer and potentate of Tin Pan Alley.

The bartender at Kernan's was raffling off a saddle horse for the benefit of something or other and pressed chances on the company. The chances began at one cent and ended at three dollars. Fields drew the four-cent ticket; Weber paid thirty-eight cents for his. The show played Kernan's Washington house the following week. In midweek Fields got a telegram, the first he has any memory of. His hands shook as he opened the message. It read:

You win horse. Will give you one hundred fifty dollars cash or send animal. Advise you take cash.

Half the horse was Joe's for it was share and share alike in good fortune and bad with Weber and Fields always. They might quarrel as to which half was whose, but the fifty-fifty never was questioned. Once with the Gus Hill show they had dissolved partnership and carried this division to heroic lengths. Weber customarily carried the firm's funds and accounted scrupulously for them. This Fields decided one day was a violation of the partnership code. He insisted that he be the custodian of the funds every other week, and Weber gave in. Lew was hazy in his accounting and Joe soon demanded a cash-on-hand statement. In answer Fields merely emptied his pockets and divided the contents into two equal piles.

"Where's the rest of it?" Joe demanded.

"What rest?" Lew asked aggressively.

"There's only $9.20 here."

"Well, didn't I give you $4.60?"

"I bet you spent it," Joe accused. "What right you got to spend my money?"

"Listen!" his partner commanded. "If I spent a dollar or so I spent it for the good of the firm. Didn't I pay half of it? Whatever I got, half's yours. That's the agreement. Whatever I spend, half's yours. That's the agreement. Take your $4.60 and shut up!"

For a week the two did not speak. Sharing the same dressing room and the same can of grease paint, this was awkward. A fictitious third party was invented as an intermediary.

"Ask him if he is going to use that grease paint all night," Joe would address the air.

"Tell him, please, to keep his shirt on," Lew would answer.

This huff would have passed off naturally in time had not Fields "accidentally" hit Weber a terrific rap over the nose with his cane during the knockabout while their relations still were strained.

Weber clutched his bleeding nose with one hand and shook the other at Fields. He would listen to no apologies. This was the end. He was done with a partner who would steal from him, even try to murder him. At this Lew flew into an equivalent rage. In their dressing room they began dividing their effects, but their joint property would not come out even. There was an odd wig, a woman's blond tresses with two long braids. Joe grabbed one braid, Lew the other, and they tore the wig in two. They owned but one trunk between them. Borrowing a yardstick and a saw from the stage carpenter, they ascertained the mathematical center of the trunk and sawed it squarely in half. Gus Hill hearing the row, intervened and forced a truce. By another week they were inseparable again, but Lew never after was treasurer of the firm.

No such halving of the horse was attempted. Lew and Joe needed few chattels less than they did a saddle horse—even a four-cent one. If they had heard of a bridle path, they thought of it as a church aisle. Their equestrian experience had been limited strictly to hanging onto the tails of the milk-white steeds in the big ring of the Burr Robins Circus, and that association had not conduced to a closer intimacy.

They had no doubt but that they should take the one hundred and fifty dollars, but the Hyde company met in executive session and decided that there was something rotten in Baltimore. Why, they asked, if the bartender was not intending to hornswoggle two inexperienced boys, was he so anxious to give them one hundred and fifty dollars in lieu of the horse? It was as plain as the nose on Lew's face that the animal must be worth much more than any one hundred and fifty dollars. They led the boys to the telegraph office and dictated their reply for them. It was: Rush the horse.

It came on Friday—with a twenty-six dollar freight bill attached—and the entire company, seventeen strong, assembled in the freight yards. Epinard was not welcomed more hospitably this year. Five dollars was needed to induce the yardmen to unload the animal without delay.

Whether the bartender switched horses on them or not still is an open question; no other solution ever was put forward. It looked the prancing palfry little enough at first glance, but when its blanket was removed it was disclosed as Exhibit A in the annual report of the S. P. C. A. Every rib in the sway-backed structure stood out in bas-relief and the rheumy eyes gazed accusingly at

Hyde's Comedians. Here was a Baltimorean that might have seen the same dawn's early light of September 14, 1814, remarked by Francis Scott Key.

It took all seventeen of them to push the four-legged misanthropist to a livery stable. The proprietor's first offer was twenty-five dollars. He had no opportunity of changing his mind. The net deficit on Weber and Fields's books was $6.42. They have lost money on horses since, but not through owning them.

From fifty dollars a week with Hyde they vaulted the next season to seventy dollars with the Australian Novelty Company, another variety road show. No theaters were open in the hot months, and the commonwealth tent show of the previous year had been no howling success. Loafing in the pool room of Miner's Bowery curb market of the variety stage, with three idle months ahead, Weber and Fields heard of a turkey show being organized by Lester and Williams, two comedians ten years their senior.

A turkey and a commonwealth are one and the same, save that the latter played under canvas. Actors clubbed together in these potluck enterprises in the slack times at Christmas, Lent and midsummer. The origin of the word "turkey" has been disputed for years to no agreement. Perhaps the equal division of the receipts suggested to some early metaphorist the carving of the Thanksgiving bird; possibly the balance remaining after expenses was thought of as a holiday windfall, or so much turkey. Lester and Williams already had arranged a booking at a Bridgeport, Connecticut, beer garden. The American Four, including Peter Dailey; Dave Marion, later of burlesque renown, and his wife, Minnie Bell; and two other well-known acts had joined up. Another turn was needed. Lester and Williams would give Weber and Fields a thirty-dollar weekly guaranty. The boys went along.

Business was bad, and Lester and Williams were the freest and easiest of spenders in a spendthrift profession. Marion, who was older in experience and had known Joe and Lew almost from their infancy, advised them on Wednesday to ask for an advance. They did, and got five dollars, which they hid in one of their shoes. All the company except the Marions slept in one large room. In the morning the five dollars was gone. Joe and Lew sniffled, and Lester and Williams were their loudest sympathizers. It was a darned shame, they asked the world to witness, and to show where their hearts were they would give the boys ten dollars more that night. The ten dollars was hidden in the same cache. Friday morning the shoe was empty again. More tears and more sympathy. Lester and Williams made no secret of their opinion of the fiend in human form who would steal from a couple of kids. In their big-hearted way they advanced a second ten dollars. What if business was bad? This time the money went under Joe's pillow. He slept fitfully, groping for the bills at each waking. Reassured, he fell off into dreamless slumber eventually.

When he woke again it was midmorning. He reached under the pillow. The money was A. W. O. L.

Lester and Williams gave them another five dollars that day, calling attention to the fact that this made thirty dollars, the week's guaranty. Joe and Lew said nothing, but on the spot they addressed an envelope, dropped the bill in and posted it home. Lester and Williams watched the proceedings with interest.

"By the way, boys," one of them said after a heavy silence, "we've been talking it over and we've decided to let you in on the turkey next week. That'll beat any thirty-dollar guaranty. Some of the others kicked, but we went to the front for you. 'Do you want to take advantage of a couple of kids?' we asked 'em."

This was out of the frying pan into the fire; a choice between a now-you-see-it-now-you-don't thirty dollars and a two-fourteenths part of an algebraic quantity known as *x*. They took a chance on *x*, the unknown sum.

Business continued poor, and there was only sixty dollars dumped on the table the second Saturday night to be cut fourteen ways. This was *x* in the Lester and Williams algebra.

A member of the company doubled for one instant as lightning calculator, then whispered to the boys, "Watch me and dive when I do." He dived. Joe and Lew dived after him. The three swept the table bare and were out of the theater door before anyone could stop them. The boys ran all the way to the boarding house. There they counted their grab. The total was twenty-four dollars. This they pinned inside the lining of Joe's vest and put the vest under Lew's pillow.

The others straggled in with reproaches and the word that the turkey would gobble no more. Joe and Lew swore that they had mailed the money home at the first post box and all seemed content to let it go at that. A Sabbath quiet lay over Bridgeport when Weber and Fields awoke. The American Four, Lester and Williams and the rest slept heavily. The vest still reposed beneath the pillow. Fields sighed relievedly and explored the lining. No twenty-four dollars! He turned the vest inside out. Only the pinholes remained as a souvenir. Easy come, easy go!

The boys were broke and the show disbanded, but they ate supper at home. To use their own phrase, they cried their way to New York. That is to say, they took their teary faces to the railway station, pulled out the *vox humana* stop and registered innocence in distress with a pathos geared up to melt the heart of a dog catcher and dissolve the boiler cake in the yard switch engine if need be. Softer material was at hand. A theatrical troupe, the James Boys' Last Ride company, rolled up in an omnibus. The women dried the boys' tears and the manager paid their fares. Jesse and Frank James were well-mannered little playfellows after two weeks of Lester and Williams's turkey show.

Weber and Fields were at liberty, as actors put it, the rest of the summer. September saw them on the road with the Australian Novelty Company, which took its name from the nativity of its stars, the Austin sisters, trapeze performers. The novelty was a human-fly stunt by Amy Austin, a thriller never since duplicated in the theater. At each performance she walked head downward without visible support on a smoothly polished platform suspended within ten feet of the very roof of the auditorium and forty feet or more above the heads of the breathless orchestra floor. Her husband, manager of the show and an ex-circus man, had devised vacuum rubber cups so powerful that, fixed to the soles of his wife's shoes, they sustained her weight. The secret of these cups died with Austin. His wife would swing herself upward by trapeze until she could plant her feet simultaneously against the platform. When the cups gripped the plank by suction Amy discarded the trapeze and slowly slid one foot before the other until she had progressed topsyturvily to the far end of the ten-foot platform. There she would pivot cautiously and return to her starting point. Often she would fall into the net stretched twenty feet below and begin all over.

Audiences fidgeted in the five to eight minutes' wait while the complex gear and tackle was fixed, tested and unfixed, and Austin sent Weber and Fields on in make-up to help the stage hands and to amuse the audience at the same time. In attempting both they did neither well. Austin tried again. Why couldn't they follow his wife with a burlesque from the same dizzy height? That the stage crew would be taking down the safety net while Weber and Fields were showing up Doctor Newton and his law of gravitation, Austin waved aside as a quibble, until they pointed out that they might fall upon and seriously damage one or more paid admissions. That was a point of view a manager could grasp.

"Well, be here to-morrow morning at ten and we'll try to work it out anyway," he ordered.

On the morrow Amy Austin's patent shoes were laced on Fields's feet and the rehearsal began. Lew hauled himself hand-over-hand up a rope to the high trapeze, swung himself higher and higher, and finally shot his upturned feet against the inverted platform. The vacuum cups glued to the plank as barnacles to a ship's hull.

There he hung upside down like a ham from a Woolworthian smokeless rafter, stricken suddenly with a paralysis of terror as his bulging eyes plumbed the yawning void below. His leg muscles turned to water. He could not move a foot forward or backward; he could not pull his feet loose and would not have dared to had he been able. But he could yell—yell so affrightedly as to drown all the jumble of shouted advice that floated up to his purpling ears.

His screams frightened even Austin, who shed his coat, spat upon his hands and scrambled up the rope to the trapeze. From this proximity he tried to soothe the boy's panic. Lew was in no mood either for lullabies or for choose-your-exit-now instructions. To every counsel he screeched one answer: "I can't."

There was only one way of getting the amateur human fly down other than by cutting a hole in the roof, and Austin took it. Gathering momentum on the trapeze, he launched a flying leap at the suspended Fields, tackled him around the waist and tore him and his trick shoes loose. Austin and Fields dropped together in close embrace. It is a feat to fall easily and safely into a net. These two just fell, dropped as a pair of mortared bricks from, a shaky cornice, but broke no bones. Fields feared the season would end before they landed. With his first returning breath he published an ultimatum.

"Hereafter," he decreed, "I act with both feet on the stage and the stage right side up."

It was during this season with the Australian Novelty Company that Fields first sank a hatchet into Weber's head, a piece of comedy business that ranks with the thrown custard pie in the pantheon of slapstick. The hatchet trick was devised as an encore bit. Its mechanics was simplicity itself—a cork cushion on top of Weber's steel-plated wig.

The gouging out of Weber's eye was another innovation of that season, stumbled upon by accident when an audience laughed at Fields's sincere efforts to remove a mote of dust that had settled in his partner's eye while the act was in progress. Weber wore a long nail in the toe of one comedy shoe and would retaliate by kicking Lew, the nail apparently sinking into Fields's anatomy and holding the shoe fast. More cork padding did the trick. Lew returned the compliment with a kick that set off an explosive cap in the toe of his right shoe. It was about this time, too, that they first sprang upon a palpitating world a gag now hoary and rheumatic but still in the ring:

"Who is that lady I saw you with last night?"

"She ain't no lady; she's my wife."

A travesty on a magic act took care of another curtain call. With the conventional hocus-pocus of stage legerdemain, they set a bottomless bottle squarely over a hole in the stage. To the audience's eyes the bottle was intact, but with the connivance of a stage hand in the basement the bottle was made to sprout a new absurdity at every flirt of Weber's handkerchief, culminating in a ten-foot steel rod and exposure of the hoax. The old knockabout was growing fatter with comedy each year, but its fundamentals were yet unchanged.

Their drawing power was such by now that Harry and John Kernell's Own Company signed them at a hundred dollars a week for their fifth and last swing around the variety circuit with a show not their own. The Kernells were rated the first Irish song, dance and dialogue team of their time. The stage has nothing quite like them to-day. The brothers were strikingly different types; John with a deep bass voice, Harry with a thin little tenor, but born comedians both. Each had been a hack driver in Philadelphia. The story is that Tony Pastor heard one of them singing from his driver's seat as he waited on a fare outside a Philadelphia saloon late one wintry night and took him up.

Ward and Vokes, later to become Percy and Harold, the stage's best-known tramp comedians, were with the Kernell show that season. Ten years earlier Weber and Fields had played with them at Bowker's Pier, Atlantic City, at ten dollars a week and board and lodging—such as it was. Bowker put his waiters and actors up in a mangy beach cottage crowded with bunks ranged in tiers three and four high like a lumber camp. Actors playing Bowker's together ever afterward had a common bond of sympathy. Ward, Vokes, Weber, Fields

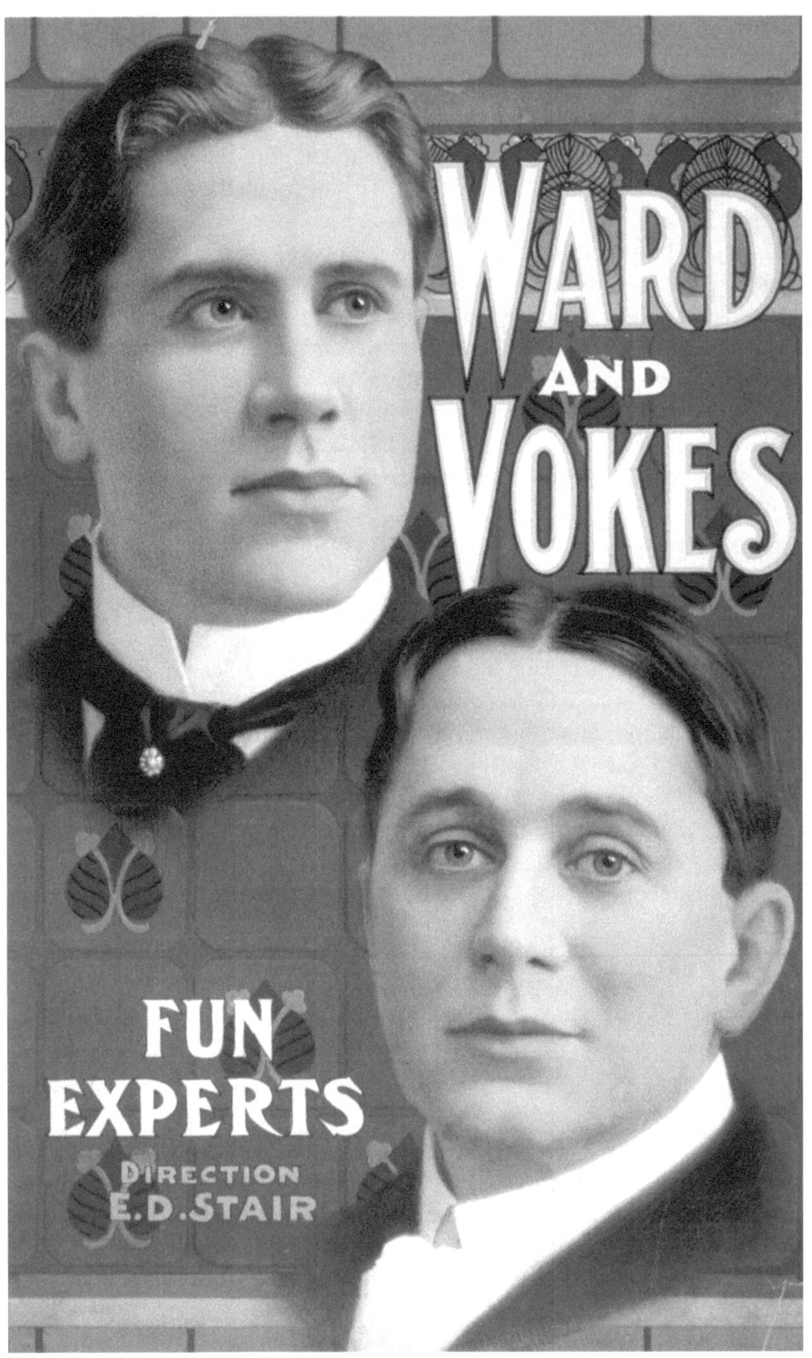

Photo 5. Ward and Vokes poster, c. 1902. U.S. Lithograph Co., Library of Congress.

and two other members of the company, Harding and Nash by name, gathered together at fifty-cent-limit poker the first week out with the Kernells and the game became a nightly institution.

When the show reached Paterson on the swing back eastward the boys had been away from home for twelve weeks, and determined to spend their nights in New York, commuting back and forth. This broke up the poker game. Ward, Vokes and Nash, who roomed together, took their meager talents to a gambling house, played the first hand to win and the rest to get even, and did neither. Paterson palaces of chance did not subscribe to that jolly old custom of refunding breakfast or drink money to the losers. Harding was the only member of the poker sextet within call and with money. One turned to Harding only in dire emergencies, but this was one such. Ward and Vokes sent Nash to Harding's room to cry until Harding should part with a dollar.

Nash wept like the third act of East Lynne and drowned Harding out. For this feat Ward and Vokes adjudged Nash entitled to a full half rather than a third of the dollar.

It was a disinterested effort on Nash's part, a bit of art for art and Ward and Vokes's sakes. He was off his feed himself and thought of breakfast with neither concern nor relish. Dropping in at the corner drug store he talked his symptoms over with the prescription clerk.

"What you need is a good tonic," the clerk told him, handing over a bottle of beef, iron and wine and dropping Nash's lone half dollar into the till. Nash sampled the bottle, found it good to the taste and improvidently drank it all before going to bed.

When Joe and Lew arrived from New York the following noon, Nash's was the first face they saw on the station platform. He was yelling their names before the train stopped. He must have five dollars at once, he insisted.

From his incoherence they made out something about owing Harding one dollar and being hungry.

"Why five dollars?" Joe objected. "You only owe Harding a dollar; you aren't going to eat four dollars' worth of lunch, are you ?"

"Ain't I?" Nash shouted. "Come along and watch me if you don't trust me. Four dollars won't buy the ham to trim all the eggs I want! I guess you never drank a bottle of appetite medicine at night and then had no money to buy your breakfast."

There was a three weeks' gap in the Kernell show booking in the late spring before it closed with a week at Tony Pastor's, New York, and a week at Gilmore's, Philadelphia. Some days before the lay-off Harry Kernell asked Joe and Lew if they wished to go out with the show again the next fall.

"Yes," Weber replied; "but we'll want more money."

"How much more?" Kernell queried.

Joe always bargained from the top downward.

"Well," he said, "we ought to get a hundred and fifty dollars next season."

Kernell showed an unaccountable rage at this asking price, and ended a tirade by saying, "If you want to come for the same money you're getting, all right. If not, all right."

Kernell was to die in an asylum, and already his company had marked the erratic moods that increasingly eclipsed his wonted geniality. His failing mind alone accounts for the feud he declared upon these two boys still in their teens.

On the Tuesday before the Monday the show was to reopen at Pastor's, Harry Kernell sent for Joe and Lew. They called, and stuck out for one hundred and fifty dollars.

"Do you know the Rogers Brothers?" he asked.

"Sure we do," they chorused.. "We put them on the stage."

"Well," Kernell told them, "I can get the Rogers Brothers for sixty dollars a week. They do an act just like yours. If you want to take a cut to sixty dollars for these last two weeks, all right. If not, I'll put the Rogers Brothers on in your place."

The boys laughed at him.

"The Rogers Brothers' act is nothing like ours," they insisted. "They do a neat song and dance. We ought to know; we taught it to 'em."

"I'm telling you," Kernell retorted, "that their act's the spit an' image of yours. The only difference is that it's a darned sight better. I'm being soft hearted to give you a chance to meet their price. Well, what's it going to be?"

They didn't bother to argue the first point longer, but warned him that they would hold him to their contract for the season.

"Maybe I will have to keep you at one hundred dollars these last two weeks," he admitted, "but it'll be a sick day for you if I do. I'll put the Rogers Brothers on ahead of you and make you the jokes of New York. I'll queer you so you won't get a show next year."

Weber thought it was his turn to bluff.

"Hop to it,' he challenged. "We'll take our own show out next season."

This was entitled to rank as the best joke of 1889, and would have been saluted as such instantly at Miner's Bowery or anywhere along Fourteenth Street; but Kernell, the pantaloon, was playing Richard III this day. He answered not with horse laughter but with more threats, and the conference broke up in showers of hot words.

Reporting at Tony Pastor's on Monday, Joe and Lew found the Rogers Brothers posted to open the bill and they were to close it. Still incredulous, they were watching from the front of the house when the curtain rose. They had not seen Max and Gus Rogers on or off stage in two years and had put Kernell's talk down as an hallucination.

Now it was their turn at hallucinations. Unless their eyes cheated them they had just seen, as in a mirror, themselves walk on the stage. There were Mike and Myer, their own flesh and blood. Facsimile costumes, facsimile make-ups, line for line and business for business, their own knockabout was done before them. No cheap counterfeit, but a photographic reproduction. The Rogers Brothers had caught the spirit as closely as the letter of the act, and they had what Weber and Fields never had—robust, resonant singing voices. It was Joe and Lew's fate to hear their own song sung so much better than they themselves could do it that they failed to recognize it until the chorus.

Weber and Fields stumbled back to their dressing room in a daze. Harry Kernell grinned fiendishly as they passed. It was too late to attempt any changes in their act. Fortunately New York variety audiences knew them so well that the house had recognized Kernell's sharp practice and resented it without understanding its wherefores. The boys could only take the audience into their confidence, promise a change by Tuesday and serve a stale repetition of an act seen an hour earlier.

Joe and Lew worked until dawn the next morning on new business, new gags, new mispronunciations, and varied their act sufficiently at the Tuesday matinée to defeat partly the conspiracy. But Harry Kernell stood in the wings taking notes on every change. That night the Rogers Brothers added each variation to the original act and anticipated the Weber and Fields turn 100 percent again.

This unequal contest of wits continued all that week at Pastor's and the next in Philadelphia. Joe and Lew slept three and four hours a night, giving the rest of their time to a feverish study of new lines and business, all memorized and used by the Rogers Brothers by the succeeding performance. Harry Kernell dropped all other work to watch from the wings, taking notes while Joe and Lew were on, rehearsing Max and Gus by the hour and prompting them when they took the stage. It became an obsession with him. Weber and Fields were in the position of a football team whose signals were being tipped to the opposition in advance of each play. They could only hammer away desperately. Had the Rogers brothers lacked real talent they never could have kept the pace set by the older team. Left-handed as it was, however, these two weeks were Max and Gus's making theatrically. Thereafter they went their own way to success.

Word of the unique duel spread and made for capacity business in both cities, all to Kernell's profit; yet he was not content. He paid Joe and Lew their hundred dollars a week, but in pennies, nickels, dimes and the dirtiest dollar bills he could collect.

In the mutual rage generated by this grotesque vendetta, Weber and Fields's sense of humor failed them. Before the first week was done they were as furiously in earnest as Kernell. Else the spectacle of two youths not yet old enough to vote, without either money or backing, organizing and producing a variety show with a weekly salary list of nine hundred and twenty-five dollars exclusive of their own, might have been lost to the theater and the later fortunes of the firm of Weber and Fields greatly different.

Now their bluff to Kernell of taking out their own show became a point of honor. That it was possible not to make money at the producing end never occurred to them. For five years they had seen the cash rolling into the box offices around the circuit. Actors always looked upon the owner as the small boy envied the street-car conductor—nothing to do but to take in the money. Presumably there were expenses, but that was mere detail. The boys' only concern was where and how they were to get their initial capital. The rest would be automatic.

Having no Wall Street connections, manifestly the first step would be to find work for the summer. That, as they had seen each year, was no easy task. Only the dime museums and beer gardens were open, and these paid starvation wages.

Why not California? In 1889 the Camino Real still was paved with gold in the imaginations of cis-Sierran Americans. The name conjured up visions, not of tourists, cafeterias, real estate, Hollywood and orange groves, but of nuggets, overnight wealth, Roaring Camp and the Golden Gate, flashing eyes and flashing guns and romance. Only forty years had elapsed since the first strike at Sutter's Mills, and the Comstock Lode and Virginia City excitements had not yet stilled.

Fields remembered that he had an uncle in San Francisco; a rich uncle, unquestionably, since he was a Californian. San Francisco!

From *The Clipper* they compiled their own mailing list and wrote by the hour for engagements; wrote everywhere, but concentrated on the city of sunshine and laughter and yellow metal. The farther from New York their letters were addressed, the better they spoke of themselves and their act. Before each letter was mailed they flipped it into the air. If it fell stamp downward, in their superstition, it would fail in its mission; but if the stamp side fell upward it would bring work. Only one San Francisco letter dropped face upward. It was addressed to Gustav Walter, the Orpheum.

A San Francisco postmark in their mail three weeks later. An ornate envelope, worthy of its California origin. Robin's-egg-blue stationery with gold lettering. Mr. Walter asked their terms!

They held their breaths and wired back, collect, "One hundred and seventy-five dollars a week." If Walter balked or did not bother to answer, they would tell him that the telegraph company had misread their figures.

A messenger boy was hammering on Weber's front door that night.

"O. K. for four weeks. Call at Southern Pacific offices for transportation," Walter had replied.

Should he have asked for more, or had the telegraph company got his message straight after all? Weber asked himself. At any rate, the tickets were waiting at the S. P.'s New York office.

Oh, Susanna! They were off to California with washbowls on their knees.

A Southern Pacific train, coasting through the snow-sheds down the Pacific Slope of the Sierra Nevadas one May morning in 1889, carried two grimy, seat-weary passengers, with twenty-five cents between them.

Eight days earlier they had set out from New York on tickets—second class—wired them by one Gustav Walter. All they knew of Mr. Walter was that they had found his name in *The Clipper*, as the proprietor of the

Orpheum Theater, San Francisco, and had written him for work. Eight nights had they curled up in day-coach seats, eight days had they whiled away in an atmosphere of train smoke, fretful babies and bananas. The twenty dollars with which they had started had been exchanged, save the final quarter, for scalding coffee in armor-plate cups, prop sandwiches and the news butcher's indigestibles.

But San Francisco was four hours away; San Francisco and one hundred and seventy-five dollars a week; San Francisco and a wealthy uncle; San Francisco and golden streets; San Francisco in Wallace Irwin's words——

She laughed upon her hills out there,
Beside her bays of misty blue;
The gayest hearts, the sweetest air
That any city ever knew.

The eight-day passengers, now sorely in need of rewinding, were Messrs. Weber and Fields, now twenty years old, knockabout German comedians of a dozen years' experience in dime museums, beer gardens and the variety theaters, bent on piling up enough money in a summer on the Coast to make good their rash boast to their last employer that they would organize their own variety show and take it on the road next season.

"You're sure about this uncle?" Weber asked for the twenty-first time.

"Like I told you, he'll be at the depot to meet us," Fields repeated. "didn't mamma write to him all about us? I'll get ten dollars from him right off. Maybe he'll take us to his house."

There was no depot. Rather, the train rolled into the Oakland Station, a terminal well out in the bay, and transferred its passengers to a ferryboat. There was a smiling, eager, rather plump citizen, a gardenia in his buttonhole and a colorful vest supporting a cablelike watch chain, who waved his silk hat and cried, 'Can this be little Lew, my nephew? My, what a fine, big fellow!

"Welcome to the Golden State," Uncle David Frank proclaimed between embraces. "San Francisco awaits you. Your names are upon every billboard. 'The Funniest Men in the East,' 'New York's Favorites,' 'The Great Eastern Stars.' Well, well, can I believe my eyes? So this is Sister Sarah's little Lew and his little partner! My nephew's friends are my friends, Mr. Weber. Take a deep breath of this air, my boys. None of your New York smoke and dust. Better shade your eyes at first. You're not used to this California sunshine. Such a big fellow, and famous too! How did you leave your good mamma and papa? This is Goat Island we are passing; off there is Alcatraz. That is Mount Tamalpais, this is Telegraph Hill, near it you see Nob Hill, where all our millionaires live."

Weber blushed to think of his unworthy doubts as he listened and looked upon this avuncular magnificence. Even relatives grew bigger and juicier and mellower in California's magic soil.

"Do you live on Nob Hill, Uncle Dave?" Lew interrupted the benevolent chatterer.

Photo 6. Joe Weber out of costume.

Photo 7. Lew Fields, out of costume.

"Not at the moment," Uncle Dave conceded. "At the moment I am living at my club, I regret to say. Otherwise I should have insisted on having you as my guests. Oh, I shouldn't have taken no for an answer!"

He edged Joe away from his partner and whispered, "By the way, Mr. Weber, could you favor me with twenty-five dollars until the day after tomorrow?

"Temporary emergency—I'm sure you'll appreciate—no necessity of mentioning the matter to my dear nephew."

Fields read the news in Weber's face. His lower jaw dropped. The Bank of England had burst in his face.

"Why, we got only a quarter between us!" he stammered. "You're just foolin', aren't you? We expected to borrow enough from you to take care of us for a few days."

It was David Frank's turn to be dumfounded. Had he nursed a viper to his bosom? True, these two hadn't the look of ready money, but he had inside information as to the untrustworthiness of appearances. Eight days on the train would account for that, anyway. Was it likely, he asked himself aggrievedly, that "New York's Favorites" would arrive in San Francisco with a paltry two bits' capital? He pondered a suspicion of a niggardly nephew, while Joe and Lew shared a great disillusion. For the remainder of the ride the scenery of San Francisco Bay was viewed in silence.

But by the time the three had emerged from the ferry building and set out up Market Street, a-roar with cable car and horse-drawn traffic, Uncle Dave had recovered his faith in a Santa Claus. "I tell you what we'll do," he said with an air of discovery. "We will get an advance of fifty dollars from Walter. Customary—quite customary! Yes, just as soon as you boys have washed up and shaved we must demand an advance. Perhaps a hundred dollars would be better."

This mention of soap and razors jogged the boys' minds back to realities.

"Where is a good place to stop?" Fields asked.

"Let me see."Uncle Dave considered. "The Palace is a very decent place. Just a step up the street now. Yes, the Palace is your ticket." The Palace was the apple of California's eye, challenging comparison with New York, London or Paris's finest. Destroyed in the holocaust of April, 1906, it was rebuilt and continued to be a hotel such as Shepheard's, the Waldorf, the Grand Hotel de Pekin or the Adlon, of which travelers speak proprietorially in steamer smoking rooms.

With an ambassadorial flourish Uncle David ushered his travel-stained protégés through its marble corridors into the famous palm patio and to the desk.

"How much?" Joe demanded in the midst of diplomatic *pourparlers* between uncle and the clerk.

"Three dollars," the clerk quoted.

Well, that was California, the boys supposed; but what New Yorker ever would have guessed that all this red plush, gold leaf, veined marble and potted palms was to be had for three dollars a week? The half, it appeared, had not been told about this Pacific paradise.

Shaving was an infrequent need with either Joe or Lew in 1889, but a thorough soaping in the Palace's basins disclosed a distinct layer of whiskers beneath the Southern Pacific's coal smoke and the soil of eleven states. A shave was ten cents universally. Only one chair was idle in the hotel barber shop when they entered. Joe took it.

A boy seized one shoe and prepared to polish it. Weber withdrew the foot abruptly.

"Don't you want a shine?" the barber asked.

"Not to-day," Joe thought.

"Might as well," the barber advised. "It goes with the shave."

Another California bargain! Weber's shoes were polished. When he left the chair, Lew was just submitting his face to the lather brush in an adjoining chair. Weber handed his quarter to the barber, who dropped it in the till and greeted another customer.

"Change?" Joe inquired.

"No change," the barber replied. "Shave, two bits. Shine thrown in. You must be from the East."

Weber's blanched face chanced to fall on a clock.

"Lew!" he yelled, making for Fields's chair. "We're late now! You haven't got time to get that shave!"

"Late? Late?" Fields sputtered through the lather, as his partner dragged him from the chair. "Late for what? Where we going?"

"The bank! The bank! It's closing!" Weber shouted an inspiration, grabbed a towel, mopped the soap from Fields's face and tore him away from the astonished barber. Fields went, waving his hands, one of which held his collar and necktie, in bewildered protest.

Once on the sidewalk, Weber explained, but not to Fields's satisfaction. "What do you expect me to do? Pull my whiskers out by hand?" Lew demanded.

"We'll go right over to Walter and get that advance," Joe soothed him. "I've got a shave and a shine, and I'll do the talking. You can leave it all to me and stay outside if you feel embarrassed."

"I left it all to you once to-day," Lew vetoed, "and you got the shave and the shine and I got some soap in my mouth. Maybe I'd feel worse than embarrassed if I left it to you again. Maybe you'll do the talking, but I'll be right alongside of you doing the listening. Else maybe you'd come out and tell me I could smell the bay-rum bottle if I'd be a good little boy all week."

In their flight from the barber shop they had shaken Uncle Dave—Fields's only consolation. This and the procession of billboards they passed, heralding "The Great Eastern Stars" and "New York's Favorites," chirked him up. The Orpheum presently proved to be a theater and saloon on the south side of O'Farrell Street between Stockton and Powell, the theater deserted at 3:30 P.M., and the saloon all but so. A bartender looked up from last week's *Police Gazette* to say, "Walter? The old gent probably is getting his beauty sleep. He ought to be in around eight o'clock."

This was the San Francisco of before the quake, a Bagdad of the Pacific, a city of ten thousand and one enchanted nights. Someone has said of Kearny Street, that Rialto of the Desperate and Street of Adventurers, that in half an hour he could raise a dozen men for any wild adventure, from pulling down a statue to searching for the Cocos Island treasure. Half the city was restaurants and all were good. It never went to bed. There was no closing law, so that the saloons and cafes kept open nights and Sundays at their own sweet will. Thirty thousand Chinese crowded into a quarter six blocks long, two blocks wide and three cellars deep. The Spanish-Mexican colony dwelt about the base of Telegraph Hill and the Italians tumbled over the hill, building as they listed. The bay was dotted with the brown-stained, lateen-rigged fishing craft of the Neapolitans. The restaurant cuisine was French, the art sense and buoyancy of the people Latin. A bonny, cosmopolitan, devil-may-care city without its like on this earth.

"The Funniest Men in the East" returned to the Palace. When they asked for their key the clerk had a question to put first—"Have you any baggage?"

"Sure," they answered. "We got a trunk. It's over at the theater."

"That won't help us much, will it?" the clerk suggested. "Guests without baggage are required to pay in advance."

"How much?" Weber wanted to know.

"Three dollars, please."

"What?" they cried in unison. "We don't have to pay a whole week in advance, do we?"

"A week!" The man behind the desk was startled into raising his voice. "Three dollars a day is our rate—our cheapest."

"I guess we don't need that key after all, mister," they decided. "We didn't leave anything in the room except some cinders."

"That fine uncle of yours again," Weber was unwise enough to mutter as they turned away, thereby reviving Lew's memories.

"That fine uncle of mine didn't spend our last quarter sprinkling rose water on himself like my fine partner!" he snapped. "Uncles I can't help, but partners I wish on myself!"

"South of the Slot," as San Francisco spoke of the wrong side of Market Street, they found a trusting landlord and board and room at six dollars a week each. Street cleaners and beached sailors were their table mates at supper. The door of their room opened just far enough to let them squeeze through. Fields argued that the door blocked the bed, Weber that the bed blocked the door. They felt more at home.

Between supper time and eight o'clock they learned much at secondhand of the Orpheum's proprietor. Walter was broke, if they could believe what they heard, his friends giving him a week, his enemies twenty-four hours' grace from the sheriff's hands. Walter had emigrated from Germany in 1865 and landed in San Francisco in 1874. There he saw the Tivoli on Eddy Street profitably mixing liquor and music, and opened an opposition resort he called the

Fountain in the basement of a building at Sutter and Kearny streets. America then had never heard the word "cabaret," but the Tivoli and the Fountain were its early progenitors. In his cellar place Walter served beer to the accompaniment of a small orchestra and a few variety acts. Among his first performers was Bob Fitzsimmons's wife, a contortionist. The price of admission was a drink. It was the waiter's job to see that the patron bought more and often if he kept his seat. Bully boys up from the Embarcadero, and other trouble shooters, occasionally tried to make one steam beer last the evening; but this exploit required not only an unaccustomed temperance, but complete insulation against insult, and above all eternal vigilance. Let an incautious hand be removed from a glass, full or empty, and it was snatched from the table and whisked away.

Walter prospered and opened a larger place called the Vienna Gardens in 1881 at Sutter and Stockton streets, then the Wigwam at Stockton and Geary streets in 1884, and finally the Orpheum in 1887.

The others had been variety saloons, but the Orpheum was a theater, built for the purpose, charging an admission, and with the bar detached from the house. True, a service shelf was set in the back of each seat to accommodate steins, glasses and tobacco, and waiters balancing trays aloft canvassed the house for orders during the show; but that was typical of the time.

He had opened his theater with a flourish, importing from Budapest a twenty-two piece novelty electrical orchestra and following this up with light opera, then the C. D. Hess Grand Opera Company, playing at twenty-five to seventy-five cents.

Rumor had it that Walter had overextended himself. Weber and Fields's letter had reached him at a critical moment, it appeared. Playing in poor luck with the low-priced native theatrical talent he had fallen back upon, he shut his eyes and gambled his last white chip on what he took to be a New York sensation, plastered the city with their names and stood off clamorous creditors with promises of prosperity to arrive from New York by the train. Possibly he had no one hundred and seventy-five dollars to meet Weber and Fields's weekly salary; but if they were as originally funny as they asserted and he sanguinely hoped them to be he would have it.

A three-hundred-pound German waddled up O'Farrell Street soon after eight o'clock and greeted the early birds at the bar—three of them bill collectors—with attempted cheerfulness, broadly accented. He got, with much puffing, on a high stool at a cashier's desk and began stacking beer checks. Each waiter bought a ten-dollar quota of these checks at the start of the night and paid with them in advance at the bar for the drinks served in the theater. The waiters supplied, Walter glanced in at the box office, then passed into his private office.

"That's Walter," someone indicated, and Joe and Lew followed him into the office, the short and shaven Weber in advance, the gangling and whisker-smudged Fields behind, but not hidden.

"Mr. Gustav Walter?" Joe asked.

"To-morrow I'll pay you," Walter said without looking up from his desk.

"You got us mixed, Mr. Wal——" Weber began.

"Positively to-morrow, or at der ladtest Monday, chentlemen," Walter promised, continuing to examine an account book. "To-morrow comes Weber und Fields, der greadt Eastern funny men. Chust you wait und see der landt-office business vot I do."

"We're Weber and Fields," Joe announced.

Walter looked up with a start. He fumbled for a pair of gold-rimmed spectacles, got them on his nose and looked again. Frowning, he readjusted his glasses and pulled himself out of his chair.

Consciously or subconsciously, Walter had formed his own mental picture of what the Funniest Men in the East—the sure things on which he had staked his all—ought to look like. Yet his eyes told him that he saw two rather pinch-faced youths, newsboys at a guess, about the age of his own Karl, a high-school junior, for neither Weber nor Fields looked his age. The taller one's face appeared to need washing. Both looked as if they had slept in their clothes on the grass of Portsmouth Square.

Walter's mind flatly refused to credit what his eyes reported. He turned the latter beseechingly about the otherwise empty office as if in the hope of seeing who really had spoken.

"We're Weber and Fields," said Lew.

Dismay was on Walter's face and choking sounds came from his throat.

"Mein Gott!" he supplicated, clutching at his collar. "You are Weber und Fields? You I pay one hundred and seventy-five dollars a week und send tickets von New York? You I bill like a circus? Tell me you are joking, please! No?" In his distress he fell back upon his native tongue. *"Du Lieber Himmel!"* was all they cared to understand.

"We just got in and haven't had time to spruce up yet," Weber apologized.

If Walter heard him he gave no sign.

"Funny men, yes?" he said, half to himself. "Veil, if you are zo funny, make me laugh!" He thumped his chest. "I bet it you'd be funny could you do dot."

Joe and Lew, in their growing discomfiture, looked more the Saddest Boys in the West than their billboard titles.

"Vell, vell!" Walter demanded petulantly. "Maybe you are Weber und Fields. Is idt my fauldt? Vat you want? Go see der stage director."

"We'd like to get fifty dollars advance," Weber suggested timidly.

Walter's worst fears were confirmed. Broke too! Swindling young bums, seeing America first on his money! He pounded his desk.

"Ven you earn fifty dollars den you get fifty dollars! Now, nod a beer check!"

Rehearsal was called for ten o'clock the next morning, by which time the scene of the night before was public property. The other entertainers, all local talent, had been coldly jealous of these well-paid interlopers billed like a three-ring circus. Now they were derisive.

"Please take a look!"

"Do you see what I see?"

It might teach Walter and the other managers a lesson.

Their scorn grew when the orchestra leader called for the Weber and Fields music. Any first-class act of the time used three or four songs; certainly an entrance number and dance accompaniment.

"We don't use any music," the boys told him.

"No music!" he exclaimed. "What the devil do you do, anyway? How do you come on stage?"

"Anything will do to bring us on,"Weber explained. "All we want is just a few strains—'The Wearin' o' the Green,' or anything like that."

"Let's get on with the rehearsal then," the stage director cut in. "Weber and Fields next!"

The orchestra struck up "The Wearin' o' the Green," and Joe and Lew walked across the stage and into the far wings.

"Hey!" the director yelled. "Your act! Whatever you do, if anything! Trot it out! It ain't a secret, is it?"

"We don't need to rehearse," Fields told him. "We've done this act ten thousand times. All we need to know is when we go on."

A guffaw exploded in the wings. Joe and Lew turned and saw their companions on the bill gathered in a mocking group and licking their lips at this Roman holiday.

"You go on at 1:30," the director instructed.

What? Did they give afternoon shows? the boys wanted to know. No, the director was talking about 1:30 in the morning. Joe and Lew broke into excited protest. What sort of a raw deal was this? Half past one o'clock in the morning! Not a minute! They wouldn't play! When the director tried to tell them that this was the preferred position on the bill they laughed in his face. He shrugged his shoulders. That was Mr. Walter's orders, anyway.

"Put us on at ten o'clock the first night," Joe and Lew pleaded. "Then if we don't make good you can stick us on with the milkman at 5:30; but give us a chance! We've got a bad enough deal here already."

The director put up a silencing hand.

"One-thirty it is. You're holding up rehearsal. I'm hungry already. Wilson and Cameron next."

"Then we don't play!" the two shouted. "And don't send for us unless it's to be ten o'clock!"

They walked out, but they did not forget, in their indignation, to make sure that their address was on file with the stagedoor man. The director went on with the rehearsal.

Another of the long succession of bluffs tossed in the face of a disdainful world by our young heroes, and the most prodigious of all. Three thousand miles from home, penniless, already in debt, their future depending on the outcome, and already discredited locally, they were at Walter's mercy if he only knew it. In their own hands were two small trumps—their unbounded faith in themselves and their belief that Walter, on the verge of bankruptcy, had staked his all on them.

Two o'clock—three—four o'clock came, and they drummed their heels in the Mission Street boarding house and watched the clock. A chill pea-soup fog rolled in from the Golden Gate and blotted out the sun. Five o'clock, and they listened tensely at every opening of the street door. Six o'clock, and they had no appetites for supper. But at 6:30 they heard their names spoken. The stage director came with a compromise. Silly as it was, Mr. Walter would humor their caprice and let them go on at midnight. It did not need the shrewdness of a street gamin to perceive that Walter was licked. Ten o'clock or bust, they reiterated.

The director slammed the door as he left, but they could eat with a relish now. Before they had finished, a messenger came with a note. Their terms were agreed to.

The circus billing had done its work. The Orpheum was chockablock by nine P.M. Joe and Lew could not, or did not, know that the place was but half awake at this hour normally. They did, however, sense the hostility of all backstage, and the heart was taken out of them. They would have no alibi now if they failed. Whipped before they started, they hugged their dressing room until the last minute.

A patter of hands when they made their nervous entrance at ten o'clock, most of it from Uncle Dave, who had insinuated his way in somehow. Folded arms from most of the house. San Francisco's address was Missouri, not California, that evening.

The audience saw a vastly different Weber and Fields from the apologetic waifs who had stuck a pin in Walter's balloon and provoked the horsy mirth of the rest of the cast. Here were two comedy Germans of any age from thirty to sixty, the little one a pocket edition, in figure, of Walter himself. The make-ups were funny, but the cold entrance and the dialect patter were novelties outside San Francisco's experience. The house was puzzled and did not know whether it liked it or not.

Early in the act Weber's lines called for him to pronounce "yesterday" explosively as "gesterday." It was Fields's business to clap a hand to one eye as if the spray had put an indignity upon him. This old spit-in-the-eye slapstick had not been done to death in that distant day. Seemingly it was new here, for the audience cackled delightedly.

"It's easy!" Lew whispered under cover of the laugh. "We've got 'em!"

They assaulted the English language with new vigor and felt the house respond. They tried a story they had used the preceding presidential year and discarded after the election. Fields declared that he had known all along that Harrison would defeat Cleveland. Weber challenged the statement. Lew pointed to the number of Harrison banners he had seen.

"Banners don't vote!" Joe retorted.

"They show which way the wind blows," was Lew's snapper.

When the house rose to this it was all over but the shouting. This grew tumultuous. Before they reached their knockabout the waiters forgot their beers and stood rapt in the aisles, watching the stage. Weber and Fields were a smash in San Francisco.

Walter beat them backstage and hugged them deliriously when they had taken their last noisy curtain call. His long shot had won. His job now would be to keep this competitors' hands off the family jewels

"Maybe you boys would like a leetle advance, no?" he suggested. "Say fifty dollar?"

He had two double eagles and an eagle in his hand, the first gold coins the boys ever had fingered. Each wanted to carry half this California money. They were saved a dispute about the odd ten dollars. Uncle Dave was at their elbow and they knew what to do with it.

The next night Weber and Fields sheepishly took the stage at 1:30, as originally scheduled. All that barking of the day before had been up the wrong tree, they had learned meanwhile. Half past one was the mere shank of the evening in San Francisco, and Walter had known what he was about in saving his best for that hour. The Orpheum began to fill up only when the legitimate theaters called it a night; and Joe and Lew, in their stubborn insistence on ten o'clock, had risked playing to empty seats. Only the stir roused by Walter's lavish billing had saved them.

Walter signed up Weber and Fields for an additional four weeks before he had finished counting his second night's receipts. Prosperity had changed her local address to the Orpheum. Unhappily, she had brought her big brother, Responsibility, with her. Last week Walter had been by repute a turnip, guiltless of a drop of blood. This week he had money and his creditors fell upon him in a body, each demanding to be paid first and in full. He paid a little here, a little there and spread his receipts out as thinly as a goldbeater.

For three weeks he paid Joe and Lew promptly and in cash that they as promptly sent home. Then, having established a reputation for solvency, he gave them a check for seventy-five dollars and one hundred dollars in gold on the fourth Saturday night. They eyed the check dubiously and said nothing, but at 8:30 Monday morning they were sitting on the front steps of the Nevada Bank and at nine o'clock they were the first customers inside. A teller nodded affably. They had met him, they remembered, with his former associate, Jim Corbett, at the Olympic Club, where the slender and pompadoured Jim was boxing instructor.

"I'll see you in New York one of these days," Corbett had told them. "I'm going to whip John L. Sullivan before long and wear that diamond belt myself."

They had smiled politely and laughed impolitely later. These Californians were too modest for their own good.

Joe tendered Walter's check. The teller consulted a ledger and returned, shaking his head. There wasn't that much money in the Walter account. As early a bird as Weber was not to be daunted by the first empty wormhole. How much money did Walter have in the bank, then? That, the teller explained, he was not permitted by banking ethics to disclose.

"What does a teller tell, anyway?" Fields punned.

Ah, that Weber and Fields! There was no resisting their drolleries. The teller beckoned them closer and whispered. Privately, confidentially and strictly as one good fellow to two others, Walter's balance was sixty-five dollars and the week-end's checks not yet heard from.

"We'll take sixty-five dollars for the check," Weber offered.

The teller was sorry. That, too, would be a breach of the banking code. A check must be paid in full or not at all. With certain customers such a slight overdraft might be condoned, but not in this instance. Joe pondered this thoughtfully, then drew a ten-dollar gold piece from his pocket and shoved it under the wicket.

"I just remembered," he said, "that Mr. Walter asked me to deposit this for him the first time I happened into the bank. No law against that, is there?"

The teller winked, made out a deposit slip and spiked it. Weber pushed the seventy-five-dollar check back through the wicket. The teller scrutinized it soberly, stacked up the equivalent in coin and shoved the cash out.

"Nice day," he observed.

"Never saw a better," Weber and Fields agreed. "Good morning."

They came and went that night with the bland and childlike innocence of Bret Harte's Chinese poker sharp, Walter watching them out of the corner of one eye. He had all but satisfied himself that he had found two trusting hearts in a wicked world, when they appeared with a casual request for twenty-five dollars advance which he could not well refuse. The next night they drew another twenty-five, and the next.

"Vot you boys doin' mit all this money?" he asked when the drawing continued. "I pay you a king's wages and efery night you are broke once more. Maybe I should keep your money for two such babes in de voods."

"Oh, we don't care anything about money," Lew startled Joe by replying. "It's just the fun of being able to brag that you get it."

All the while the two were sending one hundred and fifty dollars of their one hundred and seventy-five dollars weekly by draft to Fields's brother Max, in New York. Max paid the two mothers ten dollars each and banked the one hundred and thirty balance against the autumn and the inception of Weber and Fields' Own Company.

As they passed Walter on Friday night he shouted at them, "Hey, I find out at der bank vot shenanigans you did!"

"Then give us that ten dollars you owe us!" Weber retorted.

"Ha! Vot do you care about money, eh?" he chuckled. "Two pretty smart boys! Dot's a goot joke you play on me. But don't you belief efery ting you hear. Listen! Gustav Walter pays vat he owes. Maybe I was a leetle short for cash; but I pay, I pay. I got money before und I got it again. Don't you worry about Gustav Walter. I'll be running bigger theaters as this one ven you come to California again."

It was many years before Weber and Fields played San Francisco again, but Walter's prophecy had been fulfilled beyond his dreams, though he was dead. From his O'Farrell Street theater, and taking its name, sprang the Orpheum Circuit, which dominates vaudeville from Chicago to the coast. The name

"Orpheum" in a facsimile of Walter's rolling script is carried on half a hundred pretentious theaters.

Weathering the panic of 1893, Walter made his Orpheum a San Francisco institution. In 1896 he leased Childs' Opera House in Los Angeles and sent the late Martin Lehman to Chicago to open a booking office for the two theaters. The next year he sold an interest to Morris Meyerfeld, Jr., a San Francisco wholesale merchant, and with the additional capital sent Lehman to Kansas City to open a third theater. The Orpheum Circuit was born; but Walter died in 1898 on his return from a tour of Europe in search of new talent. The expansion of the circuit went on under the direction of Meyerfeld and Martin Beck. The parent Orpheum was destroyed in the earthquake and fire of 1906 and the present San Francisco house erected on the same site, but the service shelves on the backs of the seats and the waiters in the aisles were gone.

Weber and Fields jumped their salary to two hundred and fifty dollars for the last four of the ten weeks they played San Francisco and fattened the bank account at home. During their final two weeks at the Orpheum, Walter permitted them to play the Cremorne earlier in the evening at one hundred dollars a week additional on their agreement to take twenty-five dollars less from him. When their eight weeks with Walter ended they added the Bella Union to the Cremorne and maintained the two-hundred-and-fifty-dollar pace. The Bella Union lay near the Barbary Coast, that three solid blocks of dance halls set down in the San Francisco tenderloin for the delight of the tail-water sailors of the world—a loud bit of hell, in Will Irwin's phrase. Here on a routine night Kanaka Pete of the What Cheer House shot the Cockroach of the Little Silver Dollar in a fight in the Eye Wink Dance Hall over a woman known as Iodoform Kate. The names are taken verbatim from a police story of the time.

A balcony of curtained booths overlooked a first floor of tables. Only wine was served in the balcony, and the pay of the women habitues was reckoned on a percentage of the bottles they induced the male patrons to buy. When a waiter served an order he gave the cork to the girl with the buyer. At the end of the night the women exchanged the corks at fifty cents each at the bar. The character of a San Francisco entertainment was indicated by the hours it kept. A Bella Union night still was young at dawn in summer. Weber and Fields took the stage at four A.M., six hours after finishing at the Cremorne, and played to audiences the like of which they had not known even at Harry Hill's on the Bowery.

A four weeks' engagement at one hundred and twenty-five dollars a week at Portland, Oregon, obtained through a booking agent, followed San Francisco. They laid off a week and passed out of the Golden Gate by side-wheel steamer. A veteran variety actor, known only as the Old Soldier, bound for Portland to play on the same bill, was a fellow passenger. The Old Soldier was known from Puget Sound to Coronado Beach for two eccentricities. In four years with the Army of the Tennessee he had become so enamored with camp life that he had declared a permanent boycott on boarding houses and hotels. Tent, blankets, frying pan and fishing tackle were his theatrical baggage. He pitched his camp in the likeliest suburban spot and paid no rent. The second article of his faith was that the Pacific Coast was the Biblical Garden of Eden and he had sworn never to take a backward step across the Sierras.

Of all the rapturous Pacific Slope, give him Portland in midsummer, he asked. He invited Joe and Lew to be his guests at a spot he knew in the deep woods beside a crystal trout stream hurrying down from Mount Hood's eternal snows, and not an hour from the courthouse. The rent-free clause was an argument Weber and Fields could understand, but not the forest-primeval stuff. The Old Soldier, like many another salesman, had overtalked his merchandise. When he dwelt on the charm of being lulled to sleep by the panther's whine he lost two prospects.

The steamer bumped over the dreaded Columbia bar, churned up the mighty Oregon, turned into the Willamette and landed its passengers in a young city of forty thousand persons, still inclosed by the big timber. Its streets were wooden, its sidewalks plank, its buildings frame; the drone and screech of ripsaws smote the ear and the incense of fresh-cut pine and burning cedar ravished the nose. All Portland was wooden except its pulse; that leaped and cavorted. At a loggers' hotel, the Bixby House, Weber and Fields found lodging at two dollars a week and three-fifty commutation meal tickets at three dollars. The Old Soldier loaded his duffel into a rowboat and vanished in the Douglas firs across the Willamette.

In San Francisco everyone drank, though there were other interests in life; but in Portland life was one round of drinks after another and every man was expected to do his duty. Both teetotalers, Weber and Fields were reduced to the company of each other. But not for long.

The recruiting of Weber and Fields' Own Company had begun in San Francisco. Before leaving they had engaged two acts to come East in September to join the new show—Wilson and Cameron, black-face favorites on the Coast; and Richman and Glenroy, another California team. Selling San Francisco on the existence and glittering future of such a company was no mean feat. They did not look like producers, and there was only their word for it that they were. To live up to this role, to create the confidence needed to induce experienced actors to cross the continent to join them, often was a strain both on their nerves and the twenty-five dollars a week they allotted for all expenses. A suppostitious millionaire brother, sometimes Weber's, sometimes Fields's, and the judicious use of five dollars' worth of gaudy stationery helped, but the decisive factor probably was Wilson and Cameron and Richman and Glenroy's own eagerness to get an Eastern hearing.

Joe and Lew's loneliness was lifted unexpectedly in their second week in Portland. The San Francisco boat brought in three sun-kissed variety actors, broke and looking for work. The three had been among the many who had listened all summer to Weber and Fields brag that the lady on the dollar was their affianced bride. What more natural now than that they should wish themselves on their wealthy friends?

To have refused them would have been fatal publicity to get back to Kearny Street. Joe and Lew declared that this was the happiest of reunions, and took the three to the Bixby House, where they ate up one meal ticket the first time the dinner bell rang. With the mendacious apology that there was not a vacant room in all Portland, they invited the trio to share their one bed, and slept crosswise, five deep.

The hosts had ten dollars in paper money on them, and the honesty of their guests, though presumptive in law, was conjectural in the jaundiced eyes of experience. Since Bridgeport and the turkey show they had put no confidence in the usual shoe and pillow caches, and the sparsely furnished room suggested few alternatives. The safest appeared to be a framed oleograph of a red, blue, yellow and purple chariot race hung within a foot of the ceiling. While their visitors were out, Fields got on a chair, Weber climbed upon his shoulders and the bills were hung across the picture wire where it joined the frame.

Finishing their turn at the honky-tonk, a Portland version of the Bella Union, at 3:30 a.m., they found their guests already asleep, snaked the two pillows from under the sleepers' heads and crowded in. Fields's sleep was troubled. He dreamed that the hotel was afire, that he heard pistol shots, doors slamming, windows being raised. He tossed uneasily, then came awake. It was no dream! The Bixby House was burning! A belated pedestrian had seen the flames lapping at the kitchen walls and emptied his six-shooter in the air, bringing the sleeping street to life like a trampled ant hill.

To avoid a confusion of shoes each of the five had tied his own together by the strings on going to bed. This was no moment for undoing knotted strings. All fled for the stairs, carrying the first pair of shoes to hand. Joe and Lew were in the street when they remembered the ten dollars. They turned back into the burning building and made the room, already faintly illuminated by the advancing flames. The chariot race still went on furiously and chromatically. Fields, the taller, tried to reach it from a chair, but failed. Weber drew back his right arm and hurled his shoes at the chromo. They settled neatly over the frame by the joined strings and hung there. It was Fields's turn to shoot his shoes for the ten dollars. He broke the glass and rocked the picture for a hopeful instant, but the tied strings played him false, too. His shoes stayed with Weber's and the firm's capital. A volunteer fireman, groping his way into the smoke-filled room, found the two shaking their fists at a picture of a chariot race and yelled back to his chief that he had found "a couple of lunatics still up here." He seized one under each arm, dragged them out, and was mentioned for bravery in the *Oregonian* the next day.

In their bare feet, Weber and Fields watched the tinder-box hotel burn to the ground. They and their guests slept the balance of the morning on the floor of the theater dressing room. Scouting in borrowed shoes for a new eating place, they ran across the Old Soldier emerging from a saloon with a filled jug.

"You two boys better come out and get close to Nature with me now," he lectured them. "That fire was a stroke of judgment. Be a good thing if all houses was to burn. Mankind never was meant to live shut away from the air and the sunlight."

The chance of recovering their ten dollars and of shaking off the burdens of reputed wealth overcame their urban distrust of the forest and the panther's cry. When their next night's work was done, the Old Soldier rowed them over the Willamette by the light of the setting moon, led them through the whispering shadows of the Douglas firs by a winding path to the grassy bank of a singing stream. With a woodsman's hatchet he hewed a pile of young spruce boughs, fashioned them into two fragrant mattresses, spread blankets over them and talked the boys to sleep. They awoke to a meridian sun and the smell and sizzle of frying fish. The Old Soldier had been up for hours and snared breakfast from a pool. For two weeks the boys lived in the open, sleeping the mornings, lazing away the afternoons, fishing and listening to the veteran's talk of Vicksburg, Island Number 10, the glories of Nature unadorned and the destiny of the Pacific states, and crossing with him at night to play in the sour air of the honky-tonk. None of the three was given much to letter writing, but those two weeks in the Oregon woods left a memory with two tenement-reared youths that inspired a correspondence with their host that went on for fifteen years. They never saw him again. His last letter exhorted them to forsake the Dead Sea fruit of New York and return to the Garden of Eden, "where the sun of destiny is just rising over the purple ranges."

The summer was waning and there was eighteen hundred dollars in the bank in New York to finance the new show. Joe and Lew paid their expenses home by stopping two weeks in Minneapolis and St. Paul. Acts of any note rarely ventured farther west than Chicago, and work was to be had for the asking in the Twin Cities at sixty dollars a week.

A washout held their train up for forty-eight hours near Gloversville, New York, and the passengers had nothing to eat the second day. The Weber and the Schanfield families had made great preparations for the triumphal return of their sons, even to hiring an East Side band to greet them at the station. The welcoming party made three trips to the station to no result. When Joe and Lew arrived eventually the band had dwindled to one violin.

Again train-weary, begrimed and rumpled like two remnants at the end of a hard day in the bargain basement, they looked the conquering heroes as little as they lived up to Gustav Walter's preconception of "New York's Favorites" four months earlier. They were paraded, nevertheless, in the immodest exposure of a low-necked hack to Fields's home at 181 Clinton Street, where a public reception followed.

"I've cooked enough to feed all the East Side, God forbid!" was Mrs. Schanfield's greeting.

Laundered or unlaundered, Fields was a figure of romance to his sister Annie. She proudly introduced him, cinders and all, to her new girl chum. He did not suspect it then, still less did she, but the young woman was destined to become Mrs. Lew Fields.

"Listen to Booth and Barrett!" the Bowery scoffed when Weber and Fields, back from California with $1,800 savings, broadcast their intention of taking their own variety show on the road the coming season of 1889–90.

As a flight of imagination, $1,800 was a puny effort. The idle actors who lined the rail at Harry Miner's saloon and swapped lies by the hour about their past, present and future were irritated by such amateurishness.

If Joe and Lew liked to blow pretty bubbles, why not $18,000 or $18,000,000?

Not that a fortune was essential to the production of a variety show. Thirty years ago the emphasis was on nerve rather than capital. The acts provided their own costumes and props. The theaters furnished sets and music. The railroads did not contribute transportation, but they were not yet so exclusive with their rights of way, and tripping the light fantastic tie was a part of the trouper curriculum. It preserved the figure. Eighteen miles before breakfast on the Lehigh Valley served then for eighteen holes before breakfast at Shinnecock Hills. The Lehigh Valley was the sportier course.

There were no misgivings in Joe and Lew's minds. They were set. But one high hurdle blocked the preliminary paths of ambition. It was $1,000 high. The job plant of the Buffalo *Courier* had a virtual monopoly of the theatrical lithographing business—the printing of show posters and window cards. These had to be prepared in advance. If a show failed, the posters were so much old paper, and sad-eyed experience had erased the word "credit" from the *Courier's* lexicon. When $1,000 money had been deposited in Buffalo the *Courier* was ready to do business, and not a nickel before. If the paper was paid for as delivered weekly, the deposit would be refunded at the end of the season or when the paper on the shelf had been used.

It was a wrench, but they sent $1,000 of their $1,800 to Buffalo. With it went their own pictures and photographs of Wilson and Cameron and Richman and Glenroy, the two acts they had booked on the Coast. Pictures of the rest of the cast would follow as quickly as acts were signed up. Signing them was the rub. When Joe and Lew attempted to complete their company they learned that Matthew knew whereof he spoke when he observed that a prophet is not without honor save in his own country and in his own house. The boys at Miner's, even as you and I, believed what they saw, and they saw only two neighborhood kids whom most of them had known practically from infancy.

"Go-getters? Yes. Clever kids with a good act? Yes. Producers? I'm laughing at and with you. Why, they can't be more than eighteen! Twenty-one? They don't look it. And they'd better take half of that $18,000,000-roll, or whatever it is, and get another shirt, and their two pairs of pants pressed."

If the world believed only what its eyes told it, Joe and Lew determined to knock the world's eye out forthwith. They did it with two three-carat diamond studs, yellow white and flawed, to be sure, but flashy—and diamonds. They got them at a pawnshop not a block distant from Miner's on terms of twenty-five dollars down and ten dollars a week till death do us part, and wore their joint handkerchief down to rags that afternoon giving the stones a high polish. Two such crown jewels demanded appropriate scenic investiture. So some other part of the $800-balance was invested in what the well-dressed gentleman of 1889 was wearing, including Prince Albert coats, patent-leather shoes, derby hats, black silk shirts and black bow ties. Harry Lehr was nowhere.

Frank Bush, one of the earliest and best of Jewish comedians, was the first victim of the sunstroke that lurked in the studs. Bush was famous not only for his inimitable way of telling a joke but for the originality of his self-creations. They needed a Bush in their troupe. Two days earlier he had told them to run along and sell their papers, but it was Mr. Weber and Mr. Fields when the diamonds began to shine.

"I've been thinking over that offer, gentlemen," Bush began as soon as he could get them alone. "I'd consider it for $250 per and $100 for my wife."

Speaking metaphorically—very metaphorically in fact—Greek had met Greek. Joe and Lew would pay $350 if they had to, but it needed a better judge of poker faces than Frank Bush to guess it. They talked to him like a fatherly banker refusing to lend a young client $1,000 to buck the stock market, while Bush shaded twenty-five dollars off his price every time he gave another glance at the studs. The big news at Miner's that night was that Frank Bush and his wife, Isabelle Ward, had signed at $200 a week to go out with Weber and Field's Own Company.

The newspapers knew of the variety stage only by hearsay in that distant day; but when *The Clipper*, a theatrical weekly, gave a paragraph to the news that Bush and Ward, and Wilson and Cameron, a highly touted black-face act from the Coast, had joined up with the new venture, the trick was turned. Other sheep followed the bellwether, Bush, over the fence, and theater owners who had written that they would "try to find some time for your show" now wired in demanding that the young producers fill the booking arranged for them. Before mid-September the company and the booking were complete.

And a good company it was. In it were Frank Bush and Isabelle Ward, the Fremonts, Wilson and Cameron, Haines and Vidocq, Drummond and Staley, Richman and Glenroy, Florence Miller and Weber and Fields in person, a first-class, nicely balanced bill. The weekly pay roll, ignoring Joe and Lew, was $925. If they didn't have it, they didn't have to pay themselves. The pay roll, by the bye, was some $300 more than they now possessed.

Meanwhile, what of their own act? Their stock in trade was the same knockabout they had peddled around the circuit for five successive years with Hill, Hyde and others. Vaudeville has its perennials such as McIntyre and Heath's The Georgia Minstrels and Victor Moore's Change Your Act, which age does not wither nor custom stale; but this was hardly such a one. Joe and Lew thought of Cincinnati and Sunday-night openings at the People's Theater, where the young bloods of the town kept a death watch more critical than New York's sophisticates. One telling was the life of any gag with this audience. If they knew the answer, they raised their hands en masse and beat you to it with a mocking shout. There was the case of Lavender and Thompson and their catch line—"I knowed it first." Cincinnati had laughed the first time, let it pass in silence the second, and greeted its third appearance with the sing-song chant, "We knowed it first, we knowed it first, we knowed it first." And Florence Miller, who tried to sing a song the Queen City regarded as the rightful property of Lottie Gilson, was hissed off the stage. Miss Miller had sassed them back.

"Only snakes hiss," the indignant cantatrice retorted.

Sitting in their "office" in the pool room of Miner's Bowery ten days before the Baltimore opening, and pondering the fickleness of audiences, Weber and Fields heard German voices lifted in anger at a near-by pool table. The peppery old gallery doorkeeper at the theater and his crony, both Düsseldorfians, had been disputing every play of an interminable call-shot pool game. Their excited jargon was delighting a little group of loungers. Suddenly the smoldering quarrel burst into flames. The doorkeeper had scratched the deciding fourteen-ball and claimed a fair shot. The two old men shouted abuse in German and broken English, shook their cues at each other menacingly, then joined in battle. While butt ends of cues thrashed and pool balls smacked the walls like canister shot, Weber, Fields and the other neutrals took cover. A wildly thrown ball, ricocheting from a cast-iron column, took the doorkeeper on the temple and the birds commenced to sing. An ambulance called for him, a patrol wagon for his countryman. Fields, looking out cautiously from under a billiard table, whispered to Weber, who was beneath him, "We've got it!" Their famous pool-table burlesque had fallen plop into their laps.

Within half an hour the boys had found a one-table pool room in the rear of a half-basement saloon in an obscure side street, where, safe from prying eyes, they called their first rehearsal of their new act. The next morning before nine o'clock the rehearsal was continued in the pool room at Miner's with only a porter and a dozing bartender as an unwitting audience. When the first of the usual hangers-on sauntered in around noon, Joe and Lew racked their cues and reverted to the side-street saloon. This was precious metal, to be guarded from theatrical hi-jackers.

A week later the dress rehearsal was called in the single-table pool room. Up to now they had practiced their pretended violence softly, but here they lifted their German dialect voices and brawled hotly. As the riot in the back room waxed, the listening bartender reached for a bung starter, excused himself to his customers and burst into the room to find Lew throttling Joe with such realism that the barkeep declared himself in, and Fields barely escaped following the gallery doorkeeper to the hospital. Admitted to the secret, the bartender invited his clients to join him in the back room and the act had its first public hearing to an appreciative audience of two truck drivers, a tinsmith, a gas-meter reader and the white-aproned host.

Every pool room of the '90s was a betting station for the races, with a telegraph operator, a bookmaker's agent and a blackboard. The act, as it was seen that season with Weber and Fields' Own Company, began appropriately with a betting scene. Frank Van Ness then owned a horse called India Rubber, a regular campaigner on the Eastern tracks. Mike and Myer entered, studying the entries on the blackboard, and agreed on placing a bet on India Rubber because he was "good in the stretch." While they waited on the result, Fields, who was Myer, suggested a game of pool. A manufacturer had built a special pool table for the act in return for the privilege of having the firm's name in gilt letters across its length. Weight and bulk were reduced to a minimum by leaving out die usual slate bed and providing folding legs.

"I don't know dis pool business," Weber, who was Mike, would object when Myer suggested their playing a game.

MYER: Vatever I don't know, I teach you.
MIKE: Dot seems fair.
MYER: To make der game more interesting, I bet you dot I beat.
MIKE: Oughtn't you to beat? Ain't you biggest?
MYER: Brains in der head, not bigness, vins in pool.
MIKE: Give me otts und I bet you.
MYER: Vat you mean, otts?
MIKE: You should put up more money to my lesterest money.
MYER: I vill not! But I tell you vot I vill do. I vill put up five dollar to your ten dollar.
MIKE: Dot's what I mean.

Weber was a wistful little figure; a mild, trustful, under-sized innocent, the Mister Common Peepul or Little Jeff of the eternal comic strip, abused and exploited by the tall, bullying, brutal Fields, who told him how he loved him while engaged in gouging out an eye.

"Ven I'm away from you, I cannot keep mein mind from off you. Ven I'm mit you, I cannot keep mein hands from off you. Oh, how I luff you, Mike!" Fields was wont to declare—bending a trick billiard cue over Mike's head.

The squat Weber would guilelessly confide his ten dollars to the lower shelf of the ball rack. Fields would remove it immediately, with his own five dollars, to the top shelf. Weber, watching this maneuver, would return to the rack, raise himself on tiptoe, discover that he could not reach the money, then look questioningly at Fields.

MYER: Remember, now! Der one dot gets der money vins.
MIKE: Let me understand meinself: der one dot gets der money is der vinner, eh? (MYER, *starting to shoot*, MIKE *seizes his cue.*)
MIKE: Who made idt out you should be firstest starter?
MYER: All right, den ve choose up for it. (*They measure hands on a pool cue in the manner of boys choosing up sides for a baseball game.* MIKE *wins and starts for the money.*)
MIKE: *I vin! I vin!*
MYER: Dumbskull! You don't vin der money; you chust get shot first.
MIKE: Pardon, please. I oliogepize.
MYER: Hey! Don't get so close to dot table. You got to stand three feets away ven you shoot it."

This was the more ridiculous in that Weber's pillow padded waistline stopped him a foot short of the pool table. At this warning, he would make a blundering try at a cue's length, then reverse the cut and aim with the large end.

MYER: You can'd do dot. Always you must shoot it mit der end dot's got der sponge on.

MIKE (*EXAMINING THE TIP*): Dot's a sponge? It's very tight for a sponge!

MYER: Remember, you got to break der balls before as you bust dem.

MIKE (*PUZZLEDLY*): I got to bust dem before I break dem? (MIKE *drives the cue ball into the massed numbered balls and the fifteenth ball, by arrangement, drops into a pocket.*)

MIKE: I got him! I got him!

MYER (*GRABBING THE BALL*): You didn't call it!

MIKE: I did call it! I did call it! I called it to myself!

MYER: Dot's a bad habit, talking to yourselves, and worser in pool. Don't do it some more. Now vot ball you play?

MIKE: Do I got to tell you?

MYER: Sure, you got to tell me.

MIKE: Are you der mayor or somedings? I like to play dis one, only dot one is in de vay.

MYER: All right, I move it for you. (MIKE *also moves a ball, to his further advantage.*)

MYER: Don't do dot! Don't do dot! It ain't allowed you to move balls.

MIKE: You can move dem, und I can't move dem, eh?

MYER: Imbesilly! I moved it as a favor to you.

MIKE: Vell, I moved de other one as a favor to you. (MIKE *shoots and misses;* MYER *takes aim.*)

MIKE: Vot ball you play?

MYER: Der round one.

MIKE: Round? All is round!

MYER: Dis one is rounder. (MIKE *picks up a ball to examine it.*)

MYER: Again! Once more, ain't I told you? Drop dot ball! (MYER *manhandles* MIKE *and the game resumes.* MYER *shoots, misses and drives the white cue ball into a corner pocket. Both jump up and down exultantly.*)

MIKE: Hooray! A scratch!

MYER: Sure! A scratch! Dot gifs me four balls. Only best players can dodge all der other balls und get in der hole. I surprise meinself. (*While* MIKE *ponders this,* MYER *puts the four highest balls remaining on the table in his rack and prepares to shoot again*).

MIKE: Vot ball you shoot now?

MYER: Der colored one.

MIKE: Vich color? Dey all got colors! (MYER *ignores the question, shoots, misses, and* MIKE *takes his turn.*)

MYER: Vell, vell! Tell it vot you is playing.
MIKE: Pool aind't it?
MYER: Vat ball? Vat ball?
MIKE: Ah! So I got to play a ball?
MYER: How many times got Ito tell you got to name vat ball you shoot?
MIKE: Good! I name one Rudolph. (MYER *menaces* MIKE *with a cue,* MIKE *parrying and thrusting in fencing-master fashion.*)
MYER: Now, vill you tell me?
MIKE: Vich number is biggest?
MYER: Der fifteen ball.
MIKE: I like to shoot him. Vere is he? (*Both search the table for the fifteen ball.* MYER *finds it in* MIKE's rack, MIKE's only marker.)
MYER: Here's it.
MIKE: All right, put it down here.
MYER: As a special favor to you, I do it. (MYER *places the fifteen ball back in play.* MIKE *shoots, misses and scratches the cue ball into a side pocket. He dances jubilantly.*)
MIKE: Hooray! I vin four balls! Dot's a scratch like you told me.
MYER: Dot's no scratch. Dot's an itch. Scratches is in corner pockets, itches in side pocket. Itches is bad. One itch by you gifs me four balls more. (MIKE, *realizing that the game is going against him, jumps on the pool table, and leaps from there to the rack, grabbing the fifteen dollars before* MYER *can act. Then* MYER *attempts to take the money from him.*)
MIKE (*REMINDING HIM OF HIS OWN WORDS*): Der one dot gets der money vins de game. (*Still clutching the money,* MIKE *is dragged offstage by the scruff of his neck.*)

The pool-table act was a new thing in the theater. Until now, the usual comedy turn either was pure slapstick for slapstick's sake, or a mere volleying of quip, gag and patter, the form and substance handed down through the centuries from jester, harlequin, clown or minstrel. Weber and Fields had caught up a slice of life and put it, burlesqued but recognizable, upon the variety stage, which hitherto had left the mirroring of Nature to the legitimate theater. More or less unwittingly, they had grafted slapstick upon farce and comedy and produced a new theatrical species. The pool-table skit told a story and held a mirror up to life; a farcical story and a distorted mirror, it is true, but a long step beyond the belled cap, the bladder, the stuffed club and the topical joke. Other actors were groping along the same trail to such eventual success that to-day the $5.50 musical revues have raided the vaudeville and burlesque stages of many of the best of these turns.

The Saturday before the Baltimore opening, advances to the company and routine expenses had nibbled the firm's cash balance down to some forty dollars, with sixteen tickets to Maryland yet to be bought. In this emergency they turned to their old friendly enemy, Gus Hill, for the loan of $200.

"You dod-rotted kids have treated me pretty bad," Hill grumbled, "and your show'll surprise me if it ever gets out of Baltimore, but I'm just fool enough to let you have it."

They gave their note, and the show was got to the Monumental Theater, Baltimore. The summer hung on unseasonably and business was bad from the start. Two fortuities saved them from Hill's "I told you so." Kernan's at Washington, the second date, was only forty miles, or one dollar, away, and pay day, traditionally, was Wednesday as of the preceding Saturday. This gave three days of the following week to make up salaries.

Neither Joe nor Lew ever had sat down to the elementary problem of how much money can be crowded into a house of so many seats at a fifty-cent top, boxes seventy-five. They had taken it for granted, actor fashion, that Hill, Hyde, the Kernells and other managers were above money worries merely by virtue of being managers. Now when they counted up what had the look of a fair house and found only $260 in the box office, they thought they were being robbed. It happened that they were not, although the practice was not unknown. A show's only check on the receipts was the tickets. Tickets were hard or soft, the former the stiff pasteboards issued for the unreserved balcony and gallery seats; the latter, the thinner checks, with detachable seat coupons, for the reserved lower floor. A nimble-fingered door man could palm many a hard ticket, and the slotted boxes in which both hard and soft were supposed to be dropped had been known to have false bottoms.

But Joe stood guard in the box office beside the house treasurer, Fields kept at the side of the door man, and both used their circus-trained eyes.

Washington always was one of the poorer cities on the circuit, and the weather held hot—hot as only Washington can be. By Wednesday the company had played to only $1,000, split evenly between theater and show. This $500, added to Baltimore's offering of buttons and plugged nickels, gave Weber and Fields $810 to meet a $925 pay roll, yet it was met. Max Schanfield, brother of Lew, who had deserted the garment trade to go along as business manager, was sent by alley and back street to a pawnshop with the partly paid for diamonds. He brought back $125. The company was told that the diamonds had been sent home for safe keeping. The company had its own opinion as to that.

The second week of Weber and Fields' Own Company saw every cent of the $1,800 earned on the Coast gone, and a debt of $325 plus incurred. But their share of the last three days' receipts would get the troupe back to New York and a week at Donaldson's Bowery, where they were sure of capacity from their neighbors and friends. The Bowery rallied as expected and gave them such a reception at the Monday-matinée opening that Donaldson advanced $100 without question. With this and what was left of the Washington receipts they sent brother Max to the capital on the midnight train to redeem the diamonds. He was back in New York before dinner Tuesday.

"They must have sent those diamonds home after all," the perplexed company whispered at sight of them again.

The week at Donaldson's netted such a profit that after paying the agreeably surprised Hill his $200, and buying tickets for Boston, some $600 remained. Unable to get booking at Howard's Athenaeum, the most desirable Boston house, they had accepted without investigation an offer from Proctor's Grand Opera House. This theater lay out of the way in South Boston, played to a 10-20-30 scale, and their contract, they discovered too late, stipulated that Proctor was to get the first $1,500, they the next $1,500, and all over that to be divided equally.

When the curtain rose on the Wednesday matinée, pay-off day, the total receipts for the week thus far were $900. Proctor had $600 coming to him, and Weber and Fields had nothing. With more than $300 needed to meet the pay roll, they talked for their lives to the house manager. When talk failed they cried, bitterly and sincerely, until the manager parted with $100. A threat of double suicide on his doorstep would get no more from him, he warned.

Joe looked at Lew's stud. Lew looked at Joe's. Max looked at both.

"Again?" he asked.

By close bargaining, Max got eighty dollars on each of the studs and twenty dollars more on his own watch. Lottie Fremont, who was Uncle Dave Frank's daughter, and Lew's first cousin therefore, volunteered to wait for her salary. Thus the pay roll was met. Max was sent to New York that night to try to raise money. A letter from him came on the last delivery the next day.

"Quick work," said Joe as Lew slit the envelope.

"Dear Lew and Joe," the letter read: "I got my old job with Weinbaum back. I hope you get home all right."

Friday's night's receipts rounded out Proctor's $1,500. Saturday matinée and night were the thin core remaining to the boys. Next week they were booked for Miner's Eighth Avenue, New York, another certain life-saver if only they could make it. Jake Lewis had a jewelry store next door to B. F. Keith's Theater in Washington Street, and had known them of old. Reckless with desperation, they dropped into Lewis's shop on Saturday morning and priced diamonds. With two unpaid-for studs already in pawn, they picked out more—and better—ones at $350 each, and paid on account—two passes for the show.

That afternoon the jeweler and his son-in-law called backstage after the matinée. Already remorseful, the boys got the son-in-law to one side and poured out their story in tears—how Proctor had tricked them; how they had taken advantage of Lewis and were intending to pawn the new studs for enough to get the show to New York; how, once at Miner's Eighth Avenue they were saved. The son-in-law listened and said nothing. He went one way, Joe and Lew another, to a dreary supper at Miss Irish's theatrical boarding house. What the company did not suspect, they read in their employers' boyish faces.

The rice pudding was being served when the doorbell rang. Lewis's son-in-law asked for the boys; Jake wished to see them at his store. At the best, they anticipated, he would demand the return of the diamonds. At the worst——

"He's been telling me about the fix you're in," Lewis began. "I wish you boys had been frank with me to begin with instead of working that stud racket, but we'll forget that. I saw your show to-day and I've known you kids for a long time. You've got a good show, you're smart, and you're not lazy. That's about all any business needs. There's the safe. It's open. Help yourself to whatever you have to have and pay me back when you can. That goes for the studs, too."

How doth a good deed shine in a naughty world! Joe and Lew wept afresh as they counted $300 from the safe, but the tears that spattered upon the bills were not so salty as the tears of despair. The two Saturday performances brought in $400 clear. The $700 took the company to New York, paid Lottie Fremont her overdue salary and met the usual Saturday-night demands for advances—to the surprise of the demanders.

Miner's Eighth Avenue was a larger, better located and a higher priced house than Donaldson's Bowery, and New York jammed it to the doors all week. A $200 advance, had for the asking on Tuesday, was sent to Boston to redeem the studs and Max Schanfield's watch. After salaries had been paid on Wednesday night, $300 still remained with which to return Jake Lewis's bounty. The recovered studs were reset in two heavy gold rings. Weber and Fields now wore diamonds fore and aft, and the crowd at Miner's Eighth Avenue told each other, "I always said those boys would show 'em a thing or two."

From that day on, Weber and Fields never played a losing week. Gilmore's Central at Philadelphia followed the Eighth Avenue, then Pittsburgh and Cincinnati. From Ohio on, the Sundays were wide open and two additional performances a week brought the net profits up to $500 and $600. The first season of Weber and Fields' Own Company ended at Hyde and Behman's, Brooklyn, in April.

That same month Tony Pastor, the great Tony, who once had watched their flip-flaps in the lobby of his theater with amused disdain, sent for the two and offered them $250 a week to join his summer show. Sometime in those fifteen years Pastor had moved uptown to Fourteenth Street, next door to and part of Tammany Hall. Tammany and the theater still are there, the latter playing burlesque—the former ditto, at times. A lady might attend at Pastor's. For the first time Field's future wife, the young woman to whom his sister had introduced him on that memorable return from California, saw him onstage. Fields drove her to and from Fourteenth Street in the noblest landau ever seen in Clinton Street, while the diamond on his ungloved left hand winked at the diamond in his shirt front.

After two crowded weeks in his own house, the Pastor show took to the road. His always were all-star companies, and their coming was as circus day. Maggie Cline, then singing "Throw Him Down, McCloskey," was the particular sensation that year. In the cast also were the Russell Brothers, Jimmy and Johnny. Joe and Lew and the Russells became bosom friends. The Russells hinted that they would like to go out with the Weber and Fields company in the fall. Most of the variety actors from Boston to San Francisco were writing in to invite themselves to the same party.

What did these astonishing youngsters, so recently trafficking with pawnbrokers and crying for railroad fares, do but put two companies on the road their second season—their own and another called the Russell Brothers'

Comedians, both shows ranking not far behind Pastor's famous troupes. Their old boyhood companion, Sam Bernard—*the* Sam Bernard—was made business manager of the second company.

Supporting Weber and Fields were James F. (Young Mule) Hoey, Lottie Gilson, Filson and Earl, Johnny Carroll, Lavender and Thompson, Alburtis and Bartram, Swift and Chase, and the Bratts Brothers—a cast that sent the weekly pay roll across the $1,000 mark. With the Russell Brothers were more big names: Bonnie Thornton, Sam Bernard, Hastings and Marion, Lizzie B. Raymond, McAvoy and May, O'Brien and Havel, and Morris Kronin.

Booking was so arranged that the Comedians trailed the Weber and Fields company around the circuit, one week behind. The parent show prepared the way for its offspring. Each audience was exhorted in a curtain speech of the treat in store for them the following week, and the names of the Russells and their troupe filled the advertising squares on the in-one drop, customarily a breezy budget of the city's beauty and chivalry—The Edelweiss Chop House—Short Orders at All Hours; Fred's Palace Barber Shop—Six Chairs—No Waiting; The Alcazar Turkish Baths—Open All Night; The Capital Steam Laundry—Your Bosom Friend; The Grand Avenue Painless Dentists; The General Ulysses S. Grant Five-Cent Cigar, Thirty Minutes in Wheeling, W. Va.; and Compliments of the Queen City Baggage and Transfer Co.—We Never Sleep.

Such ballyhooing carried the new troupe through teething and the summer complaint to a small profit at the season's end. As for the parent company, observe the owners' diamonds. Gone from their wink are the red rays of shame at the secret knowledge of first and second mortgages and mechanic's liens. From finger and shirt front they heliograph the tidings that the line forms at the right of the box office and extends around the corner, nevermore to blush unseen in the dark unfathom'd corners of Shylock's safe, nor to waste their refulgence upon the hock-shop air.

This was the year in which Joe and Lew introduced Ladies' Night to a head-shaking Cincinnati. Col. Jim Fennessey's People's Theater, like the other houses on the circuit, was strictly stag. The bar to the presence of women lay not behind the footlights but in front. The entertainment was reasonably clean, but the drinking, smoking male audience was not so fastidious. Husbands, brothers and fathers carried home reports of the good things of variety and brought back the complaints of their womenfolk that the men should monopolize all this. Why not one night a week when smoking and drinking should be banned and women admitted, Fields suggested to Colonel Jim.

The Civil War veteran threw up his hands.

"Let sleeping dogs lie, son," he objected. "Let 'em in here once and they'll be pushing in regular the first thing you know, and driving the boys away. A man likes to have some place where he can get away from petticoats. Well"—the colonel gave ground grudgingly—"we might reserve the boxes for them some night and let a few in through the stage door."

"Why not do the thing up brown and get your theater talked about?" the boys argued. "Get out a lot of dodgers announcing Friday as Ladies' Night;

no smoking, no drinking, and a cut flower presented to every lady present. Give the old house a thorough scrubbing and fill your lobby with flowers. Try it once."

"It's a crazy idea, and against my better judgment," Fennessey grunted; "but have your way. You'll travel on Saturday night and I'll be left to hold the sack."

Friday morning ten charwomen attacked the outraged old theater with brushes and suds. By night it did not know itself, nor did it ever recapture all its former bachelor freedom. Ladies' Night became a Cincinnati institution.

Ed Butler's Standard was the home of variety in St. Louis. Butler had a clientele that would be described to-day as hard-boiled. It was their pleasure to chuck the doorkeeper into the street now and then just to show him his place. Frank James, brother of Jesse, appearing in St. Louis, fresh from a prison term for train robbery, and out of work, Butler hired him as doorkeeper. James was a mild-mannered, run-of-the-mill citizen, after the best train-robbing traditions, beneath whose milk-and water surfaces lurked forked lightning. His reputation alone sufficed to keep Ed Butler's customers in order, but he fell so far short of the red-shirted desperado on the blue horse, as depicted on the cover of "The James Boy's Revenge," and other volumes of that five-cent library, that Joe and Lew at first pooh-poohed his identity.

Frank was amused.

"The judge and jury didn't have no such doubts," he drawled.

On their second visit to St. Louis after Frank's advent at the Standard, he gave the boys a personal demonstration of the James family temperament. The Weber and Fields advance man was a breezy, *pushful*, back-slapping young go-getter whose brassy approach irritated the ex-train robber. James had greeted Joe and Lew amiably on seeing them after a year's lapse, then added, *en passant*, "If you send that bleating advance man around here to pester me again, I've made up my mind to kill him. He plumb annoys me." Jesse's brother may have been speaking hyperbolically, and he may not. That will never be known. An event occurred which led his employers to order the supersalesman not to cross the Mississippi the next trip out.

Joe and Lew liked to offer the last of the James boys a cigar or a drink in an effort to draw him out on his purple past. They drew him out so far on a later night of that week that he shot out the lights of a Fourth Street saloon. The bartender batted no eyelash and went on polishing a wineglass. James spared one light for illuminative purposes, flipped a bill on the bar and ran a handkerchief through the fouled pistol barrel.

"Boy, get some new bulbs," the barkeep called to the negro porter. "Let's see. Eleven times forty cents makes four-forty."

"Keep the change, Adolph,"said the sharpshooter, dismissing the incident.

It was this experience that inspired the *schützenfest* skit which succeded the pool-table turn in the Weber and Fields repertoire. A target of lighted electric lamps revolved at the back of the stage. Firing from impossible angles and ridiculous postures, blindfolded, back to the target, standing on their heads or what, these deadly marksmen, Mike and Myer, never missed. At each rifle report an electric bulb bit the dust, at the reckless cost of five dollars a performance. By comparison, Annie Oakley was a scofflaw fumbling for a galloping keyhole. The deadly accuracy, of course, was supplied by a property man who, hidden behind the target, exploded the lamps at will.

The Choking Scene

FIELDS: You look like a furnished room.
WEBER: Why do you go with me, then?
FIELDS: Why? Why? Because *I like you*! Mike, when I look at you—I have such a—a—feeling—that—oh, I can't express myself!—such a—oo-oo-oo-oo! (Chokes him, then turns to audience.) Why do I go with him? (Pointing at Weber.) When I look at him my heart goes out to him. (To Weber.) When you are away from me, I can't keep my mind off you. When you are with me I can't keep my hands off you! (Chokes him.) But sometimes I think you do not return my affection. You do not feel that—some thing that—oo-oo-oo-oo! (Chokes him again, etc.)

Weber and Fields's first real press notice was achieved in this season. The Cincinnati papers usually tossed the People's Theater bills a few lines; elsewhere the press dismissed the variety stage as beneath notice. Amy Leslie, veteran dramatic critic of the *Chicago Daily News*, then not so veteran, it was who wrote Clipping Number One in the scrapbook. One spring afternoon as the White City of the World's Columbian Exposition was taking form in Jackson Park, Miss Leslie strayed from the beaten paths of critics into the Lyceum Theater, then still Tom Grenier's property. The whisper that Amy Leslie was in the house ran backstage, but signified nothing to Joe and Lew. The pool-table act went on as usual. Fame arrived on the wings of the morrow's first edition. Chicago's principal afternoon newspaper gave a column to the poolroom skit. Its dramatic critic, turning from Joseph Jefferson, Fanny Davenport, Robson and Crane and Richard Mansfield, proclaimed the discovery, in the dim purlieus of variety, of the funniest act she ever had seen. The overwhelmed subjects of her eulogy bought out the corner newsboy's stock four times, framed one page, filled their pockets with others and packed the surplus into a costume trunk, which they continued to carry with them until the luster of the Chicago triumph began to be dimmed by their music-hall career on Broadway.

At the end of the season Tony Pastor paid Weber and Fields $400 a week to join his summer show a second season. That fall they sent three variety troupes on the road. Johnny Russell desired to manage the Comedians himself. To meet his request, Sam Bernard was detached and put at the head of a third company, called the Vaudeville Club, one of the earliest substitutions of the French word "vaudeville" for variety in America. The new troupe lost money, but its producers kept it on the road as a matter of pride.

Read the roll call of Weber and Fields' Own Company for that season: Billy Emerson! McIntyre and Heath! The Acme Four! Harry Kernell! Young Mule

Hoey! Will H. Fox! Maud Huth! And Mike and Myer themselves! The putting together of such a show is a gift. It took money to pay such a cast, tact to manage it and showmanship to blend it. An adroitly balanced vaudeville program never is an accident.

And mark the name of Harry Kernell, their former employer, their one-time persecutor, the man to whom they first made their boast of organizing their own show. He came to them one day asking for work. Joe's eyes sought Lew's questioningly. He read the answer quickly. The world was ahead of them, not behind. Oh, classic revenge!

Supporting the Russell Brothers in their second season were Montgomery and Stone, Lottie Gilson, Lizzie B. Raymond, Fields and Lewis, Herbert and Caron, Whiting and Shepherd, and Johnson, Riano and Bentley. No small potatoes, these.

Fields and the young woman he met the night of his return from California were married in New York on New Year's Day of this season. The company was playing in Brooklyn at Hyde and Behman's, and the day chanced also to be Lew's birthday. The stud and ring diamonds were reset in earrings as the groom's gift to the bride. The stones were illy matched in color and size, but not in the eyes of the bride, who knew and cherished their checkered history. The earrings are family heirlooms now.

The fourth year's cast of the Own Company reads like another vaudeville Valhalla. In it were McIntyre and Heath; J. W. Kelly—the Rolling-Mill Man; Bobby Gaylor; Capitola Forrest; Maggie Cline; Sam LeClair and Leslie; Falk and Seeman; and Weber and Fields.

And now in the eighteenth year of their stage careers, and the late twenties of their lives, we bring Weber and Fields to Broadway. At Pastor's and Miner's Eighth Avenue they were on the ten-yard line. In 1894, at Hammerstein's new Olympia, they went over the goal for a touchdown. From the Bowery at Chatham Square to Broadway at Times Square is an hour's walk. Weber and Fields had been a quarter of a lifetime on the journey.

Oscar Hammerstein was a German cigar maker turned showman, a reckless, flamboyant personality with a genius for invention and a passion for music and the stage. He began with nothing and ended with a little less; but in the interim he made and lost more fortunes than any ten other men in theatrical annals. Broadway, where a last year's reputation often is a last year's bird's nest, will not soon forget Oscar Hammerstein, now five years dead.

In 1894 Hammerstein was operating two Harlem theaters, was about to open three Broadway houses, and was paying the most prodigal salaries in the business. He wrote to Weber and Fields offering them an engagement at the Harlem Opera House for their own company at the close of their road season. The first appearance of the Weber and Fields show at a legitimate theater was such a success that Hammerstein suggested that Joe and Lew bring their own act to the new Olympia for four weeks. They asked $700 a week; he gave them $500. Blasé Broadway saw the pool-room skit and showed such enthusiasm

Photo 8. Oscar Hammerstein I, c. 1910. National Portrait Gallery, Smithsonian Institution

that Hammerstein extended the engagement and put the act on the spot, the favored position just before the intermission.

In their fourth week they lost the spot to Signor Fregoli, a lightning-change artist imported from Europe at some outrageous salary; but whatever Fregoli cost, he was worth it. The man was a marvel the like of whom the stage never saw before or since. He played by himself an entire drama with a cast of half a dozen characters, walking out one exit as an old man and entering another almost instantly as a young woman. Ten expert dressers stood on the alert back of the set and swarmed over him, changing costumes, wigs and make-ups at each exit.

Hammerstein moved Joe and Lew to the first position following the intermission and answered their howls with flattery.

"You boys are so good that they will wait for you all night if they have to," he apple-sauced.

Their nose plainly was out of joint, nevertheless. Fregoli was the toughest of acts to follow, and Broadway had dropped the old sensation for the new. Joe and Lew sat on the curb across Broadway from the Olympia, where the Hotel Astor now stands, held their heads in their hands and stared, two Thinkers.

Fields came to life suddenly.

"Hot zickerty!" he exclaimed. "My brother Nat looks a lot like me, and Bob Harris, my brother-in-law, is the image of you."

Weber saw the point at once. A hurried travesty of Fregoli's drama, with the number of characters cut to four, was contrived, and after two days' rehearsal, Nat Fields and Bob Harris were smuggled backstage. Nat was made up as a fat woman, Harris as a comic soldier, both burlesqued copies of two of Fregoli's impersonations, and the hoax was sprung upon Hammerstein and his staff without warning.

Before the rise of the curtain following the intermission, while the house still buzzed with its delight in Fregoli, Fields appeared on the apron of the stage in his familiar German make-up and addressed the audience. He was there to praise Signor Fregoli, not to bury him. The signor was a wizard, Fields was far from denying. Still and all, Weber and Fields long had done all that the signor did, perhaps more. Only Weber and Fields had had no opportunity to do their stuff on Broadway. Even now Mr. Hammerstein was opposed, but had been won over to allowing them to show three or four lightning changes. I thank you.

The curtain rose on the same set used by Fregoli. Mike and Myer entered, clowning the signor's very sober drama and substituting German sputterings for his grave Italian. The audience, not knowing what foolery to expect from these merry-andrews, waited expectantly. At a cue, Mike and Myer exited. At the same instant they entered from the other side of the stage in the guise of a fat woman and a comic soldier. If Fregoli's changes were done with a perceptible pause, Weber and Fields's were performed with no interval whatever. The Italian's rapidity was astonishing, the Americans' was a physical impossibility. As the rear halves of Mike and Myer disappeared, the front halves of the fat woman and the gendarme came into view through another exit thirty feet away. The audience gasped its astonishment. A moment later the gendarme quit the stage by the far right exit, the fat woman by the far left, and Mike and Myer reentered simultaneously from back center. The changes grew more bewildering. Now Mike and the fat woman were on. Flash! The woman was gone and Myer arrived from the other side of the stage. Flash! Mike went out one door and the gendarme came in another. Flash! Mike and the gendarme in a twinkling became Mike and the fat woman, then Mike and Myer, then the gendarme and the woman again, as deceptively as the double exposure and other trick photography of the films. In their amazement, few in the house anticipated the joker.

There was an instant of numbed silence at the end, then a storm of applause beat on the curtain. Mike and Myer came before it to take a bow. They took one bow, a second and a third. On the fourth Mike, Myer, the fat woman and the gendarme appeared arm in arm. The tricked audience sent up one mighty whoop of mingled surprise and glee and came to its feet. Up with America, down with Europe! Weber and Fields again were the talk of Broadway, Signor Fregoli the eighth day of a seven-day wonder.

The Weber and Fields Music Hall, wherein the two won their major fame, was born of this happy chance. New York palpably wanted travesty, hungered for it. If Fregoli could be burlesqued successfully, why not any reigning

Broadway favorite or show? Summer was impending and Hammerstein's show was about to adjourn from the Olympia to the roof. Prices had to be cut to attract New Yorkers to a. summer show, and cheaper admission would entail cheaper salaries.

Fay Templeton and company were playing in "Excelsior, Jr." next door in the Criterion to thinning audiences. This house had had a poor year, and Joe and Lew went to Hammerstein with the proposition that he let them have it for their own purposes. Stock burlesque with an all-star company was in their minds, not the burlesque of the stage division of that name, but a dish of Weber and Fields's own concoction; an anticipation of the music revue of to-day minus its gorgeous sets and costume dancing, both developments of recent years.

Hammerstein wouldn't hear of it

"Take the advice of an expert at losing money," he told them. "You're actors, not business men. I'm paying you $500 a week, and you have three shows of your own. Don't gamble a sure thing like that away for a Broadway wildcat. Betting on the horses is a parlor game alongside guessing which way the cat will jump on Broadway. Your idea's never been tried. You believe New York would like it. Maybe it would, maybe it wouldn't."

Sound advice! But Joe and Lew were asking not for advice but a theater. With the assurance of youth, they got it and put their last dime into the speculation.

Chapter V

A New Theater, a First Season

"The Geezer," "Under the Red Globe," and "Mr. New York, Esquire," 1896–1897

CROWNS of thorns and crosses of gold; full dinner pails and honest money; free and unlimited coinage of silver at the ratio of sixteen to one; leather lungs and flambeau clubs.

William Jennings Bryan, the Boy Orator of the Platte, Peerless Leader; Major William McKinley, the Little Napoleon; Marcus Hanna, of the dollar-marked tweeds; trusts!

The time, in other words, is 1896. We are taking our politics very seriously this year, but there is other news in the papers. The American liner St. Louis and the Cunarder Laconia are racing for the transatlantic speed record. No subways in a New York City of 2,200,000 persons. The word "automobile" has been coined, but few have seen one.

A headline reads, Prof. Bell's Radiophone—a Telephone in Which a Sunbeam Replaces the Wire, and the radiophone drops back into the limbo of uninvented things for another generation. Keith's Union Square, Tony Pastor's and Koster and Bial's music halls advertise a sensational novelty—the kineopticon, the animatograph, the biograph, the cinematograph. In another word, the movie! Flickering 300-foot shots of the Colosseum in Rome, the Avenue de l'Opéra, Paris, or the Empire State Express rocking through Tarrytown at sixty miles an hour. A ninety-day wonder, falling away presently into the obscurity of nickelodeons to reappear two decades later a full-grown competitor of the speaking stage. Hollywood, meanwhile, is the name of a cemetery in Richmond, Virginia, nothing more.

Two newcomers invade New York—John Wanamaker, the merchant prince of Philadelphia; and a young man from California, Hearst by name, bringing a thing called yellow journalism. The granddaddy of all comic strips, Richard Outcault's Yellow Kid and his fellow urchins of Hogan's Alley, appear in the Sunday paper, now beginning to grow bulky. A dollar a day is a fair wage and $100 a month a salary goal to aim at.

The country is dancing the two-step and singing "I Don't Want to Play in Your Yard," "Put Me Off at Buffalo," "With a Little Bunch of Whiskers on His Chin," and "My Pearl Is a Bowery Girl." The Cherry Sisters of Cedar Rapids, Iowa, undisputed claimants to the title of the world's worst actresses, are convulsing audiences at Hammerstein's Olympia in their New York debut. Miss Maude Adams, playing in Rosemary at the Empire, is beginning to be heard of. A young Parisienne café chantant singer, Mlle. Anna Held, makes her first American appearance at the Herald Square in a revival of Hoyt's "A Parlor Match." Melba and the De Reszke brothers, Jean and Edouard, are singing at the Metropolitan. Twenty-eight years ago, is it? Or another age?

****

On an early June afternoon in 1896 Joe Weber sat on a shoe-shine stand at the southwest corner of Twenty-ninth Street and Broadway. His partner, Lew Fields, was summering at Rockaway Beach. Weber studied a bank book as his shoes were polished by an Irish lad recently from Clonakilty. The shining of shoes was not yet a Greek monopoly.

Photo 9. Weber and Fields on stage. L to r: Sam Bernard, Faye Templeton, Weber, Lillian Russell, Fields.

Joe and Lew wanted a theater of their own on Broadway. Their recent experience at Hammerstein's had convinced them that there was a place in New York for true burlesque, and the rash of ambition had broken out in a new place. For four years they had produced traveling variety shows successfully. The past season they had had three companies out. Yet the firm's cash balance was $300. There were the figures in a pass book, recently balanced, of the Germania Bank on the Bowery. Why ask where four years' profits had gone? Fields now had a family to support. Weber, still a bachelor, had put his $5,000 savings in an equity in an $18,000 house in Broome Street. He, his mother and his brother Max occupied the ground floor and rented the upper floors to a young lawyer, Otto Rosalsky, now judge in the General Sessions Court. Three hundred dollars was no capital with which to tackle Broadway.

As the bootblack signaled a completed task with his whisk broom, Louis Robie, manager of Harry Miner's Eighth Avenue Theater, happened by, saw Weber, and stopped.

"I hear you and Fields are looking for a Broadway house," he said. "Why don't you grab the Imperial over there?" Robie pointed across Twenty-ninth Street to the Imperial Music Hall, lately operated by George Kraus. "Miner tells me that Kraus has thrown up his sublease and quit," Robie continued. "Harry owns the lease and is looking for a customer. Better look him up. He's in his office now, or was a minute ago."

Robie jerked a thumb toward the Fifth Avenue Theater Building, a block below on Broadway. Weber did not go to see Miner. Instead, he took the next street car for Brooklyn Bridge, Rockaway Beach and Fields.

As constructed three years previously, the Imperial's entrance was on Twenty-ninth Street. Kraus had added a Broadway entrance by leasing a storeroom and converting it into a lobby. The added expense, it was supposed, had lost him the theater. Kraus and Big Tim Sullivan were partners later in the Dewey Theater on Fourteenth Street. Big Tim claimed that his partner owed him a large sum of money, payment of which he persistently evaded. Sullivan plotted a revenge that still is legendary on the Bowery. Big Tim rode up in front of the Dewey one day in one of the few motor cars then in New York. It was a foreign make, glistening in new red paint and with more brass work than a Haitian admiral. A liveried chauffeur sat stiffly at the steering rod. Big Tim alighted with a flourish, acknowledged the salutes of his admiring constituents and exchanged a few commonplaces with Kraus.

"That's a fine automobile you got there," Kraus said.

"Why shouldn't it be?" Sullivan is reported to have growled. "Didn't I pay $15,000 for it not five days since? Now I'm in a tight place. I can't lay me hand on any cash, and you won't pay me what you owe. It looks like I'd have to be selling the beauty for $10,000 and pocket me loss."

Kraus's eyes glistened like the car's brass work.

"I know a fellow, friend of mine, who might give you $7,500," tradition says he offered. The same tradition has Big Tim calling his partner every name in a longshoreman's vocabulary. He concluded the tirade with: "Get me the $7,500, and may the devil fly away with ye!"

Kraus paid, still in the name of the supposititious friend.

The chauffeur alighted and walked away with Big Tim. Once around the corner, they fell on each other's necks and either laughed or cried; curious passers-by were not certain which. Kraus inspected his purchase, and knowing nothing himself of these newfangled contraptions, sent for a mechanic.

The mechanic came, poked about the car cursorily and asked, "Where did you get this fancy teakettle?"

Big Tim, it developed, had paid fifty dollars for the ruins of a French car of the Louis Quinze period, spent several hundred dollars having it repainted, refurbished and its engine doctored sufficiently to get the bedizened old fraud as far as the front of the Dewey Theater under its own power. It just had lasted the distance. That night the Dewey Theater entrance was its garage.

The morning after his chance encounter with Robie, Weber stood again at Broadway and Twenty-ninth Street, Fields with him. Their eyes roved over the exterior of the dark Imperial; they rattled its locked doors and found no watchman about. Neither ever had been inside the house. Crossing Broadway to think their problem out in the ease of the cushioned chairs in the Gilsey House lobby, they saw Leo C. Teller entering the hotel bar. Teller was Fields's brother-in-law, then a department manager in the A. I. Namm store in Brooklyn, now the Teller of the Shubert-Teller, Brooklyn, Theater. Weber nudged Fields.

"Why not Teller? He's a business man," he said, with an actor's respect for the commercial acumen of anyone outside his profession. "He's got real estate in Brooklyn. Let him in as a third partner for whatever money we need to swing the lease."

Teller was familiar with their ambition. He believed in Weber and Fields and appraised the project as a good gamble; and most of all, he desired never again to see a woman shopper.

"Done!" Teller declared, and sealed the bargain with a handshake.

The three found Harry Miner in his office a block below.

"I like to see young fellows get ahead," Miner beamed upon them. "I'll strain a point and give you boys my three-year lease on the Imperial at $20,000 a year, $1,500 down to cover the rent for the three summer months, $5,000 before the house opens in September, $5,000 on December first, and the balance in two equal payments, February and April first."

The full measure of Miner's generosity was not revealed to them for some time. Then they heard that $20,000 was double the rental that Kraus had paid.

Teller wrote a check for $1,500. The three signed the contract, Joe and Lew without reading it, and took the keys. They had bought for three years a theater of which they knew nothing definitely except that it stood on Broadway. Being a music hall, the Imperial included a bar. The new lessees entered by the cellar stairs, which served as a stage door, and through the dusty saloon. On the barroom floor as he passed through, Weber found not a face but a twenty-five-cent piece. The old fifty-fifty rule was dishonored this once. Joe kept the quarter as a luck piece, and has it yet.

A single light, as required by law, burned on the stage and lit it feebly. The body of the house was lost in windowless night. Fields and Weber advanced to the cold footlights, did a quick dance step and sang to the empty and invisible seats:

Here we are, a jolly pair,
We own a Broadway thea-ter,
We own a Broadway thea-ter!

From somewhere in the gloom came an answering miaow from the house cat, as if the deserted theater itself had spoken.

Kraus had come to Broadway via the Bowery, and had embellished his theater according to the Bowery school of interior decorating, which went in heavily for gold leaf and Turkey red. When Teller found the switchboard and threw on the house lights the sudden radiance was caught up and reflected into their dazzled vision by a sunburst of gilt rococo and flaming upholsteries. In this first enchanted glimpse, Joe and Lew got their $1,500 worth.

There was ample width and height to the stage, but only sixteen feet working depth; so little that it was necessary to paint the bricks of the rear wall to simulate a back drop, and to pass through the cellar in order to get from one side of the stage to the other without being seen by the audience. But it was a theater, and on Broadway! It lay in the very heart of the Rialto and the Tenderloin. New York City was wide open and the city's night life flowed from Fourteenth Street to Thirty-fourth. The largest hotels, the important theaters, all were within rifle shot. Daly's Theater was next door, Shanley's cafe across the street, John Daly's semi-public gambling house immediately back of the theater

Joe and Lew swept and scoured the house with their own hands. Sam Bernard, originally a paper hanger, bought a job lot of wall paper from a wholesaler and papered the dressing rooms himself, while Lew and Joe cut the deep-napped carpet that had lain on the barroom floor into lengths to fit the dressing-room boards. These touches were not lost on variety actors and chorus girls accustomed to the Spartan simplicity of a horse stall. Bernard, their boyhood friend, had been offered a partnership, but had declined out of distrust for his own business ability. No partner could have outdone him, however, in zeal for the success of the enterprise.

Sam Bernard was born Samuel Barnett. The New York City directory is rife with Colemans who were Kolinskys, Lewinskys become Lewises, Di Giorgios anglicized to Georges and Zuccarinis transformed to Flynn; but there is no other known instance of a man of so sterling an American name as Barnett dropping it for the typically foreign Bernard.

The change originated in a typographical error. Very early in his theatrical career a printer set his name and that of his brother Dick as Bernard. Unable to afford new billing, they let the error ride, and were Sam and Dick Bernard thenceforth.

Photo 10. Sam Bernard as Herman Schultz in *The Girl and the Wizard*, c. 1909. Bain News Service, George Grantham Bain Collection, Library of Congress.

By the middle of August, Teller had spent $2,200 of his own money on the music hall and announced that he was at the end of his capital. Joe and Lew, who had thought of him as rich, were shocked.

"What about all that real estate in Brooklyn?" they demanded.

"All that real estate," he replied, "is one house, and that's in my sister's name."

When they protested that $2,200 was no adequate price for a third interest in their ability, experience, foresight and good will, Teller said that he would have to get out. If they would make him manager of the house on a salary, he would surrender his partnership and wait for the $2,200 until they were able to repay him. This was done, and Joe and Lew came into complete possession of what shortly was to be one of the most profitable ventures on Broadway.

With Teller out, new funds had to be found, and at once. Five thousand dollars more would be due on the lease soon, and there would be daily expenses. At Teller's suggestion they called on the president of the Germania Bank, custodian of their $300. The banker, was a variety fan, knew them both as actors and depositors. He greeted them graciously.

"We would like to borrow about $5,000," Joe got down to business.

"How much?" asked the banker.

"About $500," Joe amended quickly.

"Surely! Surely!" the banker agreed. "Just get some responsible person to indorse your note."

"What do you mean—indorse our note?" Weber demanded. The banker explained the process.

"Do you mean to say," Fields cut in, "that after we've been leaving our money here for five years, you won't lend us your money without somebody else saying we're good for it?"

The president of the Germania spread deprecating hands. This was the universal banking custom, he pointed out.

"You haven't a glass eye, have you?" Lew asked.

"A glass eye? Certainly not, Mr. Fields!" The banker drew a cloak of dignity about himself.

"I thought not," Fields said. "Ever hear the story of the banker who had a glass eye so perfect that it defied detection? No? A client wanted a loan and the banker made him an offer. If he could distinguish the artificial eye from the natural one he could have the money. The man pointed to the glass eye at once. The banker was surprised and puzzled.

"'You're the first one to do it,' he said. 'Do you mind telling me why you were so certain?'

"'Sure,' the borrower explained. 'The glass eye looked more sympathetic.' "

Weber added his say:

"If you don't trust us, we don't trust you," he ruled.

In a huff, they withdrew their $300 and left the Germania to its fate.

Reluctantly Weber took the deed to his Broome Street home to Miner and offered it as security for the $5,000 due before the music hall should open.

Miner accepted it. Among their friends the boys were able to raise $2,000 in small loans as an operating fund. Nothing now stood in the way of the theater's opening but talent.

Joe and Lew had two years of old contracts yet to fulfill and would be compelled to take to the road soon after the new theater opened, leaving the fate of their experiment in the hands of others. With Sam Bernard in charge backstage and Teller in the front of the house, their technical and business interests would be safe; but more was necessary. The company must be selected with unusual care. The variety acts would take care of themselves. Some two dozen turns, including many of the biggest on the boards, already were under contract from previous years, and more could be had for the asking. The enterprise would sink or swim on the burlesque. The choice for principals fell on John T. Kelly, Thomas J. Ryan, Charles K. Ross, Mabel Fenton, Lillian Swain, Yolande Wallace, Sylvia Thorne, Truly Shattuck, the Beaumont Sisters, and, of course, Sam Bernard.

Photo 11. John T. Kelly and Thomas J. Ryan. National Portrait Gallery, Smithsonian Institution; gift of Leslie and Alice Schreyer.

Ross and Fenton were an ideal team, specialists in afterpieces. Kelly and Ryan were one of the prime comedy teams of the time. They had quarreled and separated, and had to be engaged individually and secretly. For weeks after they were reunited on the music-hall stage they continued to refuse to speak to each other offstage. Kelly's asking price was $200 a week. Weber and Fields offered $175. The decision was left to the toss of a penny. The penny never came down, catching and sticking on a door lintel; and the difference was split at $187.50. Truly Shattuck was billed as the prettiest woman ever to have come from the Pacific Coast. Bernard was the peer of German comedians. All were more than competent.

In their desire to give more for the money than any competitor, Joe and Lew shut their eyes and fixed the price scale at twenty-five cents to one dollar, box seats one-fifty, considerably under the tariff at Pastor's, Hammerstein's and Koster and Bial's. There were 665 seats in the house. The first newsboy in the street could have done this simple sum for them. A capacity house would not bring in more than $700, and the show would cost almost $700 a performance. Two sets of costumes did for the chorus, and costumes and scenery were rented under a six weeks' guaranty. An orchestra of eight cost only twenty-four dollars a night, thirteen chorus girls—the number was premeditated—only fifteen each a week, a quartet of chorus men twelve dollars each. The union scale for stage carpenters, electricians and property men at the hour of going to press is seventy-five dollars a week, but a stage crew of nine cost but $132 a week in 1896. Ushers usually were students and worked for fifty cents and a chance to see the show. Twenty dollars paid a stage doorkeeper. But a Broadway rental and high-salaried principals offset all this frugality.

In person, they canvassed the Bowery and the East Side, peddling tickets with such industry that the house was sold out for a week in advance before Broadway began to ask for seats. The moment it found that no tickets were to be had, Broadway's desire to see the show multiplied tenfold. The White Lights crowd rushed to the box office, waved its money in the treasurer's face and bought the house out for the second week.

Saturday night, September 5, 1896, was the date. Weber and Fields' Music Hall was a reality. The former Imperial held a family party. From the last row of the upper floor, reserved for poor relations, to the front seats of the orchestra, one graced by Diamond Jim Brady, every man, woman and child was a friend, a neighbor, an acquaintance or a relative of Joe Weber and Lew Fields, and most of them knew one another. It was an audience that came to laugh, cheer and beat its hands sore willy-nilly; as determinedly friendly and sympathetic as a high-school-commencement assemblage of papas and mammas, and as little reflecting the true value of the entertainment. Evening gowns and silk hats in some of the boxes, shawls in the back rows, cut flowers overflowing the stage, an inaugural speech by a Tammany judge, excitement in front, excitement backstage.

The curtain rose on Lavender and Thompson, sketch artists, first number on the vaudeville olio. Johnny Carroll, a singing single, followed. Then Weber and Fields in person in the favorite pool-table skit. Lottie Gilson, the little Magnet, after them. Herbert and Carron, acrobats, closed the variety bill. An intermission, an overture, and then the burlesque, "The Art of Maryland," a travesty on David Belasco's "The Heart of Maryland," in which Mrs. Leslie Carter then was starring at the Herald Square.

It was a good variety bill and a bad burlesque, but the house vociferated its approval indiscriminately. The burlesque book was the work of Bernard, Ross and Fenton; the music by John Stromberg and the lyrics by Joseph Herbert.

Stromberg's music was fair, Herbert's lyrics were almost Gilbertian at times; but the book was labored and pifflish. Stromberg and Herbert knew their respective jobs; but Bernard, Ross and Fenton had attempted a task for which they had no special fitness. The fault was Weber and Fields's, who had given them the assignment. Their plot revolved—perhaps limped is more accurate—around a cook, one Mary Land, the creator of chicken á la Maryland, and her culinary art. Even the juicy opportunity of burlesquing Mrs. Carter's curfew-shall-not-ring-to-night swing on the clapper of the church bell was missed.

The reviewers were indulgent. One of them said:

"Coupled with hits at Bryan, Justice Mott and Sheriff Tamsen, aided by such accessories as a dummy baby whose head separated from its body, and a pasteboard horse, cab and driver, and played by well-known performers of the variety stage, the burlesque promises diversion. Its language was commendably free from vulgarity."

There were digs at others than Bryan, the justice and the sheriff. The Populists and their whiskers, Coxey's Army, the Ludlow Street Jail, the Delsarte system, the Seventh Regiment and General McAlpin, Tom Johnson, Tom Watson, Mary Ellen Lease, Carrie Nation, Pitchfork Ben Tillman, Sockless Jerry Simpson, Boss Croker, David Hill and Tom Platt had their turn. Four tramps carried four banners: Free Trade, Free Silver, Free Lunch, and Free Ireland. In one number the chorus was costumed as the Yellow Kid and his Hogan's Alley followers.

If anything of "The Art of Maryland" survived its six weeks' run in the memories of those who saw it, it likely was two of Herbert's comic lyrics and a love song.

His "I Love You, Dear," was free from the mawkishness of the conventional ballad, and achieved real tenderness. Its opening stanza ran:

"I love you, dear."
There is no phrase so warm and old,
In all the world no one so sweet
To lover's lips or maiden's ear,
As this refrain, "I love you, dear.
I love you, dear."

There is a flavor of William S. Gilbert about the lines that introduced Colonel Warp—Charles Ross:

I'm the heavy-handed villain,
Who is anxious and willin',
To turn an honest shillin' when I can.

The promise of some of Herbert's later work is to be found in "Appearances Were Against Her." It went:

A little bantam rooster
    Loved a little bantam hen, ah!

They lived a happy married life
  Until one day, and then, ah!
This bantam hen for mischief's sake
  Went flirting with a gander.
The other hens made this poor hen
  A victim of their slander.

They said she was a shameless flirt;
  Their gossiping incensed her.
This little hen was pure at heart,
  But appearances were against her.

One fatal day this bantam hen
  For breakfast went out scratching.
The other hens, they stole the egg
  This henlet had been hatching,
Replaced it with a green goose egg;
  They thought it would surprise her.
This little hen was color blind.
  So she was none the wiser.

Her bantam husband paid no heed
  Unto this vicious slander,
Until one day this bantam hen
  Hatched forth an infant gander.
Othello-like, he smothered her,
  His honor all derided,
He ate a peck of carpet tacks,
  And so he suicided.

There is a footnote to stage history to be found in the second week's program at the music hall. That week the animatograph was added to the variety olio to meet the competition of the Union Square and Pastor's, where the Lumière cinematograph and the kineopticon, respectively, had been introduced a few weeks earlier, the first appearance of the films on the regular program of an American theater. Weber and Fields soon discarded the original for a burlesque of their own contriving, dubbed the lobsterscope. A revolving, many-colored screen attached to the regular calcium spotlight, when thrown on the stage while the chorus was in action, produced a curious counterfeit of the flickering, jumping, eye-straining cinematograph. Its inventors thought so little of it that they sold all rights for fifty dollars, once it had served its brief purpose in their show. The following season, when they wished to use it again in the music hall, they were forced to pay $100 for four weeks' rental.

In the third week of the music hall its owners were compelled to turn their backs upon the infant. The three road shows, Weber and Fields' Own Company, the Russell Brothers' Comedians and the Vaudeville Club began their regular season. The Own Company opened at Hammerstein's Columbus; then was off on the road, leaving behind its first week's profits to keep the music hall going. The nightly receipts at the hall had dropped below $200 meanwhile. Before leaving New York, Joe and Lew commissioned Joseph Herbert to write the entire book of a new burlesque to replace "The Art of Maryland" as soon as its minimum six weeks expired.

"We had to keep it on for six weeks because we had rented the costumes for six weeks," Fields explains unconvincingly.

Herbert looked about him for a subject. The first of all musical comedies, "The Geisha," had just been imported from Daly's London, to Daly's New York, next door to the music hall. This primacy may be challenged inasmuch as the evolution of musical comedy from comic opera and extravaganzas such as "The Black Crook" was gradual and indistinctly marked; but "The Geisha" was the first production ever to be advertised and reviewed under the name of musical comedy in the newspapers of New York. The critics spoke of it as a new stage *genre* and credited its origins to London.

The new musical comedy was Herbert's choice. The result was "The Geezer," book and lyrics by Herbert, score by John Stromberg. Succeeding "The Art of Maryland" in October, it was an immediate success, and played to capacity houses for four months, then a long run on Broadway. "The Geezer" was Li Hung Chang, Chinese viceroy and minister of foreign affairs, whose visit to America on a world tour had been an event earlier in the year. Li was represented in the burlesque as being in quest of an American heiress bride for his emperor, her dowry incidentally to pay off the indemnity, demanded by Japan after the defeat of China in the war of 1894–1895.

John T. Kelly had the rôle and Sam Bernard the companion part of Two-Hi, keeper of a Doyers Street tea house. Kelly was an Irish, Bernard a German comedian. Kelly wore the duplicate of Li Hung Chang's ceremonial robes, but spoke his lines with a peat-bog brogue. Bernard's Chinese costume was made completely ludicrous by a low-comedy Dutch chinpiece, and such Chinese-German as "Velly good, py gollies" and "One piecee beer mit pretzels." Mabel Fenton was cast as Nellie Fly, a take-off on Nellie Bly, the globe-trotting newspaper woman. "Lady Faith, Lady Hope and Lady Charity, three ballet girls who have married titles," was a play on the name of the former May Yohe, American actress, who had married Lord Henry Francis Pelham Clinton Hope. Theodore Roosevelt was head of the New York City police board, and four chorus men, garbed as policemen, were labeled A. Roosevelt, B. Roosevelt, C. Roosevelt and D. Roosevelt. Charles Ross had the straight part of Lord Dunraving, a hit at Lord Dunraven, whose cup contender, the *Valkyrie III*, had lost with some unpleasantness to the native *Defender* in the international yacht races of 1895. The locale of the second act was China, where the cast had traveled in the *Valkyrie*, with frequent sarcasm about its lack of fleetness. There were topical allusions to Doctor Parkhurst, then New York's ranking reformer; Mayor Strong, Sunday closing, high prices and small portions at the new Waldorf-Astoria Hotel; Senator Brice and Newport; George Francis Train, Professor Doremus and other topics of the day, laughable at the moment, mostly pointless now.

The show got away to a flying start at the rise of the curtain. "The Geezer" possibly is the only musical show in history, grand opera included, the opening chorus of which will bear quoting after the lapse of thirty years—or thirty days, for that matter. Herbert achieved this feat by spoofing the usual inanity of the chorus salutatory in this fashion:

Hurrah! Hurrah! We laugh and sing.
So loudly let the welkin ring.
We must admit, though far from slow,
What welkin is, we do not know;
But when a chorus laugh and sing
They always make the welkin ring
And tell you it's a holiday,
And then proceed with the play.
They clink their glasses (tin)
And drink ere they begin
To tell the tale; it's most absurd,
For who understands a word?
But we discard these methods old
And tell the tale as it should be told.
Li Hung Chang comes here today,
Hence elaborate display.
Yankee heiresses he seeks,
China's finances are weak,
Japan's war has caused a leak.

The lyrics held this pace; a negro air, "Miss Lucy," was one of the best. It went like this:

The bees hum in the blossom vine,
The birds break out in song,
The sun, he say, "Ise obleeged to shine"
When Miss Lucy pass along.

When Miss Lucy pass along,
When Miss Lucy pass along,
The red rose say, "I'll lean youah way"
When Miss Lucy pass along.

The river stops where her footsteps pass,
Tho' the tide runs swift and straight,
And says, "Ise here for youah lookin'-glass"
When Miss Lucy pass along.

The violet says, "Ise kin to you,
You must not do me wrong."
The green trees bow a how-do-you-do,
When Miss Lucy pass along.

A sell-out at every performance, the music hall still failed to make money. In December, 1896, in the middle of "The Geezer's" run, the itinerary of the Weber and Fields' Own Company brought Joe and Lew back to New York, where they were confronted with the choice of raising prices or cheapening the show. They chose to increase the top from one dollar to a dollar and a half, with box seats two dollars. The public paid without a chirp and the music hall never again had a losing week.

Another milestone in Weber and Fields's history was passed the following week. The previous June, at a party given in honor of a niece's engagement, Mr. Weber had met a young woman to his heart's fancy. She became Mrs. Joseph Maurice Weber on January 3, 1897, and their honeymoon was spent on tour with the Own Company. Fields already was the father of a daughter and a son.

There are no music halls in America now and the term is meaningless to the present generation. A music hall was a vaudeville theater in which drinks were served; or, inversely, a beer garden graduated into a theater building. Very often the bar was the main tent and the stage a mere side show, hardly better than a capper for the sale of liquor. It followed that a music hall's appeal was overwhelmingly to a stag audience. The old Imperial included a bar as a matter of course. No one ever had operated a music hall except in conjunction with a bar, and Weber and Fields had no thought of not doing so.

It was Sam Bernard who first perceived that the old order changeth; that the day was passing when a Broadway theater could prosper without catering to a general and a sober audience. At the outset he suggested that the bar be strictly subordinated to the theater, in the face of the settled belief that the profit lay in the former and the certainty that a sober spectator would be a much more critical spectator. Joe and Lew grasped his point immediately. They refused an offer of $15,000 per season for the saloon and the liquor-selling rights in the house; refused it at a time when they needed money badly; put their brothers, Max Weber and Charley Fields, in charge of the bar and stopped the sale of drinks in the theater while the curtain was up.

From the first Weber and Fields had kept their shows free from the vulgarity then associated with variety. Backstage, however, tradition died more slowly. Chorus girls, for example, were less than the dust, and a principal conducted himself as he jolly well pleased. If he pleased to curse a chorus girl or to be obscene, that had been his privilege. During the run of "The Geezer" one of the male principals appeared on the stage drunk and insulted the company. Bernard fired him on the spot. The man appealed over Bernard's head by wire to Weber and Fields in Chicago. They telegraphed back that whatever Bernard did they sustained.

The offender sulked for several days, Sylvia Thorne successfully playing his part meanwhile. Miss Thorne was a sister of Fred Titus, then six-day bicycle champion and a sport-page hero, later husband to Edna May. The principal eventually sought Bernard out and apologized handsomely.

"You insulted the others as well," Bernard suggested.

The actor was astonished. "I hope you don't expect me to get down on my knees to a lot of chorus girls!" he exclaimed.

"Why not?" Bernard asked. "They are as good as we are."

"You are just trying to humiliate me," the man protested. "I'm damned if I'll do it!"

But he did. The company was assembled on the stage and he asked their pardon individually and collectively. From that moment on the morale of the company was distinct among music halls, and no stage was conducted with more decorum. Weber and Fields agreed to remit the week's salary of $250 the actor had lost on condition that he remain sober until the end of the season. He clung heroically to the water wagon until three days before the season's close, then fell with a crash that rattled the windowpanes and saved the firm $250.

These were some of the factors in the success of the music hall. Another, and probably the most important, was the distinction of the entertainment. The Weber and Fields burlesques were unique, a patent of their own, without parallel in the theater. Gradually they eclipsed the vaudeville olio and finally displaced it entirely. A Weber and Fields burlesque was the best of advertisement for the travestied play, and producers competed with one another in sending their scripts to Joe and Lew with permission to use them as they liked. In one instance a producer gave them a special performance of "A Message from Mars" on a Sunday afternoon in the hope of inspiring successfully a travesty.

It is unfortunate that there is no other word than "burlesque" for these shows. They were true burlesque, but in the popular mind that word is associated indelibly with what is tersely and aptly known as a leg show. The burlesque show of commerce is distinctly cleaner these days than most of the $5.50 revues; it clings to mid-Victorian tights in a day of sheer veilings, censors its lines and situations, while the Broadway shows broaden both to the width of that highway at Long Acre Square, and still holds its own peculiar public; but to no effect on popular opinion, which speaks of it as burlycue, and thinks of it in connection with barber shops, Turkish baths, the *Police Gazette* and smoking-compartment anecdotes.

Leo Teller was a shining member of the Lady of Lyons Amateur Dramatic Club, and was inclined to patronize the professionals of Broadway. If the truth were known, he hinted, there was more first-class histrionic talent in the Lady of Lyons club than in some shows he might mention.

On Lincoln's Birthday, 1897, John T. Kelly, who lived at Elmhurst, Long Island, found all roads to Manhattan blocked by a blizzard. He telephoned that he might not be able to reach the theater in time for the matinée. Sam Bernard told his troubles to the business manager.

"I don't know what we'll do if Kelly doesn't make it," Bernard fretted. "We haven't anyone who can take the part on this short notice."

Teller's eyes lit up. He studied the weather from his office window. He had seen much worse storms, Elmhurst was a close-in suburb, and it was three hours yet until matinée time. Kelly would make it, he concluded.

"Shucks! I'll play the part for you," he told Bernard. "I know the lines backward and forward just by hearing the show. You actors take yourselves altogether too seriously."

Kelly's role of Li Hung Chang was the keystone of the burlesque, but Bernard concluded to risk it for one matinée. When one o'clock came and no Kelly, Teller began to be visibly nervous. He still was convinced that he would not have to make good on his bluff, but not so certain but that he felt the need of Dutch courage. He dropped in at the bar and poured a large drink.

In the next anxious hour Teller drank eight more whiskies. Two o'clock and no Kelly! The others dragged Teller to a dressing room and began to make him up as Li Hung Chang. The dressing room was beneath the stage, and hot. Between the whisky, the warmth and his fright, Teller perspired like a man in a steam bath, and evaporated not only the liquor but most of the marrow in his bones. At his entrance—a fanfare from the orchestra—he was coldly sober, but so weak that he tottered as one drunk. Leaning against a wing, he whispered hoarsely, "Push me out!"

The business of the entrance called for Sam Bernard, who was Two-Hi, to wrap a doormat emblazoned with the word "Welcome" around his body, prostrate himself and present his back and the doormat to Li Hung Chang's feet. Teller stumbled from the wings with his back to the audience and fell over Sam. He did not see the mat or anything else, and forgot even the first word of his lines. The company prompted him in hissing whispers, but all that Teller's confused ears could make out was the proper name Ki-Ki. This he mumbled over and over. "Louder!" his prompters hissed, and Teller shouted "Ki-Ki" at the top of his lungs.

"Turn around and face the audience," Mabel Fenton whispered.

"Where is it?" Teller asked in the voice of a lost child.

One of the props of the scene was a judge's gavel, one end padded and so jointed as to give off the sound of wood meeting wood when struck. The other end was a solid knob of hardwood. The action called for Li Hung Chang to rap Two-Hi on the head with the padded end. Bernard put his head in position to receive the blow, but Teller waved the gavel about aimlessly.

"Hit me! Hit me!" Bernard pleaded.

Teller granted him his boon. He brought the hard end of the gavel down on Two-Hi's head with a swipe that floored the German Chinaman for the count of nine. Bernard looked up from the stage floor at the star of the Lady of Lyons club and groaned through clenched teeth, "Oh, you Ki-Ki!" The audience was enjoying itself thoroughly. It cheered Kelly's volunteer understudy and demanded encores. Mr. Teller has owned and managed theaters for many years now, but despite this flattering debut, he never again acted in one.

In late February "The Geezer" was succeeded by "Under the Red Globe," a burlesque of Stanley Wey-man's swashbuckling story of the seventeenth century, "Under the Red Robe," first a best seller, then a dramatic success. Cardinal Richelieu turned up in this as Cardinal Fishglue, and the story was transferred from France to Gailly's gambling house at Long Branch. Gailly was Weber and Fields's next door neighbor, John Daly, thinly disguised. Daly's gambling house at Long Branch was better known than his Twenty-ninth Street place. Long Branch's glory is gone now, its giddy youth of the General Grant era forgotten; but as late as the middle '90s it, not Atlantic City, was the famous resort of the Atlantic seaboard.

On Saint Patrick's Day, 1897, Corbett and Fitzsimmons fought for the heavyweight championship at Carson City, Nevada. Joe and Lew had met Corbett eight years before when he was the unknown boxing instructor at the Olympic Club, San Francisco, and Gentleman Jim had been much about the music hall when in New York. Every member of the company was a Corbett rooter. John T. Kelly had bet two weeks' salary on his man.

As there was a special matinée on Saint Patrick's Day, Kelly suggested that a special wire be run into the big dressing room, bringing a detailed report of the battle. He passed the hat for the necessary funds and left the arrangements to Bernard. When the latter took the matter up with the telegraph company his attention was called to the fact that two P.M. in Carson City would be five P.M. in New York, by which time the matinee would be over. Bernard kept this information to himself. The wire was run in, an operator appeared and the sounder began to chatter about curtain time.

"The arena is filling up rapidly," the telegrapher announced.

"Joe Choynski is introduced and challenges the winner.

"Fitzsimmons is entering the ring. He is applauded.

"Corbett enters the ring. Terrific cheering.

"They shake hands. Round one!

"Corbett lands on Fitz, who runs away.

"Corbett feints with his left and lands a stiff right to the body.

"Corbett is chasing Fitzsimmons around the ring.

"Round over!"

Actually the telegraph sounder was reporting the livestock receipts and the grain markets at Chicago, Kansas City and Minneapolis; but only Bernard and his accomplice, the operator, knew it. The men and women of the stock company crowded around the sounder and beat one another's backs at every mention of the invincible Corbett's wicked rights and lefts. The variety acts rushed through their turns and dashed back to the special wire.

"Round two! They both rush to the center. Jim leads. Fitz ducks. Fitz misses a right swing and is staggered by a right jab to the jaw. They clinch. Corbett punishes Fitz in the infighting."

The yells of the delighted company began to penetrate the body of the house and the audience to sense what was going on. Charley Ross stopped the show to promise the spectators that the result would be made known from the stage and to hint that there could be but one outcome.

"Round three! Corbett dances around Fitz, hitting him at will. Fitz tries to clinch. Corbett knocks Fitz against the ropes. Jim drops Ruby Robert with a smash to the jaw. The referee is counting. One-two-three-four-five-si x-seven-eight-nine——Fitzsimmons is saved by the bell!"

The operator kept his imaginary fight going right through the matinée, Corbett toying with the Cornish miner, who regularly was saved from a knockout by the bell. The matinée was over at 4:40 P.M. At 4:38 the telegrapher raised his hand. A tense hush fell over the crowded dressing room. Outsiders had dropped in, including Captain Price of the Thirtieth Police Precinct.

"Flash!" the telegrapher called. "Corbett wins by a knockout! Fitzsimmons's seconds are reviving him."

The crowd has gone wild. Everybody, including the police, is in the ring. They have lifted Corbett to their shoulders.

"You can't beat that fellow Corbett; he's too quick for that Australian," Captain Price pronounced.

A telegram of congratulation was drawn up, signed by every member of the company and sent to Corbett. John T. Kelly hurried into his street clothes and made for the barroom of the Gilsey House. He found lobby and bar packed with men waiting for the result.

"How are you getting your returns—by mail?" Kelly shouted. "The fight's over, Jim won, and I cleaned up $500."

Four hundred men promptly offered to bet him that he was crazy, that the fight hadn't begun, and that Fitzsimmons would win it when it did start. Kelly waved them aside.

"I never bet on a cinch," he retorted grandly. "We had a special wire at the theater and got it all blow by blow. Fitz never had a chance."

"You poor chump!" someone called. "It's only two o'clock in Carson now, and they aren't even in the ring yet."

In support of this statement, a genuine direct wire from the ringside began chattering news of the preliminaries. Kelly went in search of Bernard with a club.

Corbett, who lost in fourteen rounds to Fitzsimmons that day, and made the solar plexus famous, came to the theater with death and destruction in his eye on his next visit to New York and demanded to know the wherefore of the telegram of congratulation.

The final bill of the 1896–97 season, Mister New York, Esquire, opened on April twenty-second, and with it the music hall began to take the form in which it won its later fame. Weber and Fields closed their road season, hurried back to New York and appeared in the burlesque for the first time; the first occasion, too, that three German comedians appeared together on a stage—Bernard, Weber and Fields. Henry Dixey also was added to the cast. He had quarreled with Koster and Bial, and accepted Weber and Fields's offer of $400 a week. Mister New York, Esquire, was a travesty rather than a burlesque. The distinction is that a burlesque caricatures a specific play or thing; a travesty is a distorting mirror that holds up the follies of the moment, a revue in the true sense of the word.

The first season of the music hall ended on June fifth. Its proprietors had not yet set Broadway afire, but they had made that haughty highway sit up and take notice. One critic, in reviewing the year, said of them, "Weber and

Fields in one season have taught a needed lesson to managers, critics and the public. It is: Establish a trade-mark of your own and do not foolishly imitate each other."

Joe's and Lew's hearts were in the music hall, but another season's contract on the road remained to be fulfilled, and the theater owners on the variety circuit refused to accept any substitutes. In their week at the Olympia, Chicago, in the season just ended, Weber and Fields' Own Company had played to $8,000 at a 10-20-30 box-office scale. With reason, George Castle, the manager, declined to swap such a certainty for a pig in a poke. He recalled too fondly the long line waiting at the box office on the occasion of Weber and Fields's latest visit. The Olympia ran a continuous performance from twelve until twelve, with a vaudeville olio filling in before and between the regular afternoon and evening shows. When business was good it was a problem to get the old audience out to make room for the new. Castle took one look at the box-office line on the Sunday afternoon when Weber and Fields opened, and hired a fifteen-dollar-a-week trained-pig act as a chaser. A chaser is an act intended to discourage the spectator into leaving the theater. The dirty work customarily is left to moving pictures in continuous vaudeville houses. The trained-pig act, as its price would indicate, was ideally calculated to thin out the house. Pigs, like cats, are very difficult to train, and in this instance the trainer was under suspicion of having recruited his company from the first carload lot of hogs to reach the stockyards that morning. The pigs paid as scant attention to the advice, cajolery and threats of their mentor as a flapper to her parents, and evidenced no bringing up better than that of the barnyard.

The pigs were sent on this Sunday afternoon before the Weber and Fields show. The crowded house watched the act in bored silence. Another variety act, then Castle sent the pigs on a second time. Some L guard, off duty, yelled, "Thirty-ninth Street! Change for the Stockyards!" But nary a seat emptied. Castle was a patient man. He waited two acts, then sent the pigs on a third time. The house began to suspect his motives. It gave the perspiring trainer and his hams and bacons an enthusiastic reception. When a pig ignored the hoop through which he was being beseeched to jump, and ambled off into the wings with a contemptuous grunt, the spectators cheered madly. And when the pig act failed to appear a fourth time the house stamped its feet and shouted, "We want the pigs! Give us the pigs! Pigs! Pigs! Pigs!" Castle was whipped and the regular bill opened fifty minutes late.

Joe and Lew's only hope of escaping their contract was to gather together such an all-star troupe that no manager in his right senses could refuse it. They had turned thumbs down on the Russell Brothers and the Vaudeville Club as substitutes, but the Vesta Tilley All-Star Company changed their minds.

The idea of the Vesta Tilley show was given to Joe and Lew by their competitors, Hammerstein and Koster and Bial. These two were conducting a billboard dispute over the present Lady de Freece, each claiming to have booked her exclusively at a salary of $1,500 a week.

"I don't believe either of them has her," Fields said to Weber and Teller at lunch in Shanley's restaurant.

Teller made an offer. He never had been to Europe, and did not feel that he could afford the trip out of his own pocket. If his employers would pay his expenses, however, he would guarantee to have the name of the famous English comedienne on a contract within a week after he landed, and at a figure less than $1,500.

"When would you sail?" Fields asked.

It was a Friday.

"To-morrow," Teller answered brashly. Lew looked inquiringly at Joe, who nodded his head. "Good Lord, they're going to take me up!" Teller said to himself.

He was about to cross the Western Ocean as lightly as if it were a Coney Island excursion. But he sailed the following noon, swallowed hard as the steamer passed Fire Island Lightship, and did not confess his qualms until he was back on American soil again.

Two days after landing in England, Teller cabled that he had signed Miss Tilley for eight weeks at $1,250 a week, and Weber and Fields began to organize a company to surround her. Between Koster and Bial and Hammersteins's quarreling billboard posters appeared Weber and Fields's exultant shout, "We got her!" They booked such acts as the Four Cohans, Lew Dockstader and Charles T. Aldrich, the comedy juggler, and sent Miss Tilley out in the fall with the greatest and highest-priced variety troupe ever gathered together, to fill the booking of the now disbanded Weber and Fields' Own Company, first using her to head the vaudeville olio at the music hall.

Joe and Lew now were free to give their undivided time to the hall, their families and the city of their birth. For the next eight years they were lost to the road and became a New York institution.

Chapter VI

The Second and Third Seasons

"The Con Curers," "Catherine," and "Helter Skelter," 1897–1899

NEW names and new faces in this second season of the Weber and Fields Music Hall. Only Tommy Ryan, among the principals of the first year, is missing. John T. Kelly, Sam Bernard, Charley Ross, Mabel Fenton and Weber and Fields are back; and with them Frankie Bailey and her legs, Bessie Clayton and Julian Mitchell, Honey Stromberg and Edgar Smith, Peter F. Dailey.

Oh, rare Pete Dailey! Inimitable Peter! Born comedian, the quickest-witted man that ever used grease paint; splendid voice; an acrobat and agile dancer despite his two hundred and fifty pounds; no performance ever the same; needing neither lines nor business, but only to be given the stage; convulsing his fellow actors as well as the audience with his impromptu sallies; an inveterate practical joker; a bounding, bubbling personality.

Dailey, the son of a New York auctioneer and politician, made his debut at the Globe Museum in the same year Weber and Fields did, and at a like age. The first of nut comedians, years before these eccentrics became a stock vaudeville type, he did on the stage of Miner's Bowery in the '80s all that they do to-day. As one of the American Four he had been Joe and Lew's companion on the disastrous Bridgeport turkey-show enterprise of ten years earlier, then had turned to the legitimate. The season of 1896–97 he had been out at the head of his own company in "The Night Clerk." His salary was $300 a week, and none would think of offering him less; yet Joe and Lew, taking a page from the practice of John L. Cancross, named $298.

"It's just a superstition of ours," they said when he lifted his eyebrows at the odd sum.

Dailey slept most of his days, stayed up all his nights and was perpetually late for rehearsals. But for matinées and rehearsals, his would have been an Elysian life. The moment a performance was over it was his invariable custom to order a quart of whisky and a quart of champagne—quarts, not pints or half pints—from the bar. Before he left the dressing room he

Photo 12. Peter F. Dailey singing "Dinah de Moon Is Shinin'" with chorus girls.

would have, unaided, emptied both, using the champagne as a chaser, and be apparently nothing the worse. Anyone happening in would be invited to join him, but should they accept, he would order a fresh bottle. The two quarts were his own. Thus fortified, Peter would set out on his nightly peregrinations.

"A workingman knocks off at six and has his evening for fun," was his defense. "When I get done work at eleven o'clock I want my fun." His wife, Mary, complained once that she saw little of him as a result of his nocturnal habits. "Come along with me then, my dear," advised Peter.

Mrs. Dailey accompanied him for three successive nights while he closed up Broadway, then returned to the hearth side, to remain without further complaint.

His foot on a brass rail or under a café table, the company of his fellow man, and the mellowing glow of alcohol. This were paradise enow for Peter, this was his fun. A highly social, gregarious creature, large-hearted, expansive, effervescent, his own high spirits did the rest. He spiked the stale beer of the casual barroom group with the old wine of his personality and yawns fled before him. When others failed him in the small hours he gathered delighted bell boys or nighthawk cab drivers about him, as did Nat Goodwin, and regaled them by the hour—Daileyan Nights Entertainments that would have opened every door in New York to him—or foregathered till dawn with the night-working newspaper men about the round table at Andy Horn's saloon at the Manhattan end of the Brooklyn Bridge.

When Peter did go to bed with the milk wagons, he demanded undisturbed repose. His wife would refuse to wake him on any pretext. When on the road it was her habit to patrol the hotel corridor in front of his door, enforcing quiet. They seldom lived further than a block from the theater—across the street if possible. On matinée days Mrs. Dailey would call him at the ultimate moment. Dashing into his clothes, Peter would burst into the theater, his eyes still heavy with sleep, his stomach breakfastless.

Dailey's impromptus were often personal and no one of his acquaintance was safe from his wit and fooling. For instance, he was in the midst of a song one evening when he caught sight of the writer entering the Music Hall. The next verse should have been, "Way down in Georgia where the watermelons grow." Instantly he improvised, "Way down in Philadelphia where the Felix Ismans grow."

A kindly wit, assaying not a trace of the arsenic of malice to the ton; but woe betide the actor who tried to discomfit him on the stage. Charley Bigelow essayed it on his first appearance at the Music Hall, but never again. Bigelow was as bald as a door knob, and wore, on this occasion, a red necktie. In the midst of a scene with Dailey, Bigelow departed from his lines to address some forgotten personal gibe to Pete. Dailey's reply, however, has not been forgotten. It was instant.

"Put on your hat," he shot back, "you're half naked." Bigelow made some feeble retort. Dailey snatched the red tie out of Bigelow's vest and roared, "Your nose is bleeding."

Both rejoinders are in the repartee of every newsboy now, but their long life only emphasizes how devastating they must have sounded the first time. The flustered Bigelow was willing to call a truce, but Dailey continued to heckle him right through the scene.

"I've a mind to report you to the Board of Health," was another of his barbs; and when he advised his victim to light his cigar in the middle, the latter forgot the lines and exited in a rage.

The name of Peter Dailey, then, had been added to the roster at the Music Hall, a comedian made to order for the Weber and Fields festivities. Dailey, Bernard, Kelly, Weber and Fields. Five merry-andrews of the first water.

But are we forgetting Frankie Bailey, whose legs go marching on? Frankie sang little and acted not at all, but what would you? Ask fruit of the magnolia? Horsepower of the butterfly? Calories of the golden apples? Frankie's legs were copyrighted at the Library of Congress. Plays were written for them. Were they truly such noble limbs, such peerless members, such nonpareils? Voice not your scepticism in the presence of your elders. They were!

In midsummer of 1897 Weber and Fields learned that Augustin Daly was dangling a London offer before Joseph Herbert, who had written the book of "The Geezer," the success of the first season. Knowing Herbert would accept, they fired him before he could resign, a typically theatrical gesture involving no ill feeling. In Herbert's place, Kenneth Lee was hired. Lee was an Englishman who had had much success as a vaudeville sketch writer. He was engaged to write the book and lyrics, with the aid of Charley Ross, to rehearse and stage all chorus numbers, and was delegated complete authority.

Lee was an Englishman of a type then more frequently met with on these shores. He copied the dress and manners of the gay Albert Edward, then Prince of Wales, and was slightly patronizing to an America that aped the every posture of England and the English. Lee appeared at rehearsals in evening dress and a cloak of reserve, tucked a bordered linen handkerchief up one sleeve and wore a wrist watch, the second ever noticed on Broadway. Walter de Freece, manager and husband of Vesta Tilley, had brought the first over some months earlier. The new director combined the decorum of his race and class with that of the more formal stage to which he was accustomed. The insouciance and go-as-you-please rehearsal methods at the Music Hall were strange and scandalous to him from the first. He and Ross labored mightily and produced an enormous book of a conventional burletta, to be called "Mr. Coughupsky." The first rehearsal was set for eleven o'clock of an August morning. At that hour the company, with the notable exception of Peter Dailey, was assembled. Lee tapped his ever-present cane in annoyance and waited. At the end of fifteen minutes he announced that the truant was fined twenty-five dollars and dismissed the company until two o'clock. On his return to the theater Lee found Dailey sitting reversed on a chair in the center of the stage.

Before the director could speak Dailey asked, "Is it or is it not your custom, Mr. Lee, in calling a rehearsal, to appear at the hour set, or an hour later?"

The director's hauteur grew more chill.

"No nonsense, Mr. Dailey," he said. "Reserve it, if you please, for the performance. I have imposed a fine of twenty-five dollars upon you for tardiness. I must insist, Mr. Dailey, upon promptness and discipline."

Dailey pretended to be outraged.

"What?" he demanded. "You call a rehearsal for one o'clock. I, I alone, arrive on time. I wait an hour, and you fine me twenty-five dollars!"

"The hour at which rehearsal was called, as you well know, Mr. Dailey, was eleven o'clock. Let us hear no more about it, please."

"There's your call board, Kenneth." Peter pointed magnificently to the slate from which he had erased one of the 1's from 11 as he arrived.

After four days of floundering about in the mazes of his involved and stilted book, the author-director threw up his hands and quit. He was accustomed to rehearsing each line, point and gesture minutely; to building a show as a bricklayer lays a wall. In the Music Hall, then and always, you saw a jumbled heap of metaphorical bricks which, at the last moment, leaped into ordered precision. When Sylvia Thorne, for example, sang a song woodenly from notes held in her hand at rehearsal, Lee assumed that she simply knew no gestures. Rapping his cane irritably, and pointing into the flies, he would protest: "The stars are up there, Miss Thorne, up there!"

"Dear me, this is most difficult," he told his employers just before he quit. "Apparently I must instruct these people in their A B C's."

"Some fragments of Lee's book and all his lyrics were salvaged from the wreck. John—Honey—Stromberg, a promising unknown who had been wasting his sweetness upon the merry-merry, or burlesque of commerce, was signed on to do the music, the beginning of a mutually profitable relationship that was ended only by Stromberg's untimely death. He was a luckier find than they foresaw. A competent orchestra leader and a musician capable of conjuring the musical trimmings for a show out of some hat, his own or borrowed, was needed. For all they knew, Stromberg was nothing more. Nothing in his previous record foreshadowed that he was to write a dozen song smashes for the Music Hall shows.

It was John T. Kelly who suggested that his friend Julian Mitchell was the very man to stage the show. Mitchell was an able actor, of long legitimate experience in both light and heavy rôles, who had turned stage manager. He was without experience, however, in stage producing, and he was deaf in one ear and deafer in the other. Weber and Fields's memory of him was of a Shakespearean actor. This and his deafness made them sceptical, but they told Kelly to have his friend look in. Mitchell came, watched a rehearsal and held a hand cupped to his better ear. As the rehearsal progressed he moved nearer and nearer the stage, and cupped his hand the more tightly. The more he strained, the less he seemed to hear. Mitchell, too, was unused to the Music Hall's methods. He heard little because there was little to hear. The principals did little more than answer "Scene over" to their cues. The chorus numbers were unrehearsed as yet and merely were indicated by the call of "Number." An outsider could not know, nor, knowing, understand that Weber and Fields and Bernard, Dailey and Kelly, Ross and Fenton were working out their own contributions to the mélange separately and independently of each other, and all that would remain to the director would be to lit the various parts together. In any ordinary theatrical troupe such anarchy would have been ruinous. Mitchell was unfavorably impressed, but he needed work. He would take the job for fifty dollars a week, he said.

"How long would it take you?" Weber shouted, needlessly loud.

"I might do it in four weeks," was Mitchell's guess.

Joe and Lew had fixed the opening less than three weeks away, and shied at time work. They offered, instead, one hundred dollars for the job, half down and half when finished. Mitchell agreed. Later, he confessed that he believed the show would die in rehearsal, and the revised terms a good gamble.

Mitchell went to work on his chorus numbers. Up to the moment of dress rehearsal, the day before the opening, that was all that he saw of the show. He had a pie crust and no filling. But now Dailey, Kelly, Bernard, Fields, Weber, Ross and Fenton brought forth the filling. Mitchell was so impressed after the opening night by the smoothness with which the apparently unrelated parts dovetailed that he told Weber he would like to join the organization permanently. Joe and Lew, in turn, had been struck with Mitchell's ability, and made him director-producer on the spot. Mitchell brought with him his wife, Bessie Clayton, the greatest acrobatic toe dancer of her day, an artist who helped to blaze the way for that great development which was to make dramatic dancing an art in its own name.

Upon the separation of Weber and Fields in 1904, Klaw and Erlanger snatched up Mitchell's services. His deft hand was also prominent in the making of "The Wizard of Oz," "Babes in Toyland" and such memorable productions. When Florenz Ziegfeld, Jr., inaugurated the Follies, it was Mitchell he chose as director. They disagreed and parted; but with the Follies showing signs of tottering from its once undisputed eminence, it was Mitchell again to whom Ziegfeld turned in this year of 1924.

The Follies was the legitimate successor to Weber and Fields' Music Hall. Each, in its own time, dominated the theatrical sky line as the Woolworth Building does lower Manhattan's serried range. Both were new and revolutionary advances in the lighter American theater, both left their mark indelibly upon our stage. The same creative talent that helped so largely to make the Follies what it is, was seen in Mitchell's direction at the Music Hall.

He found the chorus as standardized a theatrical institution as the proscenium arch. To see one was to have seen them all; they varied only as one potato from another. Its supposed function was to kindle the male eye with youth, figure and face. It did so badly and unimaginatively. Mitchell's Music Hall choruses were the largest, shapeliest and prettiest in America, but he also raised his young women to an artistic dignity to which the chorus never had dreamed of aspiring. He cast the whole dogma of chorus technic in the ash bin and made his part of the show as distinctive as the principals'. In dancing, chorus effects, costumes and settings, he put the Music Hall years in advance of the run of its contemporaries.

Where are these chorus girls of yesteryear? One hundred and fifty-three, by careful count, married from the Music Hall ranks. Helen Dunbar is a dowager of the films, Fay Tincher a movie comedienne, Lillian Fitzgerald rose to a headline spot in vaudeville, Mona Desmond to musical-comedy rôles. Bonnie Maginn, the Sweet Caporal Girl, married a Pittsburgh millionaire. Frankie Bailey is in a Los Angeles candy shop. Virgie Foltz, whose mother was the first woman lawyer in San Francisco, is the wife of a Los Angeles business man. Mabel Barrison graduated to leading woman of musical comedy. Vera Morris owns and operates a racing stable in England. Aimee Angeles married Edward Burke, owner of the Havre de Grace race track; her sister Leah is the wife of a New York lawyer, a nephew of Tony Pastor. Hattie Forsythe is married and living at Palm Beach. Allie Gilbert married William Lorraine, the composer. Goldie Mohr is the widow of a millionaire. Elaine Porter is the mother of three children. Harry Morey, now a leading man of the films, was a Weber and Fields chorus man. He was Harold Morey then. Joseph Swickard, also of the movies, began as a chorus man at the hall; similarly, Ben Hatwood Burt, the song writer, and Douglas Stevenson, the legitimate actor. Max Scheck drew twenty dollars a week one season as a chorus man at the Hall and one hundred and fifty dollars a few seasons later as an assistant to Mitchell. The late Bert Green played the piano at rehearsals.

Mitchell was a gentle soul by nature, and his traditions were those of the legitimate stage. He was a revelation to the chorus, accustomed to directors with the manners of a regular-army sergeant drilling a batch of recruits. His most vicious gesture, reserved for moments of extreme exasperation, was to dash his hat upon the stage floor. It was not in Peter Dailey to resist such an opportunity. As if the gesture lacked a little of completeness, Dailey accidentally jumped upon the hat—a derby—with both feet. Mitchell examined the crushed shell ruefully and looked reproachfully at Dailey. The next day and thereafter he wore an old soft hat at rehearsals.

His defective hearing never hurt his directorial effectiveness and sometimes it stood him in stead. Some members of the company were complaining bitterly about a ruling of Mitchell's one day. The director cupped his hand to his better ear, but failed to hear. He turned to Dailey.

"What are they talking about, Peter? I can't hear."

Dailey put his mouth to Mitchell's ear and shouted, "You're in luck, Julie, you're in luck!"

The Music Hall's second season opened the night of September 2, 1897, with "The Glad Hand" and a vaudeville olio that included Cissie Loftus and McIntyre and Heath. The book gives no hint of the wherefore of the title, nor does anyone remember the explanation, if there was one; there rarely was for a Weber and Fields title. It contained a topical Klondike sketch, the Yukon gold rush then being at its height, and a burlesque called "Secret Servants," a take-off on William Gillette's famous drama "Secret Service," just home from a London engagement, the first time an American cast had given an American play in Europe.

Read to-day, the book of "The Glad Hand" has hardly a trace of cither wit or humor. The ephemerality of topical humor accounts in part for this. The best nifties of 1924 will be sad and wall-eyed in 1951. But the true explanation lies in the fact that such a cast could make the worst drivel entertaining. Herein is adumbrated one of the difficulties of recapturing for another generation the zest and gusto of a Music Hall night.

Joe and Lew knew what was wrong and how to remedy it. The Music Hall required an author and librettist worthy of cast, composer and director. Edgar Smith was writing the books and lyrics of the shows at the Casino, the Broadway home of musical comedy. Smith was a former actor who had turned librettist and adapter. His varied trouping experience had included a season on the kerosene circuit out of St. Louis with the Dixon Sketch Club, playing a dramatization of Mrs. Burnett's "Editha's Burglar," successor to her "Little Lord Fauntleroy." The dramatization was the work of a young St. Louisan, by name Augustus Thomas, who also had a part. Editha was played by a young girl, daughter of a St. Louis photographer, her name Della Fox. Both Thomas and Della Fox preceded Smith to Broadway and to fame. Weber and Fields stole Smith away from the Casino with an offer of more money. Thereafter he wrote all the Music Hall shows and most of the lyrics.

The funniest thing in "The Glad Hand" was not in the book. Eight Italian musicians had been hired for an extra bit, and Weber suggested using them in the finale to add to the effect of the ensemble. The play ended on a duel scene between Weber and Fields. Lew offered Joe his choice of two revolvers, keeping a tight clutch on the larger. Joe retreated to the opposite side of the stage, fired the pistol into the air, Fields fell mortally wounded, and the company ran on, singing:

"Oh, what's the matter, what's the matter!
What's the meaning of this row!"

The eight Italians had been rehearsed in their added contribution for four weeks and were letter-perfect at rehearsal. But on the opening night they broke up the scene by rushing on the stage and singing:

"Oh, who's the troub, who's the troub!
Wotta da mat witta dis man!"

Smith and Stromberg's first joint production was "Pousse Café," replacing "The Glad Hand" in December. "The Little Minister," in which Maude Adams was starring at the Garrick; "La Poupée" and Anna Held at the Lyric; and Belasco's "The First Born" at the Manhattan came in for burlesques; but the main thread of the farcical story was tied to one Herr Wielshaben and a remarkable mechanical doll of his invention. Weber was the innocent Wielshaben, Fields and Bernard two low-comedy rascals bent on swindling him of his invention. To this end they organized a "skindecat" to exploit the doll, and drew up a contract. A true Music Hall fan will chortle with joyous remembrance of this contract scene. The critics all said that it was riotously funny. A fragment is inserted here to permit the reader to judge for himself:

FIELDS: Here is the disagreement papers. Now before I read them, I want to tell you that we—Fields and Bernard—are the parties of the first part.

WEBER: We are.

FIELDS: Not you! You are the party of the second part. You are lower as we are.

WEBER: Chentlemen! Please! Can't we do business mitout speaking of mein family?

FIELDS: As you wish it. Now I won't read der commencing of der contract to you because dere are a few things I wish to write in after you sign your name to it. Here I read:

"It is hereby misunderstood and mucilage agreed upon by and between the parties as if it never was, to hold any such agreement as may or may not be, so see it fit and necessary to whom it may concern; if the circumstances make it otherwise, whereby we are compelled to overreach ourselves, and necessity comes to such that everything must be arranged, consequently we leave things stand as it never was, above stated."

At one point Wielshaben was counseled to remember his etiquette. "Who et a cat?" he demanded.

Photo 13. The Doll Scene. Left to right: Willie Collier, Sam Warfield, Fields, Weber.

There was a clause specifying that Weber on the one hand and Fields and Bernard on the other should share equally the cost of transporting the doll to America. Weber furnished the ship, Fields and Bernard supplied the ocean.

When the supposedly nearsighted Weber held the contract close to his face in reading it, Bernard exclaimed, "Are you trying to lick off the date?"

And more on this order. Not so good? Possibly, but did you ever hear Fields, Weber and Bernard do it? If you'd appreciate the distinction, try setting down on paper the comedy lines and business of Al Jolson, Ed Wynn, Eddie Cantor, Bert Wheeler, Beatrice Lillie, or whoever your favorite comedian may be, or, better still, give them to some small-time vaudevillist to repeat. Or, again, ponder why the joke that convulsed you last night at the theater fell so flat when you retold it at the office to-day.

In the middle of the run of "Pousse Café" the price of the first ten rows in the orchestra was advanced from one-fifty to two dollars in an effort to keep up with the advancing costs of the shows. Still the house, popularly presumed to be a branch of the mint, earned little money.

A minor change in the bill was made in January, "The Way High Man," a burlesque of "The Highwayman," succeeding "The Worst Born," and Weber, Fields, Dailey and Bernard turning from Chinamen to road agents.

This was the patent-medicine era of American culture. Save for the department stores, the nostrum manufacturers were the surest and largest advertisers the newspapers had. The cakewalk and the bloomer girl were the pulsing, throbbing topics of the moment. Then on the night of February 15, 1898, the Maine was blown up in Havana Harbor. The town band struck up "There'll Be a Hot Time in the Old Town To-night, Ma Baby." The American public, hearing of the Philippine Islands for the first time, began to search the map for them and to denounce the atlas as a swindle because they were not to be found in the West Indies. Mothers on the Atlantic Seaboard frightened their children into taking their spring sulphur and molasses on pain of being bombarded by the terrible Cervera and his fleet.

And on Saint Patrick's Day the Music Hall established a new high-water mark in American burlesque with "The Con Curers." The subject of this uproarious travesty, one of the four or five best to the Music Hall's credit, was Paul M. Potter's dramatization of a Franco-Prussian War story by Guy de Maupassant. Under the name of "The Conquerors" it had opened in January at the Empire, with Viola Allen, Blanche Walsh, May Robson and William Faversham in the cast. It was an unpleasant play, as they said in New York in that day—though mild enough by modern standards—largely concerned with a dastardly Prussian officer and his nefarious designs upon a defenseless French maiden. Transposed to jazz time, the story became so genuinely ludicrous that the original was blown out of town on a gale of mirth.

The first real custard pie thrown on any stage is the claim made for "The Con Curers." In the original the heavy had commanded the heroine to drink a glass of wine. Instead, she dashed it into his face. In the Twenty-ninth Street version, Charley Ross, the villain of the piece, ordered his wife, Mabel Fenton, the girl, to eat a custard pie of her own making, a fat, juicy, extra-thick custard. She threw it in his face. A minor character sampled the débris later and died in agony. And Charlie Chaplin then was a cockney lad of nine.

A mere catalogue of the props in "The Con Curers" is comic. In the opening scene a bust on a pedestal had a cigar in its mouth and a military cap cocked at a rakish angle on its head. A suit of armor made of stovepipe, pots and dish pans held a mop in its hands at present arms. There was a saddle on the piano, muddy boots on the mantel, and an umbrella jar was filled with swords and muskets. Major Wolffacen, an officer of the Uhlans, spoke with an Irish brogue, drank beer from a trick stein that filled as fast as he drank. The major, in writing a dispatch to General Schloppen-hauservonauserblatzen, would dip his pen in the beer, wipe it on his whiskers and dry his whiskers with a blotter. A large bird cage held a small pig. The pig was a prisoner of war because he had rooted for the enemy. Three drunken peasants were brought in as spies. They were proved spies because they had first been seen through a spyglass. All three had been fishing. An old boot dangled from one hook and line. A dead cat hung from another. Its owner described it as a catfish. Major Wolffacen pronounced it smelt.

At one point Weber had to carry the pig under his arm. For Weber's convenience, the property man bought the smallest porker he could find, but the pig throve so on a bottle diet and the high life of the theater that Weber no longer could hold it after two weeks. Another pig was substituted, outgrew Weber's arms like its predecessor and lost its sinecure to a third. Prima donnas were able sympathize with the pigs.

The first pig was the innocent victim of Frankie Bailey's wrath. Miss Bailey was not content to rest upon her laurels, shapely as they were.

"I can act, Mr. Mitchell," she protested to the director, "but I never get any chance here. You'd think I couldn't do anything but wear tights nicely from the way they treat me here. All my public is saying that I'm not getting a fair deal."

The kindly Mitchell gave her three lines, despite the fact that her voice was so thin that it never traveled beyond Row A. The lines were to be spoken in front of a drop while the stage crew struck the previous scene. In making the change it was necessary to remove the pig from the bird cage and hand it to Weber for the opening of the next scene. The pig resented the stage hand's handling, squealed shrilly and drowned Frankie's three lines utterly. Miss Bailey hotly declared that jealous rivals in the company had twisted the pig's tail in a conspiracy to ruin her scene, and pointed to the tail's curl as damning proof.

Peter Dailey's forked-lightning wit covered up a property man's blunder the opening night. Characteristically, Dailey not only saved the situation but trebled its laugh value. He was cast as Jean Badun, alias Bumface, an innkeeper. Mabel Fenton was a guest. As she entered, Dailey's lines called for him to say, "Ah, the poor unfortunate girl, I'll give her an unlucky number," and reach to the key rack for the key to Room No. 13. He had just come to "unfortunate girl" at the first performance, when he discovered that the numbers on the rack stopped at 12. He reached for Keys No. 6 and 7, and without a perceptible pause, added, "Six and seven are thirteen."

"The Con Curers," which Acton Davies said was a great deal cleverer than "The Conquerors," ran until June first, when the company and stage crew of seventy, and everyone else who wanted to come along, were loaded into a special train and taken to Chicago for a four weeks' stand at Hamlin's Grand Opera House. John A. Hamlin was another patent-medicine prince, who had erected the theater for his greater glory. The house was managed by a son, Harry L. Hamlin. The Chicago excursion was more of a skylark than an engagement. The weather was so hot that the management served free ice cream to orchestra-seat holders, and more than one matinée was canceled and the money refunded to permit the troupe to take in the races at Washington Park.

Sam Bernard was lost to Weber and Fields at the end of the season. A producer lured him away with an offer to star him in "The Marquis of Michigan." He went reluctantly, and with the best wishes of all hands. After the final performance in Chicago the company gave him a dinner. Pete Dailey, of course, was master of ceremonies.

It was customary, Peter said, to wait until a man died to say nice things about him. They intended to tell Sam now and to his face how they all loved him and would miss him. Their only consolation was that Sam was leaving them to better himself. Pete Dailey, being Pete Dailey, a cracker on the end of the speech was inevitable. Bernard was a generous soul, but a charter member of the Dutch Treat Club. Treating was a confounded nuisance, he argued. When a man wished one drink and no more, he should not be dragooned by a fool convention of barroom etiquette to buy a round for every Tom, Dick and Harry in the place, and stand around an hour while they repaid the courtesy. The saloon keepers must have started the practice. As for himself, he wrote the name of Sam Bernard where Thomas Jefferson signed the Declaration of Independence, and if this be churlish or niggardly, make the most of it.

"As a slight token of our regard," Dailey closed, and withdrew from his vest a miniature tombstone engraved with the pious sentiment: "This one is on me, boys." It was Peter's private joke.

Bernard's going left a yawning void in the Music Hall company. Who to fill it? A young man from California was playing low-comedy Jewish types at the Casino Roof.

"That lad's an actor," some volunteer scout reported, "and he's built to order for the Music Hall."

Lew and Joe went to see for themselves, and hired David Warfield before he had changed into his street clothes.

Born David Wohlfelt in 1866, this diminutive, blue-eyed Jewish boy was selling papers on the streets of San Francisco when his future manager, David Belasco, was stage manager of Baldwin's Opera House in the same city. He entered the theater by the front door as a program boy at the old Standard and graduated to usher at M. B. Leavitt's Bush Street Theater. C. P. Hall, manager of Leavitt's house, was notoriously cagey about passes. What few he did issue were for the gallery, and it was his habit personally to call up to the gallery door tender, "All right for two up there." Not long after young Wohlfelt's advent as an usher, Hall found his gallery chockablock with boys one night.

Photo 14. David Warfield, c. 1897. B. J. Falk, New York, Library of Congress.

"Givin' a newsboys' party?" the door man asked.

"I haven't passed anyone up to-night," Hall declared.

"Go 'way with you," the door man came back. "You been yellin' up them steps all evenin'."

The following night Hall hid on a turn of the gallery stairs. "All right up there for two," floated past him in the very accents of his own voice.

It was the voice of Esau but the hand of Jacob. The new usher, it seems, was a born mimic, and every time the boss had turned his back he had franked a couple of his newsboy confrères into the show. Wohlfelt lost his job that night.

"If you can imitate so well, why don't you go on the stage?" his friends queried.

He answered by adopting the stage name of Warfield and making his bow at the Wigwam, admission two bits for two, no reduction for one, and two beer checks thrown in. According to Sol Bloom, a contemporary San Franciscan, now a member of Congress from New York City, who was present, Warfield did a personation of William Shakespeare. This is a bit of strain upon an already weakened imagination; but Congressman Bloom holds to the statement, and adds that it was worse than anything he ever heard even in the House of Representatives. The record, however, gives the personation as one of Salvini in Othello, and another of Bernhardt in the deathbed scene from "Camille," and further reports both bits as immediate local hits. Mr. Warfield himself is silent. It won him, at least, an engagement as Melter Moss, the rascally Jew in "The Ticket of Leave Man," with a California round troupe. The following year, 1890, saw him arrive in New York with three dollars in his pocket. He was saved from hunger by stumbling in his first week on an engagement at Paine's Concert Hall in Eighth Avenue, where a Broadway manager chanced to see him and offered a part in "The City Directory" with John H. Russell.

Greatness in the theater commonly demands two prerequisites. The actor must have the talent or genius to support greatness, and someone must perceive and exploit his possibilities. It remained for Weber and Fields to give Warfield his big chance, and it was not until he had proved himself on their stage that Belasco turned his glance toward the boy he once had heard singing on a San Francisco street corner, and made of him a star. Even in the tomfooleries of the Music Hall, Warfield foreshadowed that command of pathos to which the shrewd Belasco later gave full play. No other actor of modern times has so plucked at the heartstrings of American playgoers. A tear, a tear and a laugh is the formula that made "The Auctioneer," "The Music Master," "The Grand Army Man" and "The Return of Peter Grimm" personal triumphs for their star. Many an actor can alternate a tear and a laugh. Only a Warfield can summon the second tear.

Add the name of Fay Templeton, another recruit of the golden season of 1898–99, to that of Warfield. The radiant personality of Lillian Russell has somewhat eclipsed the Music Hall memory of Miss Templeton, as it has that of other talented women of the company, yet Fay Templeton was incomparably the greater actress. Miss Russell had beauty and magnetic charm in a degree probably never equaled on our musical stage, yet she never was anything but Lillian Russell, and it might be added, it would have been a captious critic who would have desired her to be. Fay Templeton's, however, was the finest feminine talent ever given to American burlesque.

Born on tour with her father, John Templeton's, opera company, cradled in dressing rooms, carried on repeatedly as an infant in arms, given a speaking part at three, she had become a light-opera prima donna of national reputation by fifteen. When only twenty-two, and supreme in her field, she had married Howell Osborn, a wealthy New Yorker known as the King of the Dudes, and quit the stage. Upon Osborn's death in 1895 she returned to the footlights in "Excelsior, Jr.," with mixed results. Her first youth had passed and her figure had matured, but her mimic powers had grown and mellowed. In the Music Hall she won a new public and fame that returned her to stardom at the head of her own company. George M. Cohan's "Forty-five Minutes from Broadway" was her last triumph. In 1906 she married a wealthy Pittsburgher and practically retired, an example later followed by Miss Russell.

Miss Templeton was in Europe when Weber and Fields decided in the summer of 1898 that the company needed another woman star to share the burden Mabel Fenton was carrying unaided. They cabled her an offer of four hundred dollars a week, which she accepted.

The Angeles sisters, Aimee and Leah, were two other newcomers in September, 1898. They were the daughters of Alex Zanfretta, the same Zanfretta who had lent Joe his skull pad at the Theater Comique in Providence back in 1881. They were useful and ornamental additions to the company, but had they been neither, Joe and Lew would have been disposed to make a place for the sisters. As boys in the gallery of the London Theater on the Bowery they had watched Aimee and Leah, then two tiny girls, perched on the great shoulders of Zanfretta, their mother balanced on his head, as he carried all three across a swaying tight rope high above the stage.

Zanfretta was a mighty drinker. Once a friend reproached him for venturing on the tight rope while unsteady with liquor.

"You are carrying all that you hold dear in the world on your shoulders. What if you should fall with them?" the friend counseled.

"It ain't as dangerous as it looks," Alex defended himself. "You see, I always see three ropes, and I just pick out the middle one."

The war was over and Theodore Roosevelt, back from San Juan Hill, was about to be elected governor of New York when the third season began, September 8, 1898, with "Hurly Burly." In his first minute on the stage Warfield coined a phrase that has been adopted into the vernacular. Fields, as Bierheister, and Weber, as Weinschoppen, admired Warfield's suit.

"Dot cost me $6.40 mitout de lining," Warfield exulted. "You see dot lining? Near-silk, it is."

Photo 15. Fay Templeton, c. 1895. B. J. Falk, New York, Library of Congress.

"Why are you so dressed up?" they asked him. It was a holiday, he explained. "What holiday is to-day?" they scoffed.

"The anniversary of the great Chicago fire,"was his reply.

A right shoe on the left foot and a left shoe on the right foot, a happy bit of comedy business sometimes credited to Chaplin, was originated by Warfield, and used for the first time in "Hurly Burly."

Miss Templeton sang "Keep Away from Emmeline," and Peter Dailey, "Dinah," the first two of Smith and Stromberg's many song hits. Weber and Fields anticipated the modern street-traffic signal system in a scene supposed to take place in Paris, and coincidently coined a gag line that died of exhaustion while serving with the A. E. F. in France. As its legal next of kin, Joe Weber claims his share of the bonus.

"So this is Paris!" Weber exclaimed.

"There is no other place around the place, so this must be the place," Fields rejoined.

A restaurant for which they were searching had been described to them as having a red light in front.

Weber saw a red light. As Fields turned to look it flashed white, and he disputed his partner. Weber looked again, the light flashed red and he offered to bet. Fields reassured himself with a glance and raised the bet. The argument grew hotter, the stakes higher and the light continued to alternate. At the climax, when they looked at the same instant, the light was green.

"We both lose; it's a station house," Weber exclaimed.

The hypnotism scene followed, the first time on Broadway of an act they were famous for in variety. Fields declared himself to be a tipnotister. Weber was sceptical. An absurd dialect argument culminated in Fields demonstrating on Weber. With a few passes he had his subject in a trance, and confirmed this state with pinches and slaps.

"You vill soon be imagination dot you are trafeling on der cars," Fields would declare. "You vill be riding fast, so hold onto der straps. Weinschoppen, you are off! You vas in Chicago. Now you're in Zinzinatty! Pittsburgh! Baltimore!" At each new city Weber, his eyes closed, would move a step to the right, then to the left. "Philadelphia! Paterson! Brooklyn!" But at Brooklyn Weber was stationary. "Hey, you're in Brooklyn now; come out of Paterson!" Fields would shout. Weber was immovable and Fields frantic. "Weinschoppen! Weinschoppen! Come out of Paterson!" he would plead, wiggling his outstretched fingers frenziedly, "My God! I can't get him out of Paterson! He must have a girl in Paterson!"

In a Shubert unit show two years ago they revived the hypnotism act, but substituted Newark for Paterson. A Paterson paper, hearing of the change, made editorial protest. The hypnotism scene was as integral a part of Paterson's fair heritage as the silk mills or the Falls of the Passaic, the editor protested, and any infringements would be prosecuted summarily.

Fields, Weber, Bernard and Arthur Dunn were standing in front of the Music Hall one evening in September when two young women stopped. One of them asked, "Who is the manager?" They were good-looking.

"I am," all four responded.

The inquirer said her name was Ethel Levey, that she was from San Francisco, where she had had some stage experience, and that she wished work.

"Can you sing?" she was asked.

She could. All six adjourned to the theater, Arthur Dunn sat down at the piano, and Miss Levey proved it. Weber offered her five dollars to appear at the next Sunday-night concert. She accepted and made such an emphatic success that her theatrical career may be said to have dated from that night. On December fourth she again was on the Sunday-concert program. The Four Cohans were on the same bill. It was the first meeting of George M. Cohan and Miss Levey, who was to become Mrs. George M. Cohan the following summer.

Julian Eltinge was another to make his New York debut at a Sunday concert at the Music Hall. The Sunday concert in New York is a peculiar outgrowth of the law prohibiting theatricals on the Sabbath. Long ago some slippery manager discovered that he could evade the law's intent by calling his Sunday vaudevilles sacred concerts, having the performers appear in street clothes, and adding some such number as "My Rosary" for verisimilitude. Once the evasion was well established, the blasphemous "sacred" and "The Rosary" were dropped, and the Sabbath desert became dotted with vaudeville oases. It was a part of a Weber and Fields contract that every member of the stock company must do a specialty once every four weeks at the Sunday show. Some of the stars were without variety experience and had no specialties in their repertoires. Their objections led shortly to the abandonment of the Sunday-night performances. The vaudeville olio with which the Music Hall shows were opened the first few years were dropped for a different reason, the public showing its indifference by arriving about nine o'clock, when the olio was ending. When this became apparent the main performance was extended to a full evening's length, and the Weber and Fields house lost its last resemblance to the Music Hall of previous New York tradition. By 1900 the Weber and Fields show had become and remained a first half of musical nonsense and a second part of burlesque.

Lee Harrison, of whom more anon, came into the cast in early October. The first burlesques of the season were added in November. Richard Mansfield in "Cyrano de Bergerac" and Viola Allen in "The Christian" were the butts. At Twenty-ninth Street the titles became "Cyranose de Bric-a-Brac" and "The Heathen." Neither was especially funny and both were displaced in January by "Catherine." If "The Con Curers," the previous spring, had established the Music Hall as a New York institution, "Catherine" clinched the title. Echoes of the roof-raising hysterics at Twenty-ninth Street carried even to the ivory towers of the highbrows, who began to "discover" Weber and Fields. Parenthetically, our more serious thinkers in New York continue from time to time to "discover" vaudeville and burlesque turns that have been convulsing audiences from Harlem to Bellingham, and return via Tampa, for a dozen seasons. *Harper's Weekly*, then the dominant national weekly, reviewed "Catherine" at length. *The London Era* ran a column report of the burlesque.

As for the New York dailies, where Weber and Fields's had been lumped with the other music halls, vaudeville and the merry-merry in a perfunctory summary in one corner of the Sunday dramatic pages, the house now moved up to the tops of the pages on even terms with the classic Empire, Daly's and Wallack's. The same critics who pronounced upon the Jovian Mr. Mansfield were godfathers at the Weber and Fields christenings, and gave the Music Hall, if anything, a trifle more space. Alan Dale complained that he no longer could enjoy a new play for wondering how it would burlesque at Weber and Fields'.

Like "The Conquerors," "Catherine" was of French origin and Continental morality. The original was the Comédie Française drama played by Annie Russell at the Garrick earlier in the season to the scandalization of a not yet so sophisticated New York. There may be a secret of successful burlesque in the fact that the funniest of the Weber and Fields travesties were take-offs of plays of dubious morality. The formula was simple; substitute flawless virtue for timid apologetic vice; turn the original wrong side out, stand it on its head, and leave the rest in the competent hands of the Weberfields, as the company had come to be known. Other plays of the Parisian school, such as "Zaza," "Sapho," and "Du Barry" fell victims to the method.

Warfield, as the father who found any effort beyond playing an electrical piano too exhausting, escaped for the first time from his stock characterization of a Jewish-peddler and Fields, too, dropped their dialect, stepped out of their standard roles and make-ups and were even funnier as "Catherine's" younger brothers, Weber in curls and a Little Lord Fauntleroy suit. Fay Templeton, as an irreproachable Catherine, determined to make the world sweeter and more wholesome for her presence, was a delicious parody of Annie Russell's more-sinned-against-than-sinning heroine.

Miss Russell and her company were guests at the opening night. They asserted that they never again were able to give a completely serious performance of the original for recollection of the counterfeit. By now few plays on Broadway could pretend to success until they had been travestied at the Music Hall. Special matinées were played for the Weberfields to induce burlesques, but managers objected to their players attending the result for the reason cited by Miss Russell. Richard Mansfield made an exception to his rigid rule of permitting no one to watch a rehearsal of a play of his, and let the Weberfields in to watch a dress rehearsal of "Cyrano." Mansfield rarely ever attended the theater as a spectator, but he was a regular at Tuesday matinées at the Weber and Fields house, shedding his austerity, mainly assumed, and visiting backstage. George Edwardes, a famous London musical-comedy producer, made a special trip to America to see a Music Hall performance, and offered the company a London engagement, which was refused.

Photo 16. Richard Mansfield, c. 1897. James M. Hart & Co., Library of Congress.

The final bill of the season was "Helter Skelter," opening April sixth. "Catherine" was retained, and to it were added burlesques of "Lord and Lady Algy," in which Faversham was playing at the Empire; Mrs. Leslie Carter's "Zaza" at the Garrick; "The Great Ruby" with Ada Rehan next door at Daly's, and E. H. Sothern's "The King's Musketeer" at the Knickerbocker. Miss Templeton had a new song, "What? Marry dat Gal?" Dailey added "Loves My Lou to Dina." John T. Kelly sang "Maud."

As ever with a Weber and Fields first night, the performance ran until long after midnight, and half an hour more of flower presentations and curtain acknowledgments followed. Joe and Lew always were missing from these felicitations. With the same modesty with which they regularly gave others of the company better parts than their own, they effaced themselves completely from the flower-and-speech love feasts.

On stage, a Weber and Fields show always was at its worst on a first night. It was a prevalent custom then, since become almost invariable, not to bring a show to Broadway until it had been smoothed and polished in try-out performances at Wilmington, Atlantic City, Bridgeport, or some such "dog" town. The Music Hall fiestas always opened cold, and showed it. Having a peculiar public, Weber and Fields could not be guided by the verdict of Atlantic City or New Haven. Only Broadway could say what Broadway wanted. Julian Mitchell, Weber and Fields would wait for the opening night returns, tabulate the laughs, then prune the waste material accordingly. A week later the show would be fit and down to weight.

Who cared how long or uneven the performance might be? On opening nights the company played second fiddle to the audience. The spectacle was in front of the footlights. One went to a Music Hall first night to mingle, to see and be seen, and returned a week or two later to watch the show. To be there the first night was to rub elbows with celebrity, step on the feet and trains of the elect, to have one's own corns honored by being trod upon by peers of the white-light realm, and to inhale an atmosphere heavy with cigar smoke, patchouli and musk, serene in the conviction that one had not lived in vain. On the first night of "Helter Skelter" a reporter noted, among others in the house, Boss Richard Croker of Tammany Hall, Mayor Van Wyck, Chief of Police Bill Devery, Sheriffs Dunn of Manhattan and Buttling of Brooklyn, Stanford White, Augustin Daly, Tony Pastor, and the exquisite Clyde Fitch.

Both Miss Rehan and Mrs. Carter were actresses of marked mannerisms, and Fay Templeton and Mabel Fenton, respectively, took them off delightfully in burlesques of the sleep-walking scene from the Drury Lane melodrama and the big act from "Zaza."

In the original, Zaza calls at her lover's home to demand that his wife give him up, falls in with his little daughter and is dissuaded from her hellish purpose by the child's artless prattle. In the burlesque, the daughter became a large French poodle, with Richard Garnella as the insides. The conversation between Miss Templeton and the poodle was hilarious. Peter Dailey, Zaza's steady company, reproached her for having invaded his home.

"I could have forgiven you for speaking to my wife"—he beat his chest—"but my poor, innocent little dog—never!"

The presumably free-and-easy Music Hall public was strangely censorious of both lines and situations. In Mrs. Carter's scene with the daughter, the child asked her, "Were you ever a little girl?" At the music hall the poodle plaintively inquired of Miss Templeton if she ever had been a little dog. "No, I've been a cat all my life," was her answer. The propriety of this speech was questioned so strongly that it was cut. Objections were made, too, to Zaza's innocuous line: "You have no right to bring your wife into the same restaurant with me and make me look like thirty cents," but it was retained over protests.

The salary list by now had climbed to the then staggering figure of six thousand dollars a week, exclusive of Weber and Fields's, in a pint-sized theater seating only six hundred and sixty-five persons. Even after marking the balance of the first floor up to two dollars, the proprietors were never drawing more than two hundred dollars each a week, against a certain salary of one thousand dollars a week they could command as an independent attraction. But they had set Broadway afire. The acclaim was sweet on their tongues and they thirsted for more.

Then in the midst of their summer vacation they lost their only woman principals, both nearly irreplaceable. Fay Templeton, restored to first magnitude by her season at the hall, resigned to star; and hard on her heels departed Mabel Fenton, who quit to give all her time to the Ross-Fenton farm on the Jersey shore.

A canvass of the available comediennes was discouraging. The list was not long, and included not one actress of the proved versatility necessary to fill the vacant shoes of either Templeton or Fenton. The Music Hall was no place for a specialist; a principal had to be prepared to play any position on the team, and play it well. In this dilemma Fields was so daring as to give a thought to Lillian Russell. Miss Russell was the most beautiful woman on the American stage, its highest-priced woman star, never had appeared in burlesque, and very likely would not consider doing so, even if Weber and Fields could meet her terms.

"Well, why not Lillian Russell?" Weber replied to the faint-hearted suggestion, and surprised at his own words.

"Could we afford to pay her price?" Fields doubted.

"No; but we will, if she has one," was Joe's decision.

"Who's going to ask her?" Lew asked breathlessly.

"Why not you?" Joe suggested. "She's at Sheepshead Bay every afternoon at the races, and you're always there."

"Is that a nice way to ask me?" Fields grumbled.

Fields met Jesse Lewisohn in the paddock at Sheepshead Bay the next day. Miss Russell was sitting in Lewisohn's box that afternoon. The copper man had a straight-from-the-feed-box tip on the second race and shared it with Fields. Lew was more concerned with nerving himself up to approach Miss Russell than with the races, and listened abstractedly. After the race they met again in the paddock.

"Sorry about that bad one I steered you on," Lewisohn apologized.

"Give me some more of your bad ones," Fields said. "That one paid fifteen to one."

"What one?"

"Smilax," said Fields.

"I didn't say *Smilax*," Lewisohn exclaimed. "I told you to get down on *Ajax*, and that galloping glue pot isn't home yet."

Fields slapped his knee.

"I knew it was something with an 'ax' in it." Smilax had won, and so had the absent-minded Lew.

Here was his opportunity.

"Web and I have been thinking we would like to have Miss Russell in the company," he led. "Do you suppose she would consider it?"

"Why not ask her?" Lewisohn countered. "She's in my box."

"Would you introduce me?"

"I would," said Lewisohn, and led the way.

Miss Russell was pondering over the entries for the fourth race. Her method of picking a winner was to collect the inside information of everyone from stable boy to stable owner, discard it all, shut her eyes, jab a hatpin through her program, and bet on the horse whose name the hatpin chanced to pierce. As good a system as any, it might be remarked in passing. She was using the hatpin when Lewisohn and Fields entered the box. She explained the method to Lew, after introductions.

"Why not use a fork and pick them one-two-three?" Fields suggested. Miss Russell laughed so appreciatively at his nifty that he popped the question then and there.

"Oh, but you boys couldn't possibly pay my price!" Airy-Fairy Lillian laughed.

"What is your price, Miss Russell?" Lew asked, and held his breath. He lost it a moment later.

"I'm dreadfully flattered, really," she answered; "but my terms are twelve hundred and fifty dollars a week, a guaranty of thirty-five weeks for the season, and all gowns and costumes to be paid for by the producer. You see, it's quite impossible in your tiny theater."

Fields blinked.

"That's quite satisfactory," he gulped. "Just write your own contract. We'll be expecting you in August." It was Miss Russell who blinked then. She never had broken her word. She had played tag and she realized she was it.

Chapter VII

The Fourth, Fifth, and Sixth Seasons

And "Whirl-i-Gig" and "Hoity Toity," 1899–1901

Give place, you ladies, and begone!
Boast not yourselves at all!
For here at hand approacheth one
Where face will stain you all.

I think Nature hath lost the mold
Where she her shape did take,
Or else I doubt if Nature could
So fair a creature make.

Truly she did so far exceed
Our women nowadays
As doth the gillyflower a weed;
And more a thousand ways.

—John Heywood

LILLIAN RUSSELL! Airy-Fairy Lillian. A lovely lady! Salute her memory! By the calendar that tapes the years of common mortals, she was thirty-eight when she came to the Weber and Fields Music Hall; but what had calendars to do with her? This was no mortal woman, or so it seems to us. She was the Queen to all the company within the first month, and in death she remains the Queen. First at rehearsals, last to leave, asking no privilege or indulgence; as unassuming as a new chorus girl; the most beautiful and the highest salaried woman on the stage, and as gracious and merry as beautiful.

She was born Helen Louise Leonard in Clinton, Iowa, in the first year of the Civil War, her father a country editor, her mother an early crusader for women's rights. She studied as a young girl in Chicago and New York for the grand-opera stage, and by the advice of her teacher and for the sake of experience, she made her debut in the chorus of Edward E. Rice's "Pinafore" company. The musical director, Harry Braham, instantly fell in love with her, married her after an ardent two months' courtship and swept her back into private life. The marriage was not a happy one, and Miss Russell returned to

Photo 17. Lillian Russell, c. 1920. Bain News Service, George Grantham Bain Collection, Library of Congress.

the stage at nineteen to sing "The Kerry Dance," "Twickenham Ferry" and like ballads for Tony Pastor at fifty dollars a week. It was Pastor who christened her Lillian Russell. By the charm of her voice, her radiant beauty, graceful presence and considerable ability as an actress, she conquered first light opera, then musical comedy; America, then England. The years never rested more lightly upon a woman's head. At thirty-eight she was unique, unrivaled, the Queen of Song.

The seats for the opening performance of the fourth season were sold at auction, such was the demand. Sam Bernard, Peter Dailey and Lee Harrison knocked the seats down from the stage a week before the opening, and all Broadway was there. Jesse Lewisohn bid $1,000 for two boxes in what was called the Horseshoe Circle. Stanford White, the Fish family, Mrs. Herman Oelrichs, Louis Sherry, J. B. Martin, Richard Croker, William Randolph Hearst, Abe Hummell, James R. Keene and Senator William H. Reynolds paid from $750 downwards for other boxes, and orchestra seats were bid in at as much as $100. Thereafter first-night seats at the hall always were auctioned off. The total receipts for an opening show ran as high as $10,500, a figure never approached in any other theater of twice the seating capacity, benefits possibly excepted. Weber and Fields had tried for three years to keep all seats out of the hands of ticket speculators. Failing, they appointed an official speculator of their own, Louis Cohen. Working on a salary for the house, Cohen disposed of a block of choice seats for each performance, in the lobby and on the sidewalk, at supply-and-demand prices. But for this additional revenue Joe and Lew would have been pressed to meet Miss Russell's $1,250 salary in so small a theater.

The crush at the doors was so great the first night that many of the audience were ushered in through the stage door on Twenty-ninth Street. If there were fire rules for New York theaters in 1899, their fiat did not run these nights, and New Yorkers got a foretaste of rush hour in the Subway. The house was newly decorated, Turkey red and gold replaced by pink and buff. Alan Dale likened the interior to a salmon mayonnaise. As always, the curtain was not lowered finally until past midnight. Then the flower show, the ovations and the speeches.

"Never in the palmy days of the stock companies of Wallack, Daly and Palmer, nor yet in the present one of the Frohmans," the *Herald* critic wrote, "were members greeted more enthusiastically in new plays. Each, down to the chorus, had his and her own ovation."

The play was "Whirl-i-Gig," the second part a burlesque of the first of bedroom farces to come from Paris, "The Girl from Maxim's." None but Weber and Fields would have had the effrontery to attempt to burlesque a farce. At the Criterion the heroine was a questionable person let loose in prudishly conventional society. The topsy-turvy methods of the Music Hall made of her a prim innocent plumped down in the superheated atmosphere of Newport. The virtuous spiritualistic wife of the original became a virago addicted to spirits in liquid form. The rise of the curtain disclosed Lillian Russell in bed in what

Photo 18. Bessie Clayton in *The Merry Widow*. Private collection.

appeared to be a night dress, with a plug hat on her head. When she emerged from the covers, it was discovered that she was wearing a low-cut evening gown. O tempora, O mores, O Avery Hopwood! Letters began to arrive from patrons complaining that the scene was suggestive. It was changed.

The production was two shades more gorgeous than anything Broadway had seen until then. Pete Dailey sang Stromberg and Smith's newest hit, "Say You Love Me, Sue." Only Charley Ross, among the males, was permitted to look handsome. Come what might, the matinée girls could depend on Ross to be handsome. Powdered temples and a little grease paint, and Ross was ready for any role.

In the first half of "Whirl-i-Gig," Warfield was Sigmund Cohenski, a millionaire Jew vacationing in Paris. His daughter, Uneeda, was in love with Charley Ross, the dashing Captain Kingsbridge, U. S. N.

"The captain is my ideal of a hero," Uneeda told her father.

"A hero! Is dot a business? A tailor is a business, a shoemaker is a business, but a hero? Better you should marry a bookkeeper!" Warfield exclaimed.

"A bookkeeper? I suppose you think the pen is mightier than the sword," the girl sneered.

"You bet you my life," said Papa Cohenski. "Could you sign checks with a sword?"

The scene in which Cohenski bought wine and dinner for Lillian Russell followed. The lines, with one exception, were nothing; but Warfield made the scene convulsingly funny. The one exception was:

FIFI: You might bring me a demi-tasse.

COHENSKI: Bring me the same, and a cup of coffee

This and every other joke quoted in the last six paragraphs still are in active service. You run an even chance of hearing them the next time you enter the theater.

For the first time in her career, Miss Russell sang a coon song, "When Chloe Sings Her Song."

Incomparable drawing card that she was, Miss Russell could not stop the gap made by Fay Templeton and Mabel Fenton's absence from the burlesques. Again Weber and Fields lured Miss Fenton back from the Jersey shore in December to take the title in "Barbara Fidgety," a burlesque of Clyde Fitch's drama, based upon the Whittier poem, in which Julia Marlowe was starring at the Criterion. Miss Russell thereafter gave all her time to the first part of the bills.

Charley Ross was running for mayor of Frederick on the platform of "To the victims belongs what is spoiled." Weber and Fields were stray privates from the Union Army. Weber had been promised the job of tax collector by Ross.

"I have to go along the street and whenever I see a tack, I should collect it so the bicycles wouldn't get punctuated," he explained to Fields.

The excavator of the buried ruins of the Weber and Fields Music Hall turns up an old friend at every stroke of the pick. Another such a one was the scene in "Barbara Fidgety" in which Lew had a nickel and a thirst and Joe only the latter.

"Listen!" Fields drilled his partner. "It wouldn't do for us to look poor with these unicorns on, so we will walk in and when I ask you what you will have, you must say, kind of careless, like this"—stretching—"'I don't care for it.' Then I will have a beer, and they will not get onto us that we are impecurious."

The two parted the swinging doors, and Dailey and Ross took the stage. As the latter finished a scene, high words came from the barroom, and Joe and Lew emerged, gesticulating furiously.

"You are a false friend to me," Fields accused.

"What did I do?" Weber demanded.

"When I asked you what you would have, what did you say?"

"I said what you told me. I said"—stretching—"'I don't care if I do.'"

Over at Wallack's, across the street from the Music Hall, Olga Nethersole was engaged in the spring of 1900 in the diverting and dual task of playing "Sapho" and keeping out of jail. Magistrate Mott, Police Inspector Thompson and a horrified public opposed the former and endeavored to expedite the latter. Miss Nethersole spoke at length and often of her great moral purpose, the press agent rubbed his hands—and the horrified public stormed the box office.

Having seen the original, by now considerably disinfected, the public waited for the burlesque that was certain to follow across Broadway. Miss Nethersole was an actress of many mannerisms and a ripe subject for burlesque. To make certain of doing the job adequately, Joe and Lew borrowed May Robson from Charles Frohman for the title rôle. Few incidents better illustrate the prestige of Weber and Fields than that Mr. Frohman should have lent so distinguished an actress for a burlesque and that she should have gone willingly.

There was no Wednesday matinee at Wallack's, so the Music Hall canceled a Saturday afternoon performance and sacrificed a certain $1,200 house to permit the company to watch Miss Nethersole's performance on that afternoon. Although the play and star were sure to fare roughly at the impious hands of the Weberfields, the manager of Wallack's, who knew free publicity when he saw it, reserved the four lower boxes for his visitors.

Peter Dailey was living at the time in the Norfolk Apartments, Broadway and Thirtieth Street, less than a block from either theater. At curtain time everyone was on hand save Dailey, who was to have the leading male role in the burlesque. Joe and Lew hurried to the Norfolk. Snores proceeded from Peter's room, outside of which Mrs. Dailey stood guard. Nothing less than a fire would cause her to wake him, she declared. Peter must have his sleep.

"Either you get him up and over to Wallack's in fifteen minutes, or he can sleep forever as far as we are concerned," Weber declared hotly.

Dailey stumbled into the box inside of the fifteen-minute limit, resumed his interrupted sleep and did not hear three lines of the show. But on the opening night of the burlesque he was letter-perfect, and contributed more original business to the travesty than any two other players. Miss Robson, in contrast, was frantic and despairing, and pleaded for her release at every rehearsal. To an actress of her training, the Music Hall at rehearsal was a madhouse.

"I always had a cue to work on; I don't know where to start my lines," she complained. "I'm sure I shan't know what I am doing the first night, nor any night. I never know what the others are going to do or say next, particularly Mr. Dailey."

But she was persuaded to stay, did her part perfectly, and came to enjoy it as much as any of her temporary associates.

The Music Hall merely reserved the character of the Daudet heroine, and rechristened her Sapolio in token of her having consecrated her life to the task of making Paris a spotless town morally. Dailey was Jean Gaussin, the unwilling victim of Sapolio's high moral purpose. Warfield had the role of Uncle Cæsaire, who ate moth balls to conceal his alcoholic breath from his wife. Fields was a comedy servant girl who, ordered to serve the capon en casserole, cooked it in castor oil. Joseph, Fanny Le Grand's perfect little gentleman of a child, became, in Weber's hands, a kicking, brawling, tobacco-chewing brat. Harry Morey, now a Hollywood hero, had the small part of a concierge with an Irish brogue.

"If you only will let me stay, I'll black your boots," Fanny, or Sapho, had pleaded with Jean in the original. Peter Dailey dragged out a shoe-shining stand and the curtain fell on the travesty as May Robson opened a boot-black's kit and began on Dailey's shoes.

The Music Hall closed on May fifth and the company took to the road by special train. The season was late, but Philadelphia, Baltimore, Washington, Cincinnati, Indianapolis, Chicago, Toledo, Buffalo, Syracuse and Boston were waiting. The Weberfields' fame was becoming national. In these ten cities "Whirl-i-Gig" piled up profits greater than those of the entire season at home. In the Music Hall the margin between the overhead of the show and the revenue of a capacity house was slender. Outside of New York, the company played in theaters of two and three times the capacity of the little house at Twenty-ninth Street. Joe and Lew perceived where the big money lay and decided to give more time thenceforth to the road and to shorten the Broadway season accordingly.

Stardom claimed Peter Dailey that summer. He signed a contract to head a musical comedy company of his own, and Joe and Lew scurried about the Rialto seeking a successor. They found a happy one in De Wolf Hopper. As these lines are written Mr. Hopper is heading a musical stock company in Washington and tempering the heat of a capital summer to a panting populace. Yet he was sixty-six last March. Lean, perhaps, but no slippered pantaloon, he.

Weber, Fields, Warfield, Dailey, Kelly and Ross came up from obscurity. Will Hopper, as his name really is and as his friends know him, was born in New York City, but of the socially elect. His father tried to make a lawyer of him, but an amateur performance left the son fatally footlight-blinded. With the $50,000 that came to him on his father's death, De Wolf organized his own company and made his professional debut in "Our Boys," a comedy that had made a smashing success in London. It made a smashing failure on this side. With what remained of his inheritance he financed and managed a tour of the South and the West of a company playing "One Hundred Wives," a record that

Photo 19. Cast members during the season of 1899: Fields, Fritz Williams, De Wolf Hopper, John T. Kelly, Lee Harrison, Sam Bernard, Weber.

Mr. Hopper so far has not quite equaled. The company stranded, Hopper lost his all and returned to the ranks with Edward Harrigan. Studying music with the intent of taking up grand opera, he fell into a small part with the McCaull Opera Company. In Philadelphia the chief comedian was taken ill. Hopper was shoved into the role of Pomeret in "Desiret" and walked off with the show. By 1891 he was a star. That was the first season of "Wang," with Della Fox. He was just back from a flattering engagement in London in Sousa's "El Capitan" when the Weberfields snared him.

Mabel Fenton was gone again, but Fay Templeton was back in the fold after a year's absence. Russell! Templeton! Bessie Clayton! Fields! Weber! Warfield! Hopper! Kelly! Ross! A chorus of forty-two! Their number, not their age. Julian Mitchell directing! Edgar Smith and Honey Stromberg doing the words and music! The like will not be seen again.

If Elsie Janis, Fannie Brice, Will Rogers, Ed Wynn, W. C. Fields, Walter Catlett and Joe Cook, just for example, could be induced to share the honors of one stage, which they jolly well couldn't, what would the harvest be? A "Follies" chorus and the rest is assumed. At a $6.60 top and the Hippodrome to do it in, the demented producer might survive a week. Times have changed. Weber and Fields did it with 700 seats. But their weekly overhead in 1900, with nominal wages for themselves, was less than $6,000, theater rental, stage crew, house staff and an orchestra of twenty included.

This was the company that opened in "Fiddle-dee-dee" on September 6, 1900. Hopper was as nervous as a bridegroom at the altar, and all the congenital idiots in the audience yelled "Speech" at his first entry. The Music Hall was

Photo 20. De Wolf Hopper and Viola Gillette in *The Beggar Student*, c. 1910. Bain News Service, George Grantham Bain Collection, Library of Congress.

a new environment to Hopper, and particularly was he dazzled by the proximity of Lillian Russell, with whom he never had appeared until then. In an early scene the two had to sit in the branches of a stage tree in full view of the audience for four minutes without a line to speak, until Fields should perpetrate the pun, "Ah, I seem to hear a rustle"—Russell—"in the trees." The minutes were forty to Hopper. Lillian was serene as always. Her awed vis-à-vis fixed a frozen smile on his twitching face and sat like a small boy at his first party.

As Fields exploded his pun and Miss Russell and Hopper rose to descend from the tree, the serenity abruptly left the fair face. She clutched frantically, then whispered in anguish, "Will, have you a safety pin? My bloomers are coming down!"

Warfield, Weber and Fields were back in their familiar Jewish and German low-comedy rôles. Weber and Fields were proprietors of a life-sized mechanical doll they hoped to sell to Hopper, who was Hoffman Barr, a Wall Street magnate.

"What is a magnate?" Lew asked.

"Something that eats holes in cheeses," Joe explained.

Warfield broke the doll and was compelled to impersonate it in a scene as ludicrous as the Music Hall ever knew.

In the second scene, laid in the Paris Exposition's Swiss Village, Weber, Fields and Warfield emerged from a papier-mâché mountain pass, to be confronted by a growling St. Bernard dog, played by George Ali. A chance sally of Weber's in this scene exploded the first-night audience. As rehearsed, Warfield was to attempt to conciliate the dog, then Fields to try. Both failing timidly, Weber was to lack the fearsome animal contemptuously out of his way.

Warfield began.

"Here, Abie," he called. The dog snarled. "Nice Mose. Cute little Izzie," he tried again.

"Whoever heard of a dog called Abie or Mose?" Fields scoffed.

"Maybe he would be a kocher spaniel," said Warfield.

Fields tried it.

"Come, Otto," he wheedled. The dog showed its teeth. "Hans? Rudolph? Adolph? Schneider?"

As Weber waited for his cue, a possible line occurred to him. The Music Hall method was to try everything on the audience. If it laughed, the joke stayed. Weber made the experiment doubtfully. He said, in place of his rehearsal line, "Maybe it's not that kind of a dog." George rose brilliantly to the occasion. At "Julia," spoken endearingly by Weber, he barked, pranced joyfully and wagged his tail. The impromptu drew the show's biggest laugh.

A small cask was attached to the dog's collar. Fields explained learnedly how the monks of the St. Bernard hospice sent their great dogs out, each with a small cask of brandy fixed to the collar, to succor wayfarers lost in the winter storms. Warfield smacked his lips in anticipation, but Weber turned the cask around, disclosing the word "Powder" painted on it.

"Powder?" Warfield exclaimed. "What kinds of powder? Seidlitzes powder? Talcums powder? Bang-bang powder?"

"Flea powder," said Weber. "What else would dogs want?"

The second half of the show was given over to "Quo Vas Iss?" a burlesque of "Quo Vadis," the theatrical best-seller at the moment. Liberties were taken with Sienkiewicz's plot. As translated by Edgar Smith, the W. C. T. U., having closed the saloons of Antium, threatened next to burn rum, to the alarm of the Emperor Zero and others. Zero ordered the lovely Lythia, of the Rome W. C. T. U., tossed to the wild borax in the arena, in reprisal. The mighty Fursus, depended upon to rescue her, turned out to be a whited sepulcher of a strong man once his leopard-skin robe was removed. He failed even to burst the chain of pretzels and link sausages with which he had been bound, but Lythia got saved somehow; just how, no one recalls.

Ross plumed himself on his rich orotund voice, and not unjustifiably; but he could not sustain it through i long scene. In "Quo Vas Iss?" he was thrown against Hopper in a long scene, and few such resonant speaking voices as Hopper's have been known on our stage. Hopper, moreover, had a figure and personality that would permit him to play straight parts. All this was a threat at Ross's four-year monopoly of the Weber and Fields concession of looking and acting handsome. Others in the company waited interestedly.

On the opening night Ross's voice began to pinch down in the middle of his long passage with Hopper. As the newcomer began to take the stage away from him, Ross tried the old trick of the legitimate stage of dropping his voice half a tone under Hopper, thereby forcing him to take a higher pitch. Hopper knew the trick, and dropped half a tone below Ross. The latter tried again, and Hopper again outmaneuvered him. The round was Hopper's by a wide margin. The next day Ross buttonholed Edgar Smith.

"You know, Edgar," he confided, "I think I'll play this part a little lighter. I was too heavy last night." Which, translated from the patter of the stage, means that Ross knew when he was licked.

Augustus Thomas's "Arizona" had opened early in the season at the Herald Square to immediate success. The Weber and Fields burlesque of it was ready by mid-October. Warfield, minus Hebrew dialect and make-up, was the villainous captain who had set out to corrupt the womanhood of Arizona, and especially his colonel's wife, by teaching them to smoke cigarettes. Fields was a German sergeant, Weber his wistful daughter Lena, hired girl at the Aridvapor ranch, presided over by Hopper as Henry Cannedbeef. Kelly was scarcely recognizable as Colonel Bunjam. Sarsparilla, wife of the colonel, daughter of Cannedbeef and sister to Beneather—Fay Templeton—was Lillian Russell's role. Charley Ross played Lieutenant 'Tention, and was glad to be rid of "Quo Vas Iss?" Hopper, in the Theodore Roberts rôle, no longer competed in manly charm.

A trick cow, the ranch's only livestock, concealed George Ali, whose face was doomed never to be seen in a Music Hall show. The cow laughed rudely at Warfield's approach. Lena apologized.

"It makes him laugh whenever he sees an army officer," she said. "Since the Cuban war any fresh beef has the laugh on the Army." Is it so long since Santiago that the canned-beef scandals must be retold for a new generation?

Lena aspired to give up the life of a Kitchener and become the daughter of the regiment. Fields would have none of it.

"I'm your fader, ain't it?" he chided her. "If you vas the daughter of the regiment, I would have to be the regiment's husband."

"Remember, Lieutenant 'Tention," Lillian Russell declaimed, "that you are in the presence of your colonel's wife, in your colonel's wife's father's house and in the apartments of your colonel's wife's husband."

"I am glad," Ross answered, "that you remember that speech, madam. At rehearsals I sometimes doubted that you could do it.

When the colonel intercepted the fatal letter from Sarsparilla to the captain, Cannedbeef intervened to protect his daughter's name.

"Hold on!" he cried. "The cow stamped upon this letter. The cow belongs to the Government, hence it is a government stamp. I reckon you wouldn't obstruct the mails, colonel."

"There's nothing male about a cow," retorted the colonel.

"I guess I made a bull of it," the ranchman said sadly.

"Put down both gags," ordered the colonel. "They may get a laugh in the War Department."

At two o'clock on the afternoon of December nineteenth, at a dress rehearsal for a new burlesque, a composite of "A Royal Family," "Floradora" and "Gay Lord Quex," Charley Ross came down with an attack of temperament. He knew his part thoroughly, he said, and refused to rehearse. The opening performance was only thirty hours away, but this was a defiance that Joe and Lew could not overlook. They gave Ross his choice of going on or of getting his salary. Ross drew his money and departed.

Ross's real name was Kelly. He had been a jockey in early life, and took the name of Charley Ross on going on the stage. It was a shrewd bit of showmanship, for Charley Ross was the best-known name in America at the moment. It was that of the boy who was kidnaped from his parents' home in Germantown, Pennsylvania, on July 1, 1874, and never more heard of, the most notorious crime of its kind in our annals. Ross had met Mabel Fenton in a Deadwood, South Dakota, dance hall, where both were playing. They married and came East with a straight-comedy act that attracted attention, straight-comedy sketches being a novelty to Eastern variety patrons.

At one o'clock of the next afternoon, with the opening now but seven hours off, Joe and Lew found an actor to take Ross's place. Charles Frohman loaned them Fritz Williams from his Empire Theater Company. Theatergoers of to-day will recall Williams as the doctor in "Rain," which still was playing to full houses after two years when the Equity dispute closed it on June 1, 1924.

From one o'clock to five o'clock Williams rode in a hansom cab in Central Park and studied his part. John T. Kelly rode with him and coached him.

"If you miss any line, I'll throw it to you," Kelly assured him when they parted at five.

Williams was letter-perfect that night. Kelly, who was notoriously slack on first nights, stumbled twice, and was prompted by Williams on both occasions.

Kelly did get off a nifty, however, congratulating Williams on how well he kissed Miss Russell on such short preparation.

It is the boast of Weber and Fields that they never once discharged a man or woman from the Music Hall, that Ross was the only member of the company, one chorus girl excepted, to leave under unpleasant circumstances, and that those who left to better themselves always departed with the good wishes and blessings of the proprietors. Broadway called the Weber-fields the Happy Family and marveled at how the lion lay down with the lamb.

Fields put the secret in eight words once in reply to a question from Joseph Jefferson. The creator of the stage "Rip Van Winkle" and his crony, ex-President Cleveland, were often at the Music Hall, Jefferson frequently backstage.

"How do you boys keep the peace among all these stars?" Jefferson asked, voicing the general wonder.

"We're always wrong and they're always right," Lew replied.

Mr. Isman asked De Wolf Hopper the other day what memory of the Music Hall was most vivid to him after twenty-four years.

"The fact that I enjoyed every moment I was there," he said. "The Ross incident excepted, I can't recall an unpleasant word, look or gesture. Yet there never was another stage so cluttered up with the high explosives of temperament. Half a dozen stars managed by two other stars! There is no parallel for it in my knowledge of the theater.

"I don't know how it was done, but one for all and all for one was achieved at Twenty-ninth Street, and against the most unlikely odds. I do not say that there was no jealousy; that would be absurd. Had there been no jealousy, there would have been nothing remarkable in the harmony. The astonishing thing was that everyone kept a tight rein and curb bit on his or her envy. If anyone had a gag or a bit of business he could not use at the moment, it was nothing for him to pass it along. With six or seven exceptions—my wives—those were the happiest moments of my life."

Fay Templeton sang "I'm a Respectable Working Girl" for the first time in this burlesque. Miss Templeton did not fancy the song, and was so certain that it would not go over that she memorized but one verse. The first-nighters made her respond to four encores. At each she could only sing the first verse over. By the following night she knew the entire song. She had few more popular ones.

On the other hand, much was expected of "My Japanese Cherry Blossom," which was the Oriental setting for a Templeton coon song, and it failed flatly at the Music Hall. The coon song had been raging for five years and more. Stromberg and Smith believed that it had been done to death and that the moment had arrived to ring a change on it. But they found that the Weberfields' public wanted just what they thought it had tired of. The Japanese song really had a lovely melody, and was the success of the season in Europe. "Rosie, You Are My Posie" was substituted hurriedly for it at the Hall. There must be those who remember the polka-dot costumes of the chorus that helped Fay Templeton sing it. Of all that long succession of song hits that Stromberg and Smith wrote for the Music Hall, "Rosie Posie" probably led the list. The sheet music of the Music Hall shows carried the fame of Weber and Fields to the farthest village. The grocer boy in Corpus Christi, Texas, was whistling "Rosie Posie" within the month and the young ladies of Paradise, Montana, were trying it on the parlor organ. Echoes of it are heard to this day. Stromberg composed the air originally for some dance music for Bessie Clayton, but she and Julian Mitchell did not like it. When "My Japanese Cherry Blossom" failed, Stromberg and Smith dug the other out of the discard.

Another bad guess was made in the burlesque of "Arizona." In this the chorus was costumed in one scene as a company of dusty campaign-stained troopers, and drilled in the manual of arms and squad formations for weeks by an army officer. The effect was expected to be the talk of the show, but the audiences turned thumbs down. They did not want to see the girls dusty and drab even for a moment; a chorus was there to look pretty.

The burlesque of "Floradora" was confined to a parody of the famous sextet by Warfield, Weber, Fields, Bonnie Maginn, Allie Gilbert and Belle Robinson. Only a photograph can suggest how risible it was. Stromberg's music was a remarkable bit of work. He succeeded in the rare feat of imitating all the musical tricks of "Tell Me, Pretty Ladies" without repeating the melody.

The horseplay backstage at Weber and Fields was continuous. One of its forms was the writing of fictitious mash notes and oilers of fabulous salaries to one another. Warfield received such a letter signed David Belasco, and tore it up.

"Why do you always pick on me?" he grumbled.

This particular letter happened to be genuine, and Belasco was accustomed to prompt and grateful responses to his overtures. When no reply came he was on the verge of dropping the matter, but his business judgment conquered his pride. He called in person and repeated the offer to make a star of Warfield.

The business methods at Weber and Fields's were sketchy. Contracts usually were verbal and no thought taken of next season until next season arrived. Joe and Lew had marked Belasco's frequent presence in the theater, however, and his interest in Warfield. As they stood in the wings one night waiting for their cues, Warfield came up.

"Is it all right for next season, Dave?" Fields asked.

"I'm sorry, boys," Warfield answered. "I'm going with Belasco in the fall. It's a big opportunity for me; but if it's all right with you, I'd like to feel that I can come back if I fail. Failure in the theater isn't like failure in business. If I go starring and do not succeed, I will be worth more money than before, because my name will have been up in the electric lights for a season."

"Go to it, Dave, and the best luck in the world," his bosses told him.

Warfield put himself under Belasco's tutelage at the end of the season. In September, 1901, he made his appearance in "The Auctioneer," under a contract that gave him $300 a week and 20 per cent of the net profits the first season, 25 the second, 30 the third and 50 per cent thereafter. He never has left the Belasco management since.

"Hoity Toity" opened the sixth season on September 5, 1901, a hot, a noisy and a gala night, to a $10,500 house, and no standing room sold, an average of

Photo 21. *Twirly Whirly* poster, showing Mabel Fenton and Charlie Ross, 1904. J. Ottman Lithographic Company, lithographer, Library of Congress.

something like $15 a seat. Sam Bernard was back to take the place of Warfield, the only missing face. Fritz Williams became a regular and had the song hit of the piece, "The Pullman Porters' Ball." Lillian Russell's gowns and the chorus costumes, designed by Will R. Barnes, gave Broadway a new mark to shoot at. Julian Mitchell marshaled a company of sixty without confusion on the smallest stage but one in New York. Russell and Templeton had fasted all summer to gratifying results. Russell, Bernard, Templeton, Williams, Kelly and Harrison made speeches, and the house called vainly as in previous years for Honey Stromberg, Weber and Fields. Pete Dailey and Charley Ross were out front beating their hands sore.

"There is only one dull moment in 'Hoity Toity,' "Robert Edgren wrote the next day, "that being the interval in which you step out to puff a cigarette, take a deep breath and get ready for another scene." The *Evening Post* critic said that there was "nowhere else in the world where you see such a droll pageant." *The World*, borrowing the English of Weber and Fields, wrote, "What's the use of asking anybody to write anything about something that there is no use writing anything about?"

"Hopper was General Steel, a billionaire widower at Monte Carlo with six debutante daughters, Bonnie Maginn, Mayme Gehrue, the Moyer Sisters, Belle Robinson and Goldie Mohr, who demanded frequent parental kisses.

"Who wouldn't be a Weber and Fields papa?" Hopper asked the audience.

Verily, the life of a good joke is longer than Methuselah's. A favorite anecdote of the postwar period has been that of the Jewish soldier who lay dying on the trenches, when an Irish priest came by and administered absolution.

"Do you believe in the Father, the Son and the Holy Ghost, my son?" the priest asked.

"I'm dying and he asks me riddles!" the soldier complained. It has a modern sound, but it is to be found in a joke book called "Anecdotes of the Rebellion," published in the '70s.

All of which is preliminary to the unearthing of more old friends in "Hoity Toity." One of Hopper's daughters lisped her discovery that her beautiful silk dress came from a poor insignificant little worm.

"Yes, I'm the worm," was Hopper's line.

Another daughter asked, "You would not go so far as to marry again?"

"I'll go as far as any father, and I may go a step farther and give you a stepmother," papa answered; adding, "But as actors frequently say after pulling one of the author's best lines, let us return to the book."

Many will remember "Hoity Toity" best for the put-in-and-take-out banking scene and the poker game, two of the best bits in the Weber and Fields anthology. The idea of the banking scene came to Weber, Fields and Bernard as they were lunching at Shanley's during the rehearsal period and a newsboy passed their window crying an extra. Another bank cashier had absconded with a large sum. Why not a banking scene? They passed the bare bones of the idea along to Edgar Smith, the author. The bit ran for only five minutes the first night. Before the end of the season, Sam, Lew and Joe had expanded it to twenty-five-minute length, the longest and much the funniest scene in the show.

Like most Weberfieldian humor, it loses much in any attempt to reproduce it in type. The three comedians were East Side delicatessen dealers who had cornered the sauerkraut market and come to Monte Carlo to spend their money. Weber was entranced with the beauties of the Riviera. What a heavenly spot! What smiling skies and sea and shore! He would settle here and sell sausages. Fields and Bernard argued for starting a bank.

"But I don't know anything about this banking business," said Weber.

"So much the better; we would teach you."

"Is it a good old-established business like the sausage business?" Weber asked.

"Older! The sausage business only dates back to Cincinnatus, while there have been banks since the days of Pharaoh."

The fundamentals of banking were explained to Weber. A bank examiner was described as one who "comes around occasionally and overlooks the books." Weber was to put up all the money, Fields and Bernard to give him their joint notes for their interests.

"A joint note," they told him, "is a note signed by three or more people who all become unreliable for the full amount." Weber wanted to know who the third signer was to be. He was it.

The bank opened, Weber behind the barred window, the bars to remind him of his finish, Fields explained. As the initial transaction, Fields borrowed ten dollars from the bank. He gave half to Bernard, who approached the window.

BERNARD: Mornings.
WEBER: Mornings. Put in or take out?
BERNARD: I wish to make a posit of five dollars.
WEBER: I got back five dollars anyhow!

Bernard asked for a check book and left the window. Fields approached.

FIELDS: Evenings.
WEBER: Evenings. Put in or take out?
FIELDS: Push my name in the book for five dollars.
WEBER: That's ten dollars I never expected to get!

Fields received a check book and left the window. Bernard meanwhile wrote a check payable to bearer for $200 and presented it for payment.

BERNARD: Mornings.
WEBER: Mornings. Put in or take out? Huh? Do I have to pay this?
FIELDS: Don't ask the foolishest of questions.
BERNARD: If you please, hurry. Time is money.
WEBER: Have some time then.
BERNARD: The check reads for $200, not hours.
WEBER (*passing out bills reluctantly*): Don't grab!

Bernard was for making out another check at once, but Fields declared that it was his turn. They struggled for the one pencil. Fields wrested it away and made out a check for $200, which Weber likewise cashed. Sam and Lew hugged each other; but Joe, who had been sweating over his books, announced the discovery that each was $195 overboard. He demanded payment.

"Will you take a check?" they asked.

"Sure! Checks are good. Didn't I already give you money for them?" said Joe.

Bernard drew a check for $302, pushed it through the window and asked for $197 change. Weber balked, but was silenced scornfully.

"What do you know about banking, anyway?" Bernard sneered. "Only what we teached you. Anyway, it's the principle, not the money, with me. Money means nothing." To prove it he wrote a check for $1,000,000, tore it up and blew the fragments from his hand—pouf.

"This banking ain't quite clear to me," Weber admitted. "I get on to it after a while, maybe."

Fields paid his overdraft with a check for $502, demanding $397 in change. When Weber's funds appeared to be exhausted, the sketch ended in a run on the bank, Bernard and Fields running offstage.

Lillian Russell made the fourth in the poker game that followed, she fleecing Fields and Bernard of all they had taken from Joe and what they had overlooked. Fields boasted that he was the champion long-distance pokerer of the world, to which Bernard retorted that he meant that he could play longer for less than anybody. On the first hand Lew asked Sam if he had stacked the cards.

"Sure! I was trained by a gambler."

"You must have been overtrained," said Lew. "I've got five aces of spades."

Fields heightened the comedy by crouching low to examine his hand card by card in the manner of a suspicious player. As he jerked each card from the table he would flash the ace to the audience. It was Bernard's job to arrange the deck and hand it to the property man before each performance. Props nodded one night and Fields was incensed at drawing a Weehawken straight, jack high, instead of his five aces. He accused Bernard of treachery and would not be consoled. At the next performance Weber happened to experiment with a new bit of business in the poker scene, and drew a laugh from the spectators. Fields, whose face was averted, heard only the laugh and jumped to the conclusion that Bernard was up to more trickery. When the unaccounted-for laugh came again the following night, Lew called in his brother Charley.

"You stay out from to-morrow and watch Bernard," he ordered. "He's slipping something over on me."

Charley stood watch, detected Weber's new business and harmony was restored.

Charles Hawtrey's "A Message From Mars" at the Garrick arrived at the music hall in burlesque form in November. The original told the story of an acutely selfish man reformed by a supernatural visitor from Mars. In the travesty, the Martian A. D. T., Hopper, came to cure Fritz Williams of his morbid generosity. Hopper made an explosive entrance from the Subway, the blasting for which was shaking Broadway in the autumn of 1901, to find Williams listening to the pitiful story of a Floradora sextet maiden clad in a pink opera coat and seventeen eighteen-carat diamonds. Her mother, she wept, had turned her out of doors until she should bring home a motor car. Williams bought her one instanter. Hopper, explaining the hatred of humor on Mars, suggested that this was why she and her sister planets were favored locales of comic opera.

Fields made a straight character portrait of the tramp inventor and carried off first honors in the reviews. Broadway discovered tardily, as in Warfield's case, that it been underestimating an able character actor. The inventor had just left the hospital "eight dollars short of having forty cents." His most notable achievement was a locomotive cowcatcher that not only picked up the cow but milked her and tossed her back unharmed into the pasture.

Pink pajamas were prominent in the costuming, in deference to Pauline Chase, who was making those garments famous in "The Liberty Belles." Both Miss Russell and Miss Templeton had entirely new wardrobes, replacing the Rue de la Paix creations which the "Little Duchess" company had copied.

When the critics wished to speak superlatively of a burlesque they said it was as good, or nearly, so, as "Catherine," that triumph of the third season. This was the verdict on "The Curl and the Judge," a travesty of Clyde Fitch's "The Girl and the Judge." Annie Russell, it happened, was the star of each of the originals, and Fay Templeton had both the corresponding rôles.

Frankie Bailey, whose fatted calves had been on tour with Peter Dailey and Anna Held, was home again, her return made glorious by a brand-new pair of geranium tights. And while Bonnie Maginn stepped into trousers to play a minor speaking part, all the men save Hopper were in skirts. Sam Bernard put aside his dialect and did Mrs. McKee Rankin's rôle of the garrulous boarding-house landlady who had seen better days and whose lodgers had seen better boarding houses. Her pension was furnished in what Fields called the Louis-the-Fourteenth-Street period. Large red lobsters rampant on a bright-green field was the wall-paper motif, and a passion for cretonne had been carried to the length of draping the washbowl, pitcher and coal scuttle.

Fitch's play was all about the theft of a jeweled brooch by a presumably respectable woman who proved to be a kleptomaniac. In the burlesque, Fields was Mrs. Tankton, who had been told by her doctor that she had kleptomania and was "taking things for it." Fields had been on the stage minutes before the audience penetrated his make-up. He stole a false curl from Fritz Williams, who had the part played at the Lyceum by the venerable Mrs. E. H. Gilbert, then in her 80s, and the fidelity of his copy was astonishing. Bernard first was suspected of having pilfered the curl to add to the hash. A moment earlier he had inquired if anyone had found the can opener in the hash; he required it to nail down the matting. Bernard served coffee in the rooms. It would be extra in most boarding houses, he said, but he threw it in.

"It would be thrown out anywhere else," Fields said.

John T. Kelly, as Tankton, was Fields's husband and Fay Templeton's father, a drunkard who would drink anything, but had decided to stick to mucilage.

Hopper was a judge to whom the Tanktons took their marital difficulties. Kelly's first act was to drain the ink bottle on the judge's desk. This habit, Fields told the judge, had made her husband a black-hearted wretch who deserved to be sent to the pen. Kelly demanded a divorce and rested his case on Fields's face.

"What'll you have?" the judge asked Fields.

"I'll have the same, and a little alimony on the side," was the answer.

Fields accused Kelly of having given him a black eye. The court was sceptical.

"What? That physical wreck?" Hopper exclaimed.

"He wasn't a physical wreck until he gave me the black eye," Fields came back.

Weber was a Jewess pawnbroker and fence who persecuted the court with pleas that her son be sent to the penitentiary.

"Didn't I tell you the last time that your boy is too young to send to state's prison?" the court demanded.

"Ah, but he's been studying so hard since then!" Weber implored. "Now he's a regular thief, even if he is young. Ain't you, Micky? Steal something for the nice gentleman! Judge, you wouldn't believe what a life I've led trying to bring that boy up to walk in his father's footprints and be a credit to us. He's too lazy to be a good thief. If you don't send him up the river this time he might grow up an honest man and break his poor mother's heart."

"I'm sorry, but the reformatory is the best I can do," the court ruled.

The boy was insulted.

"Gee, the gang would give me the laugh!" he complained.

"Take it or leave it, madam." Hopper rapped with his gavel. "If your boy can't learn to be a thief in the reformatory, then he's no good. If you bring him in here again I'll send him to the House of Refuse."

"Constructed without the slightest regard for historical accuracy and performed by the following daring cast," read the playbill of "Du Hurry," a burlesque of Belasco's "Madame Du Barry," which closed the season. The authorship of Du Barry had been taken into court, both Belasco and Jean Richepin, the French poet-playwright, claiming it.

"Any author who thinks he wrote 'Du Hurry' need not bother to enter suit," the Music Hall program announced. "He is welcome to it."

Genevieve Dolaro, of the chorus, had been cast for the rôle of a gypsy hag. When Julian Mitchell criticized her reading of her five lines at dress rehearsal she quit, and Mitchell had to take the part himself on the opening night.

Sam Bernard was Louis Quince, King of France. On his taking a flying leap from the center of the stage to the throne, Fritz Williams remarked, "That's a big jump."

"Yes, from the third act to the fourth," said Bernard, and the action of the play proceeded accordingly.

Jeanette Vaubernier, the doll of the world in Belascoese, became Jeanette d'Auburnhair at Weber and Fields's in token of Mrs. Leslie Carter's locks, and the *pièce de résistance of the travesty was the frying of an* egg over the flaming hair of the bogus Mrs. Carter, Fay Templeton. Bonnie Maginn held the frying pan, Frankie Bailey dropped in a lump of butter and Fields broke the egg into the sizzling skillet and produced it fried forthwith. Fay sat up in bed and ate the egg. Weber was Du Barry's aristocratic and wounded lover whose blue blood discolored his frilled shirt front. Hocking the Kaiser, done to death in the late war, made its appearance in "Du Hurry." It was not, however, original, having been lifted bodily from "Mr. Dooley."

Which brings the Music Hall to its seventh and next to the last season. Great changes were afoot.

Chapter VIII

The Seventh and Eighth Seasons

An Ending and Then a Reunion, 1902–1904, 1912

THE story of Weber and Fields nears its end. The separation of the team still was two years away when the Music Hall's seventh season began with undimmed brilliance in mid-September, 1902, but the horizon already was clouding. Broadway saw only the sun blazing from the zenith and thought of Weber and Fields as fixtures. No hint reached even to members of the Music-Hall company for another fifteen months.

In midsummer of 1902, John Stromberg, whose music had been one of the Music Hall's distinctions, died. All Broadway was at his funeral and all Broadway sobbed when an orchestra played the dead composer's "Come Back, My Honey Boy, to Me." Stromberg had written part of the score for the new season's show. One of these posthumous numbers, "Come Down, My Evenin' Star," was sung by Miss Russell in "Twirly Whirly," and brought more tears to Broadway eyes. A successor was found for Stromberg, but the music of the Weber and Fields show never again was quite the same.

De Wolf Hopper had gone starring. It cost Joe and Lew $15,000 outright to procure a successor they deemed worthy. This was the sum they paid to obtain the release of Willie Collier from a contract with Jacob D. Litt, then a figure in show business. Collier and his wife, Louise Alen, drew a stiff salary in addition."

Sam Bernard, too, left again to head a company of his own, and in December Julian Mitchell dropped out to stage, direct and buy an interest in "The Wizard of Oz." With him went Bessie Clayton, his wife. But Peter Dailey was back; Charles A. Bigelow, a first-rate comedian, was a newcomer; and Miss Russell, Miss Templeton, John T. Kelly, Frankie Bailey and Bonnie Maginn were present and accounted for. It was no weak company.

From a stage box the opening night the real Mary McLane watched Mrs. Collier spoof her in a bit called "I, Mary McPain." That soulful young woman of Butte is one with yesteryear's snows now, but she had her crowded hour.

Miss Templeton had a song, "My Intimate Friend," written for her by Wilton Lackaye, the actor. "An intimate friend of a friend of mine is an intimate friend

Photo 22. Sheet music from *Hoity Toity* showing Weber, Fields, and Lillian Russell. New York Public Library, Digital Collections.

of his," Miss Templeton sang, describing why she, a stage-struck maiden, was sure of a job in one of Charles Frohman's companies. Mr. Lackaye thought so well of his own work that he recited the lyrics around the Lambs' Club all summer to great applause. "Sally in Our Alley" opened two weeks ahead of "Twirly Whirly," and lo and behold, Marie Cahill presented herself as a stage-struck maiden from Arkansas who sang a song to the effect that she was

Photo 23. William Collier and Louise Allen, c. 1905.

assured of a Broadway engagement because "an intimate friend of a friend of mine is an intimate friend of his." Mr. Lackaye and the author of "Sally in Our Alley" exchanged compliments, but both stars continued all season to claim the same intimate friend.

This was the year in which Weber and Fields ceased to speak to each other offstage except when necessity demanded. At one time that winter they were on the point of immediate separation, but the lawyers who were called in argued so vigorously against it on the ground of business expediency that a truce was worked out. A contract was drawn up leaving the management of the front of the house entirely to Weber, the region behind the footlights exclusively to Fields.

They continued as they had for a quarter of a century to use the same dressing room, and not a whisper came to the ears of the company. Such was the business acumen of the two that when a vague rumor did get loose, Joe and Lew killed it quickly and cunningly by sitting for three hours on a shoe-shine stand at Twenty-ninth Street and Broadway and eating peanuts from the same bag while all the Rialto passed. It was the same stand upon which Weber had sat the day Louis Robie strolled by seven years earlier and spoke to him of the chance of leasing the Imperial Music Hall. Their purpose accomplished, their silence was resumed.

It would serve no purpose here to revive this long-buried quarrel except to say that it had its inception in the burlesque of "A Message From Mars," produced in their sixth season. Fields's characterization of the tramp inventor brought him high praise. Weber's was an inconspicuous role. Fields believed at the time that outsiders had stirred his partner to jealousy. Weber resented Fields's suspicions. Relatives and friends took a hand and the coolness grew. The wound probably would have healed naturally and easily as had the spats of their youth had not complications, none personal, set in.

The first of these complications was the changing state of the theater. Weber and Fields had won their unique place on Broadway by setting an unprecedented pace. They had given Broadway something new. They had put six and seven stars into one show and paid them lavish salaries. But now, and partially because of their own precedent, salaries were leaping yearly. The Music Hall, to hold its eminence, must always press forward. To stand still was to seem to fall bade. The time was at hand when enough business could not be packed into the little theater to pay the soaring costs.

Weber and Fields could have had any theater in New York, including the largest, for the asking; but every adviser they had, and this included virtually everyone in the business, argued that their peculiar entertainment would fail in a larger house. It needed, all agreed, the intimacy of such a bandbox as the Twenty-ninth Street house, where the audience almost could reach over the footlights and shake hands with the company. Everyone was wrong, of course. Their road experience was there in disproof; but that is more easily perceived in 1924 than it was in 1904.

It is highly probable, too, that the Music Hall could have raised its prices half again and held its public; possibly even stimulated New York's interest by so doing. New York will pay any price for what it likes, but two dollars for an orchestra seat and a half a dollar more for a box seat looked like the point of diminishing returns in a time when 25-50-75 had only just ceased to be the prevailing scale in the theater.

Weber always had been the business manager of the partnership, and he had unquestionably the better money sense. He saw a prosperous enterprise endangered by outrageous costs and was for leaving well enough alone. Fields's was the better theatrical vision. He foresaw the changing times and wished to meet them with altered tactics. Actually, both were right. The Music Hall was doomed if it stood still, but to advance farther was to court disaster. What the enterprise needed was a man who combined the business caution of Weber and the artistic foresight of Fields. Had the two put themselves under the management of such a man as A. L. Erlanger, for example, they might well have become and continued to be an international attraction the like of Sir Harry Lauder.

When Collier and his wife left at the end of the seventh season, attracted by bigger money and a company of their own, and Charley Bigelow followed, Fields was for engaging Nat Goodwin and his then wife, Maxine Elliott, two of the legitimate stage's most notable stars. They could be had for $2,500 a week, he said.

"Where are we going to quit?" Weber said. "I guess we could pay them $2,500, but each season we pay more. We can't keep on at this rate."

Fields dropped his negotiations. Louis Mann, Carter de Haven and the McCoy sisters were engaged to strengthen the company. But when Fay Templeton was lured away once more and no adequate successor could be found, Weber listened to Fields's amazing suggestion that they angle for Lillian Nordica, then the leading prima donna of the Metropolitan Opera Company.

"We're both going crazy; but all right," Weber agreed.

Madame Nordica's talents obviously were not particularly adapted to Weber and Fields burlesque, but that was not the issue. Would the public talk? Would the public come? The public would, indubitably.

Six thousand dollars was the sum named by Madame Nordica's pianist, who also was her business manager.

This was four times the wages of Lillian Russell, the Music Hall's most expensive ornament. It is an unheard-of salary to-day. Joe and Lew grit their teeth. They would try raising prices.

"Look at the talk it will make," ventured the sanguine Fields.

"Who said talk was cheap?" Weber groaned.

The pianist arranged a meeting with the prima donna at her home in Ninth Street. Joe and Lew walked down Ninth Street on tiptoe, were ushered in and sat in that hushed silence accorded to death and important money. Ten slow stiff minutes elapsed. Then the pianist entered, moved directly to the grand

Photo 24. A. L. Erlanger, c. 1919. Bain News Service, George Grantham Bain Collection, Library of Congress.

Photo 25. Lillian Nordica, c. 1910. Bain News Service, George Grantham Bain Collection, Library of Congress.

piano and struck a thumping chord. At this, one of the portières parted and Madame Nordica, in jewels and evening dress, swept through. The pianist leaped to attention, clicked his heels and bowed from the waist Joe and Lew endeavored to copy the grand manner, but succeeded only in bowing their heels and clicking their waists. Madame smiled graciously.

The conversation passed from the amenities to business. Madame had considered the offer of $6,000 to appear at the Music Hall and would accept. It would be a bizarre experience for her, but she trusted, a pleasant one—mutually pleasant.

"We are deeply honored," Weber and Fields murmured. "Just make out your own contract."

"But I am puzzled," madame went on. "Yours is a very small theater, I understand. They tell me that it could be tucked away in the last gallery of the Metropolitan. And surely your prices are modest How then is it possible, I ask myself, that you can pay me $6,000 a performance?"

Some minutes later Messrs. Weber and Fields emerged benumbedly into the fresh air of Ninth Street and laughed weakly. There had been a slight misunderstanding. $6,000 or any other sum in the theater means weekly. The week is understood. In grand opera $6,000 would mean per performance. The performance is understood. Madame Nordica did not join the Weber and Fields company.

The last-minute choice fell upon Evie Stetson, who outweighed Miss Templeton, at any rate, such being no mean accomplishment. There was no perceptible falling away in the brilliance of the opening-night spectacle. True, the advance auction of first-night seats had not brought quite the prices of other years, but everyone that mattered was there. Frankie Bailey's and Bonnie Maginn's copyrighted legs were missing, and mourned, but Miss Russell stepped into the breach, as it were, sang one song in male evening dress, and was prettily embarrassed. The opening had been postponed for two weeks while she subdued a summer cold—not because, Peter Dailey told the first-nighters, the tailor had not finished her trousers in time.

In this number the fair Lillian dawdled with a cigarette.

"Her lighting and smoking of a cigarette claimed admiration for true naturalism and ease," the *World* reported with a straight face the next morning. And this was only twenty years ago!

Peter Dailey, as always, was master of ceremonies at the love feast and flower show that followed the final curtain, though Louis Mann strove to edge him out of the center of the picture. When his turn came, Mr. Mann delivered a carefully rehearsed impromptu speech.

Louis Mann is a character. He is an undisputed artist in his field; no one probably ever has excelled him as a German comedian. He knows every dialect and colloquial mannerism of the German states, and how best to use them.

When Weber and Fields approached him with a music-hall offer he declined to talk business informally. They must wait upon him in his home, he ruled. Accordingly, Joe and Lew presented themselves at the Mann residence off

Riverside Drive immediately after a night performance. After ringing the doorbell for what seemed an interminable time, a figure appeared in the rented livery of a butler and showed them into the drawing-room, where Mann, in immaculate evening dress, greeted them.

Fields, who was tired, rudely began to talk business. His host ignored this breach of etiquette, and a pleasant quarter of an hour was passed in social chat, until Mrs. Mann—Clara Lipman—joined them. Dinner was announced by the butler. It was a very correct meal, two hours in the eating. At two o'clock the four arose and repaired to the drawing-room, where coffee was served. When each had been supplied with a demi-tasse, and the men with tobacco, Mr. Mann cleared his throat.

"Now, gentlemen," he said, "to what do I owe the honor of your company?"

At 2:30 A.M. an agreement was reached with Mann to join the Weber and Fields company for thirty-five weeks at $1,000 a week, exactly what he had been offered at the first meeting.

During the Equity-Fidelity fight Mann affiliated with Fidelity and presided one night at a meeting at which George M. Cohan gave a large sum to the cause. If Equity members may be believed, Mann waved a bit of paper above his head and declared, "I hold in my hand an anonymous check for $100,000."

Mann's father bred prize Saint Bernard dogs and sold two of his best to the late James Gordon Bennett, of the late New York *Herald*. The dogs became ill and Bennett sent for the senior Mann to doctor them. The father mentioned the incident in a letter to Louis, who was on the road at the time with "The Girl From Paris" company, which was to open at the Herald Square Theater a week later.

On receipt of the letter Louis wired his father:

"When you next see Bennett arrange that I get good notice in the *Herald* when the show opens in New York."

The father followed instructions and was met with a curt refusal from Commodore Bennett.

"A good notice for Louis or I don't doctor the dogs," the elder Mann threatened.

"The Girl From Paris" reached the Herald Square as scheduled. Whatever the other papers said, the *Herald* had none but kind words for the show and Louis. The dogs got well.

Mann liked to tell the Weberfields of how he had acquired an education by dint of extraordinary perseverance and industry against pathetic odds. He was playing the old tune with variations in the barroom of the Baltimore Hotel in Kansas City during the 1904 road trip of the company when a fellow actor, who had confined his speech hitherto to brief cash exchanges with the bartender, cut in.

"Louis, if you're so well educated, tell us where Lincoln delivered his Gettysburg speech," he said hoarsely. "And who delivered it," the hoarse voice continued before anyone could titter.

Mann strolled into Weber and Fields's dressing room one night as the latter were killing time by cutting cards. There were no stakes.

"What are you playing for?" Louis asked.

"Fifty dollars a cut," said Lew.

Fields cut the high card and won, and Weber, catching the former's wink, suggested making the next cut for $100. Joe lost again and suggested redoubling the stakes.

"Write your own ticket."

Lew flicked the ash from his cigarette boredly. The stakes climbed to $200, $400, $800, $1,600. For once Mann was silent. He watched pop-eyed as $3,200 wavered on the cut of a card. When Weber's imaginary debt to Fields reached $50,000, Mann was perspiring like a lawn sprinkler.

"One cut for $100,000 or nothing!" the ruined Weber shouted.

"You're on!" Fields hissed.

Mann seized Weber and dragged him back. Joe escaped and reached for a card. Mann begged him to remember his family. Joe pushed him aside.

"Seven!" Fields yelled, without looking at his card.

"Nine!" Weber exulted, without a glance.

"Thank God!" Mann breathed.

In the first scene Fields played with Mann in "Whoop-dee-doo," the latter backed Lew upstage and blanked him, stealing the scene, an old stage artifice. Louis did it again the second night, but on the third Fields got the jump on him and kept one step ahead. In the middle of the scene the two reached the back wall of the theater, which, by reason of the stage's shallow depth, had been painted to resemble a set.

"What do you think you are doing?" Mann demanded.

"I'm going to back you right through that brick wall if you start that crowding again," Fields warned.

After the separation of Weber and Fields, Lew and Edgar Smith were in Pittsburgh with Marie Dressier in "Tillie's Nightmare." On an after-dinner stroll they passed a theater where Mann was playing in "The Man Who Stood Still." Fields studied the billing a moment and read the name of the play aloud.

"Huh!" he grunted. "That must be some other Louis Mann."

The McCoy sisters were Lizzie and Nelly in 1903. Lizzie changed her first name later to the more euphonious Bessie, and her last name still later to Mrs. Richard Harding Davis. Their mother was their constant companion. Carter de Haven, who still was a mere youth, also was accompanied by his mother at all times.

At the first meeting of the two mothers at an early rehearsal, as is the wont of stage mothers a difference of opinion arose. Mrs. McCoy gave as her frank and unbiased opinion that her daughters were the stage's most gifted dancers. Mrs. de Haven no less disinterestedly intimated that her Carter could dance more giftedly on one leg than Mrs. McCoy's daughters on four. The feeling grew cooler—or warmer—at each succeeding rehearsal.

In the midst of the trying ordeal of the "Whoop-dee-doo" dress rehearsal a thud and a scream came from offstage. Mrs. McCoy had fallen down a flight of stairs in hurrying to help her daughters in making a change. The dress rehearsal scarcely was under way again when a louder crash came from the opposite side of the stage.

"What now?" Fields exclaimed.

"Don't bother," Edgar Smith advised coolly. "That's probably Carter's mother falling down two flights of steps. She isn't one to let Mrs. McCoy get the better of her."

This was an era of ping-pong, pyrography, peg-top trousers and more important things. Little Japan was thrashing giant Russia. A new Italian tenor, Enrico Caruso, made his bow at the Metropolitan. And on December 17, 1903, two young bicycle builders of Dayton, Ohio, Orville and Wilbur Wright, fluttered perilously over the sands of Kitty Hawk, North Carolina, in the world's first airplane flight. Less than a month later a man from Michigan, whose name did not break into "Who's Who" until eleven years later, drove a motor car of his own making over the frozen surface of Lake St. Clair, Michigan, in the fastest mile ever attained by man until then. This was Henry Ford, not unknown to his generation, but not known as a maker of racing cars. His time was thirty-nine and two-fifths seconds, a record lowered later in the month to thirty-nine seconds flat by W. K. Vanderbilt, Jr., in a foreign car on the beach at Ormond, Florida.

In these same months the first New York subway began operation, the Hudson tubes were joined, the Pennsylvania Railroad announced its purpose of coming into Manhattan by other tunnels under the Hudson to a great new terminal to be built in Thirty-fourth Street, and the New York Central began building its new terminal on the site of the old Grand Central Station in Forty-second Street.

The world, America, and New York in particular, were on the threshold of a new, fantastic age. The young twentieth century had its foot on the gas and the cut-out wide open, and the destinies of the least of us were scrambled. In 1904 the Flatiron Building at the intersection of Broadway, Fifth Avenue and Twenty-third Street was the hub of New York and the city's most famous skyscraper. The great stores lay in and around Twenty-third Street, and there, it seemed likely, they would stay indefinitely. It had been understood for years that when the Central road got around to building its new passenger terminal it would come down to Twenty-third Street by tunnel under Park and Fourth Avenues.

Now New York's retail district shifted overnight, so to speak. The great stores rushed for Thirty-fourth Street, driving the theaters northward before them. The displaced white lights settled in and around Times Square, made a pivotal point by the new subway. Four-fifths of the Broadway theaters were overwhelmed in this tide rip of trade and traffic. Of the first-class theaters of 1903–1904 only the Casino, Empire and Knickerbocker survive in their original character, and all lay on the northern fringe of the old Rialto. Wallack's,

Daly's, Weber and Fields', the Herald Square, the old Bijou, the old Princess, Hammerstein's Thirty-fourth Street, Manhattan and Madison Square are gone. The Savoy, Grand Opera House, Academy of Music and Broadway are picture houses. The Garden is a Jewish theater and the Garrick a Theater Guild plaything. Twenty-ninth Street and Broadway has been left in a backwater. Three-story taxpayers now stand on the site of the music hall.

Inside the American theater another revolution was in full swing. This was the season in which musical comedy came into its own. It brought to Broadway the "Wizard of Oz," which elevated Montgomery and Stone to stardom; George Ade's "Sultan of Sulu"; the "Prince of Pilsen," the "Merry Widow," "Mr. Bluebeard" and "A Chinese Honeymoon"—six of the best remembered musical comedies of our stage—all in twelve months. The music comedy form was no novelty, but these were bigger, brighter, fresher—break-aways from stereotyped forms. The public turned to them, and the music hall was face to face with formidable competition for the first time in its history. Fields believed that the day of the Weber-fields shows was passing. He was for going over to the enemy. Weber studied the ledger and held back.

The final blow fell on December 30, 1903. On that afternoon 575 persons lost their lives in the Iroquois Theater fire in Chicago. Their old friend, Eddie Foy, played the hero in real life. With the flames bursting through the curtain at his back, Foy stood upon the apron and clowned in furious earnest in a desperate effort to stop the panic-stricken stampede for inadequate exits, narrowly escaping finally with his own life. Every American city revised its theater-building code at once. New York enforced drastic changes calling for new fire walls, asbestos curtains, increased exits and unobstructed alleyways on each side of a theater. The music hall would have to be rebuilt or abandoned. Fields was for abandoning it; Weber opposed.

The skies had smiled upon Weber and Fields continuously for eight years or more. Were two men who virtually had lifted themselves by their own boot straps from mean and hungry streets to a stage box on Broadway to collapse like turkey chicks in the first shower? They had capital, prestige and youth—they still were in their thirties. Their success had been won with only the last of these assets. The answer is to be found in an old adage. United, Weber and Fields stood; divided, they fell.

Joe and Lew would have found a larger theater, changed their show to suit the times, jockied their way back to the rail and gone on. Mr. Weber and Mr. Fields went their separate ways. The music hall closed on January 30, 1904, never to reopen as Weber and Fields'. Two nights later the company, augmented by Charley Ross, Mabel Fenton, Frankie Bailey and other music-hall alumni who returned to make the transcontinental junket, left for San Francisco by special train. The rest of the season would be spent on tour, it was announced. Broadway and the company believed that this was done to give time for remodeling the music hall or for procuring a new theater. Weber and Fields still kept their secret.

Photo 26. Eddie Foy in Hopsy Topsy Turvy, 1898. Strobridge & Co. Lithographers, Library of Congress.

Klaw and Erlanger controlled the first-class theaters of America so closely in 1904 that it was next to impossible to book an extended tour other than through their office and at their terms. The heads of the Shuberts, Sam, Jake and Lee, who were to challenge this monopoly, were just showing above the horizon. It so happened, too, that K. & E. were producing the Rogers Brothers shows, old rivals of Weber and Fields.

When Joe and Lew went to K. & E. to book their show to the coast and return they stumbled over the outstretched feet of Max and Gus Rogers a second time. Weber and Fields asked for 80 per cent of the gross receipts, not an unusual division for a show of their pretensions. What is more, they carried their own stage crew and orchestra, making the theater's share of the box-office income almost net. The syndicate countered with a lower offer, which Joe and Lew refused.

"Take it or leave it," said K. & E., and added, "We've got a better show in the Rogers Brothers anyway."

This slur called for defiance. Joe and Lew left it. Booking independently, they managed to patch out a tour to begin in the Stair and Havlin houses in the West. Marc Klaw and Abe Erlanger were not the lads to let such finger-snapping go unrebuked. They promptly made a pooling agreement with Stair and Havlin, who canceled Weber and Fields's route in the middle of the show's second week in San Francisco. Joe and Lew were left 3,000 miles from Broadway with a company of 103 persons on their hands.

Their memories of names, dates and localities normally are poor, but ask either where the Frying Pan River heads, what the mileage from Ash Fork to Flagstaff, or what the seating capacity of the Bird Cage Opera House at Tombstone, and they will answer correctly offhand. This is the fruit of the intensive study they gave to maps, railway folders and the Billposter's Friend in their final three days in San Francisco. An independent house was found in Los Angeles and booked at once. But from there to Denver, 1,400 miles, the route was blank. In all that territory there were just four recognizable theaters, and K. & E. had roped and branded these.

The Weberfields had their option of a 1,400 mile dead haul, of buying a tent and wildcatting, or of trying to crowd Lillian Russell, Peter Dailey, Evie Stetson and Broadway's most famous chorus into sagebrush opera houses where the star's dressing room once a year houses the bloodhounds of an "Uncle Tom's Cabin" troupe or into town halls usually given over to the Knights of Pythias drill teams and the Ladies' Auxiliary of the Anti-horse Thief Association.

Came at this juncture, as the boys and girls in Hollywood say, a caller from Albuquerque, New Mexico. The Elks of Albuquerque, he stated, were just completing a handsome new theater and the boys hoped to open it with a splurge that would set the Rio Grande and the Sangre de Cristo range afire. Weber and Fields were just the sort of outfit they would admire to corral. The man from Albuquerque was in Los Angeles to talk business.

"Where is this Albercookie?" asked Weber. "Al-bu-ker-kee, sir," corrected the New Mexican, "is the seat of Bernalillo County and the largest city in New

Mexico. Located on the right bank of the Rio Grande, division and junction point on the Santa Fe railroad better than halfway from here to Denver. The state university is located here, important cattle and sheep center, and——"

"How big?" Fields cut in.

"Well, the last census gave us only 6,238, but we've been growin' fast since," the Albuquerquean defended. "The chamber of commerce estimated the population at 10,000 on January first."

"What'll you give us?" Joe asked.

"Whatever's right. Half the round-up is the usual split, isn't it?"

Weber shook his head.

"Sixty-forty, then," the caller raised his bid.

"It will cost us $3,000 to stop off at your town," Weber countered. "As Brother Elks of Brooklyn Lodge No. 1, we'll play your theater for cost, cash in advance, just to accommodate the brothers."

"Done," agreed the other. "I'll wire the boys."

"Ever been in Albercookie?" Weber asked a Californian when the visitor had gone.

"Many's the time," the Californian admitted.

"What sort of a place is it?' Joe wanted to know from an impartial source.

"Well, it ain't any Los Angeles, brother," the native son told him. "Seven or eight thousand, maybe."

Weber congratulated himself.

"If nobody but one of those Navy-joe Indians and the girl at the Harvey House lunch counter shows up at the theater we've got our $3,000 and we've broken the jump to Denver," he exulted.

"Oh, there'll be a plenty there," the Angelino thought. "Albuquerque ain't any slouch of a town at that."

"It don't sound like any Lillian Russell among cities to me," Joe retorted. "If they slapped a dollar head tax on everybody there they couldn't raise more than $6,000. It's a wonder they didn't want us to take our share out in town lots. A fellow has to keep his eyes open out here in the West.'

At Albuquerque the Weberfields were greeted by an official reception committee bearing a certified check for $3,000, a brass band and the larger part of New Mexico. Punchers had galloped in from range and ranch to see if Lillian and Frankie looked like the cigarette cards tacked on the walls of every bunk house in the West. The governor and all the territorial officials had come from Santa Fé in a body. Delegations of brother Elks were there from El Paso, Las Vegas, Phoenix, Tucson, Bisbee, Santa Fe and Trinidad. There was a carnival parade in the afternoon with costumes funnier than anything in the show. Every seat in the fine new theater had been sold at auction at prices equaling the best Broadway ever had paid for a music-hall first night.

The receipts for the one performance were $12,500. The show's share at 60 per cent would have been $7,500. Weber and Fields had lost $4,500 by their insistence on a $3,000 lump-sum guaranty.

On the journey out to the coast Fields had overheard a group of chorus girls complaining of the cost of eating in dining cars. He spoke to Weber and the two decided to pay for all meals eaten by the chorus while en route. The first statement from McBride, the business manager, reached Weber's eyes just as K. & E. cut the ground from under the show at San Francisco. The total was staggering.

Photo 27. The company embarking on a tour by train.

Coming into Los Angeles several mornings later, Weber watched one of the chorus at breakfast. She began at the upper left-hand corner of the à-la-carte menu and ordered it all. A waiter staggered in with more than six dollars' worth of breakfast, at which the young woman pecked casually, then told her companion that food annoyed her in the morning.

That ended the Chorus Girls' Free Lunch Counter. On the first morning out of Los Angeles, Weber kept an eye on the same young woman at breakfast. She glanced at the card and said to the waiter, "Bring me a pot of coffee and an order of buttered toast."

From Albuquerque the company jumped to Denver, arrived at eight P.M., began the show at nine, and were on their way East again at one A.M. From Chicago east the Shuberts were able to give the show regular booking. It had reached Pittsburgh in March when the first credited report of Weber and Fields's separation came to Broadway. John T. Kelly had discovered the truth. He sent notice to New York by wire that he would not be with the music hall the following season and hinted at the real reason. Joe and Lew denied the report categorically. In New Haven on April twelve Peter Dailey admitted that this would be his final season with the show and the rumor revived. Despite

Joe and Lew's disclaimers the story now was credited generally along the Rialto.

The partners still were denying on April eighteenth in Boston, but on the following Sunday they slipped away from the show quietly for New York. They met on Monday morning, April twenty-fifth, in the office of Abe Hummell, Weber's attorney. Fields's lawyer accompanied him. In twenty minutes' time an agreement was concluded ending the partnership of twenty-eight years. Joe gave Lew his check for $40,000 and took over the music hall.

The two returned that afternoon to Boston, where Fields fell down a flight of hotel stairs two days later. The first examination indicated a broken hip, and Weber was about to close the show then and there, when the doctors concluded that Fields's injuries were less serious and that he could return to the cast inside the week.

The end would have come at Boston with the completion of the local engagement, but mutual friends intervened. The New Amsterdam was the newest and costliest theater in New York. On their own initiative, these friends rented the future home of the Follies for a Weber and Fields farewell and persuaded Joe and Lew to keep the engagement.

The New York newspapers of the morning of May 30, 1904, tell the story: "The Weber and Fields partnership was dissolved last night with the final performance of 'Whoop-dee-doo' at the New Amsterdam, closing that theater's first season," said the ever-flippant *Sun*. "Everybody in the company made speeches, including Peter Dailey, Lillian Russell, Louis Mann, John T. Kelly and Charley Ross. The chorus girls wept. Ross told the audience that it was business suicide for Weber and Fields to break up, and the audience agreed vociferously. Miss Russell shed real tears, and it was twelve o'clock before the obsequies ended and the mourners departed."

The *Herald* wrote in a different vein:

> A demonstration unique in theatrical history marked the ringing down of the last curtain. An audience which filled the large new theater, and composed of representatives of society, clubdom, the world of first-night, the theater and every walk of life, called for the curtain to rise again. Then in response to demands, speeches were made by members of the stock company in which the two men who had made Weber and Fields a household word were told that they were committing business suicide; were told that they were making a grievous mistake, amid cries of "Right! Right!"

A Broadway audience is not particularly sentimental, but the tears that streaked the painted and powdered faces of the stage were multiplied many times in the audience as "Auld Lang Syne" became the final musical number.Among that tear-stained audience the *Herald*'s society reporter noticed Mr. and Mrs. Orme Wilson, James Hazen Hyde, Mr. and Mrs. Howard Gould, D. Phoenix Ingraham, W. H. Neilson, Dr. and Mrs. Frank Northrup,

Mrs. Hermann Oelrichs, Mr. and Mrs. Ernest G. Stedman, J. Sayre Morton, Frank Crowninshield, John Forrester, Chalmers Daly, Jr., Jesse Lewisohn, J. P. Whiton Stuart, Judges Levintritt and Dugro, of the Supreme Court, and all the charter members of the Music Hall First Night Club.

Willie Collier and his wife rushed "The Dictator" through its evening performance and hurried to the New Amsterdam to pay their tribute. Fay Templeton and Sam Bernard were out front. Aimee Angeles came from the Majestic. Warfield, who was on tour, sent a telegram. Frankie Bailey burst into tears when her name was called and ran off the stage sobbing.

The audience stood and refused to leave the theater until Weber and Fields responded. They appeared together from the wings at last, both visibly moved by the demonstration.

"Speech!" shrieked the house.

When Weber spoke his voice carried only to the front rows.

"We can only say that we are sorry," he murmured,

"Fields!" the house cried.

"I can only echo Mr. Weber's sentiment," Lew's trembling voice answered.

"Shake hands," a gallery voice demanded.

They shook hands.

"Both members of this club," shouted some anonymous wag.

Joe and Lew smiled wanly and the curtain fell slowly.

The partners had dressed in the same room the last night as they had the first. The stage was crowded with friends and fellow players as the two climbed the winding stairs to their joint quarters, but none had the poor grace to follow. Their farewell said in the privacy of their dressing room, Joe and Lew emerged in their street clothes and passed separately out the stage door.

The history of theatrical teams dissolved by death, agreement or disagreement is a melancholy one. Success demanded in the beginning that they merge their individualities in the team. Having ceased to be individuals professionally, accustomed for years to achieve all their effects cooperatively, few have been able to readjust themselves when the union ended. Smith and Jones become, in the public mind, Smithandjones. Smith is no one, Jones is no one, Smithandjones is everything.

Only one notable exception occurs to the writer. Stuart Robson and William H. Crane went separate ways successfully, but they were of the legitimate stage. Montgomery and Stone, however, came up from the circus, partners for thirty years or more. Dave Montgomery died and Fred Stone continues to be a star of the first magnitude. On the other side of the ledger is a long list, Siamese Twins of the stage who failed to survive the operation that severed them. Max Rogers passed out of the picture when Gus Rogers died. Harrigan and Hart were supreme together. Tony Hart lost his mind and Ned Harrigan fell off into mediocrity. Evans and Hoey were great in union, ordinary singly. A bolt of lightning killed Bert Savoy on a Long Island beach a year or so ago. Jay Brennan has found a new partner, a competent vaudeville comedian, but the old savor is gone from the act. Scanlon and Cronin once were a team of note.

Scanlon lost his mind. Some old memory in the back of Fields's mind was stirred one night at the Broadway Theater, about 1910, by an old man among the fifty-cent-a-night supers. Fields asked the derelict his name. It was Cronin. Lew put him on the salary list for the rest of the season.

"Every time I saw Fields's name on a show poster after our separation," Weber recites, "I thought of a one-legged man. If I used the telephone the conversation would run something like this:

"'This is Joe Weber speaking.'
"'Who?'
"'Weber—Joe Weber.'
"'I don't get the name.'
"'Joe Weber, of Weber and Fields.'
"'Oh, yes, Mr. Weber?'

"Lew and I have answered either to Weber or to Fields for forty years. 'Glad to meet you, Mr. Weber,' a man says on shaking my hand; and 'Good-by, Mr. Fields,' when he leaves. My wife and I are used to being introduced as Mr. Weber and Mrs. Fields. We were in Florida last winter. A young woman from a Palm Beach paper interviewed us. Her story in the next day's paper read correctly until the last line. 'Mr. and Mrs. Fields will be in Palm Beach for several weeks,' it concluded.

"Lew and I sometimes wonder if they'll get our names straight on our tombstones and on the judgment morning. Probably not. For one thing, his real name is not Lew nor mine Joe. Both of us were born Moisha, the Hebrew of Moses."

In this story of Weber and Fields, as in all proper tales, the darkest hour precedes the dawn, and the curtain falls upon a happy ending.

The music hall reopened in the fall of 1904 with Weber's name alone in the electric lights. In order to procure Anna Held for his company, Weber took Florenz Ziegfeld, then Miss Held's husband, into partnership. The show was "Higgledy-Piggledy," built on the old music-hall recipe. Marie Dressier, Charley Bigelow, Sam Marion, Bonnie Maginn, Aimee Angeles and Aubrey Boucicault were in the cast. Ziegfeld withdrew after one season and invented the Follies.

Fields went into partnership with Fred R. Hamlin and Julian Mitchell. A new theater Oscar Hammerstein was completing on Forty-second Street, now called the Frazee, was christened the Lew Fields. There he opened on December fifth, an independent star and producer, in "It Happened in Nordland." Victor Herbert wrote the music. May Robson, Bessie Clayton, Marie Cahill, Pauline Frederick were in the cast. Hamlin died on the eve of the opening and the brief partnership ended. The show, however, was a success.

For more than seven years Weber and Fields pursued their separate paths, each with his successes and failures; more, it is pleasant to record, of the former than of the latter. They wished each other well, but they met only once, at a benefit performance in which both took part.

Early in January, 1912, Fields's father died and Weber attended the funeral. He and Lew rode together returning from the cemetery. Their route led through the Bowery. There was Miner's, here Donaldson's London, farther down the street the old Bowery Theater, there what once had been the Chatham Square and the Globe Museums; a moving panorama of their youth. Newer immigrants had displaced their generation from these crowded tenements. They saw themselves in the urchins that played in the noisome streets and fell silent.

'So you're giving up the old music hall, Web?" Fields asked at length.

"Yes," Joe said. "It has been losing money in recent years. It has seen its day."

"We ought to go together again, Web."

Lew read Joe's answer in his eyes.

That was the reunion of Weber and Fields. Their first thought was of Lillian Russell. She met them at the door of her home, took their hands and clasped them together.

"This is a sight for sore eyes," she rejoiced. "Most certainly I want a part in the reunion. Try to keep me out of it! Pay me what you like."

They paid her $2,000 a week. Fay Templeton, much more of her than in the old days, was the next to enlist. Then Willie Collier and his wife; John T. Kelly, Ada Lewis, George Beban, Bessie Clayton, Frankie Bailey. Many of the old Weberfields, Sam Bernard and De Wolf Hopper included, were under contract for the season and could not break away in mid-year. Ross and Fenton were celebrating their own twenty-fifth anniversary at Hammerstein's Victoria. Edgar Smith returned to write the book, a potpourri of Weber and Fields's reminiscences, and called it the "Weber and Fields Jubilee."

On the night of February 8, 1912, at Felix Isman's Broadway theater, Noah Webster's worst enemies returned to the stage together. The seats had been sold at auction as of old. Boxes brought as much as $900, orchestra seats $35! There was $13,700 in the house the opening night, a new Broadway record. Fields and Weber were offered $1,250 each for the two lower boxes, but saved them for their families. Weber's mother, ninety-three years old, was in his box, her first time in any theater.

Ten years before, Lillian Russell had been the victim of a Felix Isman joke. He had substituted the name of a chorus girl for that of Miss Russell on a gorgeous floral piece handed over the footlights. Lillian knew the flowers had been intended for her.

"You did that," she accused him quietly as she passed him in the wings.

The subject never had been mentioned again by either. Now Mr. Isman commissioned a florist to drape the proscenium arch and the orchestra pit with entwined American Beauty roses, to weave a carpet of American beauties for the floor of Miss Russell's dressing room and to hide the walls of the room with bowers of the same flower—American Beauties in compliment to her stage title. She gasped when she saw it and threw her arms around Mr. Isman.

"You got even," she said. Only the two understood the remark.

Peter Dailey, dead four years, alone was missing when the orchestra struck up John Stromberg's "Dinah" as an overture, and the show was on. Time and tide had waited on Frankie Bailey's legs, it appeared. Lillian made her entrance in a gem-bespattered gown that tinkled like a glass chandelier when she moved. Her fiancé, Alexander P. Moore, Pittsburgh publisher, now ambassador to Spain, and her daughter Dorothy were out front. Another Pittsburgher, W. J. Patterson, husband of Miss Templeton, sat near by. There were William A. Brady and Grace George, here ex-Sheriff Tom Foley, Al Woods, Ziegfeld, Fire Chief Croker, Commissioner Daugherty, Frank McKee, David Belasco, Morris Rose, E. J. Conley, Julian Mitchell, Clifton Crawford, Olive Wyndham, Gertie Vanderbilt, Diamond Jim Brady, Arthur Brisbane, William R. Hearst and family party, Sam Harris, Augustus Thomas, A. E. Thomas, Will Irwin, Charles Dana Gibson, J. J. Shubert, Thomas F. Ryan, Mrs. Willie Collier and Willie, Jr., Mr. and Mrs. Ralph Pulitzer, Mr. and Mrs. Conde Nast, Mrs. M. Sheldon Fuller, Miss Marjorie Curtis, Mr. and Mrs. W. Forbes Morgan, Jr., Mr. and Mrs. J. Stewart Barney, Mr. and Mrs. Herbert Rawlins, T. Pearsall Thorne, Louis Larocque, Thomas B. Clarke, Jr. Justice James W. Gerard excused himself from Ambassador Whitelaw Reid's dinner and arrived during the first act.

"Don't poosh me, Myer!"

Weber's voice from the wings! Enter Mike and Myer sputtering the old hashed German-English to a reception the like of a stampede in a national convention. Fields resumed the gouging-out of Weber's eye where he had left off eight years earlier. In its affectionate enthusiasm the audience made such a racket that the comedians' lines were drowned out repeatedly. What matter? All knew the lines by heart.

Russell, Collier, Weber and Fields were in the midst of the old poker game from "Hokey Pokey" when a cry came from offstage.

"Bine Gollies!" said the voice.

"Sounds just like Warfield," the audience whispered.

Collier, Russell, Joe and Lew turned in amazement as a Jewish peddler emerged from the wings, rubbing his hands and chattering in the almost forgotten accents of the pre-Belasco Warfield.

"A perfect imitation of Warfield," the audience whispered. The whisper changed to a shout.

"It is Warfield!"

It was Warfield! He had shortened his usual performance of "The Return of Peter Grimm," slipped out of the character of that ghostly Dutchman into the old make-up of his East Side peddler, jumped into a taxicab and popped in at the New Amsterdam to add his bit to the jubilee—as graceful a deed as one actor ever did for another. Warfield spoke, Belasco spoke. A quarter of an hour passed before the delighted house permitted the show to go on.

The gay, excited crowd was spilling into Forty-second Street by midnight, the show over. Backstage, the company hurried into other clothes to attend the dinner the Friars were giving to Weber and Fields, a signal honor to any actor.

Photo 28. Nora Bayes, c. 1920. Bain News Service, George Grantham Bain Collection, Library of Congress.

Photo 29. Weber and Fields in their heyday, c. 1900.

Caruso was one of the party at the head table. The tenor had been a constant patron at the music hall in its last season and his first in America, visiting backstage and drawing his cartoons of everyone in the troupe.

When a speech was demanded of him this night, he rose and convulsed the diners by saying, in a purposedly thickened Italian accent:

"At the Metropolitan Opera House we study so hard all our lives to learn to sing. Mr. Gatti-Casazza gives you an all-star cast. We sing like the angels and you pay $10,000. But Fields here, who sticks his finger in Weber's eye, plays to thirteen-fourteen thousand dollars. How is that?"

Road bookings forced the show to close its Broadway engagement while New York still was paying fancy prices to speculators for tickets and crowding the theater to capacity. On tour, the Jubilee duplicated its New York triumph, playing in the largest theaters to be had; in Chicago the Auditorium, in Kansas City Convention Hall. The season closed in Pittsburgh in June. Miss Russell and Mr. Moore were married the following night in the Hotel Schenley in the presence of the Weberfields.

Weber and Fields' New Music Hall, now the Forty-fourth Street Theater, opened the following fall with an all-star stock company that included Frank Daniels, Marie Dressier, Norah Bayes, Jack Norworth, Helena Collier-Garrick, Bessie Clayton, Arthur Aylsworth and Joe and Lew. It lived only one season. The venture required patience. Broadway needed time to adjust itself to the new location, the new principals and the much larger theater. Joe and Lew, deceived by the sentimental outburst of the Jubilee, expected to resume where they had left off at Twenty-ninth Street in 1904. When the season ended with smaller profits than they might have earned independently, they gave the new music hall up.

Mr. Fields returned to musical comedy and still is actively on the stage. His sense of comedy is perhaps more acute than ever. In his last play, "The Melody Man," he has a situation where he has lost his job and he and his daughter are at the end of their financial resources. A lady clerk of his former place of employment had just called on his daughter. She would like some ice cream and offers him the money which he refuses. "No guest can pay," says he. The room is brilliantly illuminated. He takes a few steps towards the door and then hesitates, opens his pocket-book and peers into its recesses. What he saw was disturbing. "How dark it is," said he, still fishing in the pocket-book.

Mr. Weber has given more of his attention in recent years to producing. You may see them, Mike and Myer again the coming winter in vaudeville. Should you hear a plaintive voice offstage saying,

"don't poosh me, Myer,"

they will be next on the bill.

THE END

www.ingramcontent.com/pod-product-compliance
Lightning Source LLC
LaVergne TN
LVHW050152080826
844660LV00002B/184

* 9 7 8 1 4 3 8 4 9 0 5 1 9 *